Threshold

CALIFORNIA SERIES IN PUBLIC ANTHROPOLOGY

The California Series in Public Anthropology emphasizes the anthropologist's role as an engaged intellectual. It continues anthropology's commitment to being an ethnographic witness, to describing, in human terms, how life is lived beyond the borders of many readers' experiences. But it also adds a commitment, through ethnography, to reframing the terms of public debate—transforming received, accepted understandings of social issues with new insights, new framings.

Series Editor: Robert Borofsky (Hawaii Pacific University)

Contributing Editors: Philippe Bourgois (University of Pennsylvania), Paul Farmer (Partners In Health), Alex Hinton (Rutgers University), Carolyn Nordstrom (University of Notre Dame), and Nancy Scheper-Hughes (UC Berkeley)

University of California Press Editor: Naomi Schneider

Threshold

EMERGENCY RESPONDERS ON
THE US-MEXICO BORDER

Ieva Jusionyte

UNIVERSITY OF CALIFORNIA PRESS

University of California Press, one of the most distinguished university presses in the United States, enriches lives around the world by advancing scholarship in the humanities, social sciences, and natural sciences. Its activities are supported by the UC Press Foundation and by philanthropic contributions from individuals and institutions. For more information, visit www.ucpress.edu.

University of California Press
Oakland, California

Library of Congress Cataloging-in-Publication Data

Names: Jusionyte, Ieva, 1983–
Title: Threshold : emergency responders on the US-Mexico border / Ieva Jusionyte.
Description: Oakland, California : University of California Press, [2018] | Includes bibliographical references and index. |
Identifiers: LCCN 2018008950 (print) | LCCN 2018014229 (ebook) | ISBN 9780520969643 (epub and ePDF) | ISBN 9780520297173 (cloth : alk. paper) | ISBN 9780520297180 (pbk. : alk. paper)
Subjects: LCSH: Emergency medical services—Mexican-American Border Region. Rescue work—Mexican-American Border Region. | Mexican-American Border Region—Emigration and immigration—Social aspects.
Classification: LCC RA645.7.M58 (ebook) | LCC RA645.7.M58 J87 2018 (print) | DDC 362.180972/1—dc23
LC record available at https://lccn.loc.gov/2018008950

Manufactured in Canada

27 26 25 24 23 22 21 20 19 18
10 9 8 7 6 5 4 3 2 1

To Bojo, Alex, Capt. Lopez,
and all fellow firefighters
who save lives
on both sides of the line

CONTENTS

Plates between pages 88 and 89

Introduction

The US-Mexican border *es una herida abierta* where the Third World grates against the First and bleeds. And before a scab forms it hemorrhages again, the lifeblood of two worlds merging to form a third country—a border culture.

GLORIA ANZALDÚA,
Borderlands/La Frontera

DEAD END

"Vámonos?" Alex was waiting for me in the truck, ready to start the engine.[1]

The fire was in Mexico. We were a few miles north of the border, in the United States, wearing navy blue T-shirts with logos of the Nogales Suburban Fire District. Concerned that the blaze could jump the line into our jurisdiction, the chief instructed us to go and check it out.[2]

We didn't need to hurry. Heading south, we passed an area known as the Buena Vista Ranch: a handful of houses cradled in the desert, its pale skin barely covered by a stubble of mesquite trees. I could see why back in the day John Wayne made movies here: the scenery was an ideal stage for a Hollywood Western. Several hydrants, their red paint beginning to fade, pointed to another story, one about plans to develop the area. But the ranch happened to be on a route of intense drug and human trafficking. Locals say that fear of violence associated with illicit trade scared potential homebuyers away, squelching their dreams of building a community. We passed a yellow "Dead End" sign perforated by bullets ("target practice," Alex reassured me), unhitched a gate with a barely legible sign warning "no trespassing," and after a few turns found ourselves on a dirt road running parallel to the border wall.

From afar, the wall is but a squiggly dark line following the contour of the hilly landscape; close up, it resembles the spiky spine of a stegosaurus, low curves giving shape to menace and fear. Stretching as far as the eye could see, to the east and to the west, the road next to the wall served as the US Border Patrol highway: federal agents, in search of unauthorized border crossers, steer a fleet of white trucks with green stripes up and down these slopes, expecting spectacular, newsworthy captures of marijuana, cocaine, or methamphetamine loads, but more often encountering tired migrants with tattered clothes and blistered feet.

The fire department could use the road too, at least in emergency situations. Driving along the wall, we continued scanning the sky for smoke. Only a few days had passed since I chased fires with the crew of Mexican firefighters—the bomberos—in Nogales, Sonora. It was May, more than a month until the summer rains would arrive, and fires were so abundant that the bomberos might go from one call to the next without taking a break. On this side, in Arizona, fires were less frequent, but once they started, they could expand rapidly, fiercely devouring the dry vegetation and often requiring the US Forest Service to bring in helicopters and elite firefighter crews—the hotshots—to battle them for days or even weeks in remote canyons. The average temperature in Arizona has increased by over 2°F since the 1970s, making wildland fires in the region both bigger and more severe.[3] Down by the wall looking for smoke that morning, Alex and I didn't yet know that later in the afternoon La Sierra Fire would start in Sonora and cross the border about 17 miles west of us, on the opposite side of Nogales, burning thousands of acres and requiring joint efforts of Mexican and American firefighters to contain it. Binational cooperation in such situations was common—emergency managers and frontline responders recognized that the border did not stop fire. Nor, for that matter, did it halt flash floods, toxic fumes, or any other natural or manmade disaster.

We reached a place where the metal wall abruptly ends and gives way to several strings of barbed wire and a low-lying steel beam construction, known as a Normandy barrier. Even though it may not be obvious during the dry season, when all you see are lush green trees and occasional puddles of water, this is the bed of the Santa Cruz River, which crosses the border perpendicularly, running south to north. It is an important path for migratory wildlife—deer, javelina, mountain lions, ocelots, and the only known wild jaguar in the United States, El Jefe, who lives in the Santa Rita Mountains. The engineers didn't build a wall here since a solid barrier would threaten endangered species and cause damaging floods.[4] Unauthorized pedestrian traffic, involving migrants and drug mules, know about this gap, too. Dry arroyos are convenient paths across the undulating desert terrain: capillaries circulating life without regard to who is legally entitled to it.

We still didn't see any smoke. Nor, surprisingly, did we see any Border Patrol.

Alex was not fond of the Border Patrol. Though he meets them regularly on the job, when he goes through the checkpoint on I-19 they often look at him with suspicion. "These guys, they come to Nogales from somewhere over there, say Montana—the 'Holy See' of white people—and at the checkpoint they see Hispanic people, Mexican people, driving up and down all day long." Alex has been pulled over regardless of whether he drove his personal vehicle with firefighter union decals and his bunker gear thrown on the backseat or an official city truck with government license plates. They would still ask him: "Is this your vehicle? Do you have anybody in the trunk?" Short and stocky, with black hair and a thick mustache, he knows he looks like a stereotypical Mexican. He orders chilaquiles with a side of tortillas, making young Sonoran waitresses smile. He is also stubborn. "I just laugh. I never answer," he says, referring to the questions by federal agents. I believe him, for I saw how it played out at the station, where Alex's blunt remarks were habitually taken as offenses. He had no intention to change. One time, after a joint exercise held in the tunnels under Nogales, he even had the guts to tell the Border Patrol that had it been a real emergency, he would not have stayed to rescue an injured federal agent; he would have grabbed his partner and they would have run for their lives. "I'm an honest asshole," he admits. The agents at the checkpoint must sense his defiance: they send Alex into secondary inspection, again and again. A price he's willing to pay for feeling righteous.

With the rescue truck obediently tracing the difficult topography of the desert terrain, we reached the easternmost limit of our jurisdiction and stopped to consider the rusted bollard fence spanning far into the horizon. "They used to smuggle chicken into Mexico through here," Alex told me. Chicken in Spanish is *pollo*. I dwelt on the cruel irony: the only pollos crossing the border these days pay several thousand dollars to *polleros* (the "chicken wranglers") for a chance to work long shifts in poultry-processing plants in Ohio, Missouri, or the Carolinas.

Though it had been a full year since I arrived at the borderlands, I was still eager to hear Alex's stories about life on the frontlines. On what we call "slow" days, between station duties and vehicle check-offs, we would spend hours talking without being interrupted by dispatch. This rhythm—alternating between action and boredom—was familiar to me. Trained as an EMT, paramedic, and wildland firefighter, before I came to Arizona I had spent several years volunteering as an emergency responder in Florida. As far as fire departments go, Nogales Suburban was on the quieter end of the spectrum. The number 74 written on the board in the day room meant that, about five months in, we were only waiting for the seventy-fifth call of the year. Unlike during my time as a rookie, I was no longer anxious to run with lights and siren to structure fires, rollovers, or cardiac arrests—I had learned to appreciate the absence of emergencies. Slow days were good for ethnography.

It looked like we would have another one of those: there was still no sign of the brushfire.

Once we started heading back, we spotted a Border Patrol vehicle. The agent did not notice us immediately. "We must have tripped off one of their sensors when we got off the road making a turn," Alex reasoned. We drove slowly and watched the agent head toward the area where the fence cut across the dry riverbed, then pause and inspect it. He probably heard our engine because suddenly he made a U-turn to face us. As the fire truck approached him, Alex raised a hand to greet the agent, but neither of us saw whether he waved back. Sometimes they do.

In the vocabulary of the Border Patrol, the Sonoran Desert is known as "hostile terrain." It is an obstacle course that migrants have to complete in order to enter the United States. Those crossing near Nogales or Sasabe will walk for three days until they reach Green Valley or Three Points, the first semi-urban settlements north of the checkpoints; Tucson is about five days away. But that's only if they go straight. Abandoned by their guides, thirsty and disoriented, people get lost and walk in circles. It's a cruel and prolonged game at wilderness survival, where improperly equipped human beings try to avoid being lethally wounded by the sun and the ecosystem. Ever since the government constructed the new taller fence (hypothetically a more effective barrier against unauthorized crossing) and adopted cutting-edge technologies of surveillance, human traffic has rerouted from border towns to the desert—a grueling terrain that precludes taking life for granted. Since 2001, nearly 2,500 human remains have been recovered in the Border Patrol's Tucson Sector alone.[5] Most of them were unauthorized migrants from Mexico and Central America. But nobody knows how many more have died, their corpses yet to be found and identified. And nobody knows how many have survived, but must deal with debilitating effects of traumatic injury or illness caused by the journey.

The "killing fields," "a neoliberal oven," and "a massive open grave" are phrases that capture the cruelty and tragedy of this desolate stretch of the earth.[6] "Gorgeous despair rattles the land like a great serpent's tail, warning of the deadly bite behind the greeting-card sunrises," Luis Alberto Urrea wrote of the treacherous beauty of the desert landscape.[7] This is the homeland of thorny plants—jumping chollas, nopales, saguaros. Rattlesnakes and scorpions, javelinas and wildcats inhabit the rocks and ravines, invisible at night. I know a paramedic who once treated a migrant attacked by a mountain lion—he had deep lacerations on his neck left by the animal's claws. But it is the weather—temperatures that rise to over 110°F during summer days and fall to below freezing on winter nights—that hurt most border crossers taking the route through the desert.[8] Security strategies, from fences to checkpoints, superimposed on the perilous landscape have turned terrain into a weapon that maims or murders those who commit the civil offense of entering the territory of the United States without proper documents.

"I can't even begin to count how many people we picked up in the desert," Alex tells me.

One time he hiked for six hours looking for a toddler who wandered off when his exhausted mother fell asleep under a tree. Desperate, the woman gave herself up to the Border Patrol, pleading them to help find her son. Border Patrol brought in a signcutter—an agent who specializes in detecting and interpreting disturbances in natural terrain that indicate the passage of people, animals, or vehicles, and after hours of arduous hiking in the hills following footprints, they were able to locate the child.[9] "They found him without a scratch. Six hours alone in the desert and nothing was wrong with him, no medical need," Alex said. Rare luck. Migrants who get lost may never be heard of again or, if they are, they may be in grave condition. Alex saw people so severely dehydrated that their bodies shut down. "Once we found a woman over here and, when we were helping her out, we noticed ants inside her mouth. The ants got inside the mouth because it was still moist. They were looking for water. It was bad."

Alex has collected men's fingers and limbs either cut off by the wheels of the freight train that undocumented migrants caught for a ride north to Tucson or amputated by the sharp edges of the border fence. He has participated in rescue and (more often) body recovery attempts when people across the line got swept away by the turbulent waters of the Nogales Wash. Tossed around with such force, they hit their heads on the rocks or heavy debris floating downstream, and by the time they reach this side of the border, they are either unconscious or dead. "Most of them, they were coming to work," Alex said, and we rode in silence for a while.

Firefighters along the Arizona-Sonora border are routinely dispatched to save people in the life-threatening situations that Alex describes, often with the coordinates of "out there in the middle of nowhere." But they have also performed other tasks that are unusual elsewhere. The presence of the border adds peculiar dimensions to the work of emergency responders, already equipped to manage the most extraordinary of scenarios. For example, customs officers habitually asked Nogales firefighters to use powerful rescue saws to open gasoline tanks, rims of vehicles, or tires stacked with marijuana. Sometimes, as the saw cut into the metal, sparks ignited the pot. They wouldn't be wearing airpacks and, back in the day, nobody cared about filling out exposure forms. "We laughed our heads off," a captain later told me about one such incident. "We had the munchies." Not everything was funny, however. When Alex started working at the Nogales Fire Department in the mid-1990s, he found bulletproof vests strapped to the seats of the ambulance and was told to wear a Kevlar helmet on calls to the border. "We used to get shot at, thrown rocks at." Incidents related to drug trafficking posed danger to emergency responders, who, when providing care on scene, were easily mistaken for law enforcement. "They didn't care much who was who. Government is government."

Back at the station, Alex called our chief to report that we did not spot any fire on either side of the border. We finished the morning routine: inspected and washed the trucks, checked the equipment. The rest of the time passed slowly in this isolated building on the edge of the desert, beige like its surroundings, with a flagpole in the front and a basketball hoop in the back. When they blasted the solid rock to make room for the construction of the station, the soil was not pressed hard enough and now cracks were appearing on the floor: the firehouse was slowly sinking. We were not allowed to stay inside overnight.

Later in the afternoon, as the day was winding down and the heat was more bearable, we stood at the open bay and watched an occasional vehicle pass by on Highway 82. The place was so serene, the webs linking it to state violence and the criminal economies south and north of the border imperceptible to the naked eye. But we knew better. Smugglers, migrants, and federal agents have all dropped by the fire station: smugglers requesting to make phone calls to arrange pickups; migrants seeking water and directions; agents passing time while monitoring the road. On our last shift, a DPS-led task force used the station to stage an operation. They stopped and arrested a suspect right in front of where we were now standing, and I was relieved when the lead officer changed his mind about questioning the man inside the firehouse. They left, nine unmarked vehicles in single file. Alex, whose brother worked in a similar interagency task force, was not surprised by what we witnessed. Nothing on the border seemed to surprise him.

"They have asked me to hide drugs in the truck," he confided. Some years ago, a man came to the station to recruit Alex. The plan was to set a brushfire in the Buena Vista Ranch and, when Alex came to put it out, they would load the fire truck with drugs. Alex said no. But not everyone could resist. The appeal of the drug economy, at an arm's length, was strong and the use of official insignia as a disguise for trafficking seemed clever. In fact, it was common practice.[10] Police officers and firefighters from the local communities were logical targets for recruitment. Even Border Patrol agents have been charged with taking part in such camouflage operations.[11] Formal duties tangled up with side hustles; law meshed with crime.

The border put some lines into focus and blurred others.

TREACHEROUS TERRAIN

In the US-Mexico border region, sovereignties are anything but settled. Here, political topography competes with other claims on the landscape: indigenous forms of governance, neoliberal networks of profit-making, criminal economies, desert ecosystems. After the signing of the Treaty of Guadalupe Hidalgo, which ended the US-Mexican War in 1848, the Joint United States and Mexican Boundary Commission spent more than seven years trying to survey and map the new jurisdictional divide. The borderline not only cut through territory that was previously claimed by Mexico, but also split the homelands of the Tohono O'odham, Pima, and other peoples who had lived there before the Europeans arrived and took over.[12] Even the environment rigorously resisted the commission's attempts to inscribe one nation's victory and another's defeat onto the surface of the earth. The survey report mentions "the bleached barrenness" of the region, where both Mexican and American teams endured temperatures of over 100°F, shortages of food and water, and rough terrain.[13] Imposing "state definitions on the ground" was no easy task.[14]

More than 150 years later, national territories carved out of the contiguous physical landscape remain a fragile achievement. In recent attempts to strengthen their titles against rival uses of this space, the US and Mexican governments declared it a zone of two militarized conflicts—the "war on terror" and the "drug war" (*narcoguerra*)—justifying legal exceptions and the deployment of lethal weapons that ended up targeting migrants and refugees.

As if that wasn't enough, this vicious cycle of security buildup and accumulating atrocities unfolds under volatile environmental conditions. With temperatures in the area steadily rising, extreme weather events have become more frequent.[15] Even when reinforced with steel and concrete, the arbitrary boundary cutting across the desert does not prevent intensified wildfires or flash floods, nor does it stop toxic chemical spills. These are the times of multiple emergencies; yet they are all subordinate to the primacy of homeland security. To speed up the construction of the wall in the aftermath of 9/11, DHS was authorized to waive thirty-seven federal laws, including the Endangered Species Act, the Clean Water Act, the American Indian Religious Freedom Act, and the Native American Graves Protection and Repatriation Act, as well as regulations preserving clean air, migratory birds, national forests, and rivers.[16]

Such an inauspicious misalignment of politics and ecology, compounded by warfare and lawfare, keeps the border in a perpetual state of alert. Emergency can result from any combination of potential threats: a migrant may suffer a heatstroke while taking a remote route through the desert in hopes of avoiding checkpoints; a train carrying hazardous materials to the copper mines may derail, polluting the washes that supply water to communities on both sides of the border. Or a security barrier put in place to prevent trespassing may exacerbate the destructive effects of summer rains. In 2008, without notifying the International Boundary and Water Commission, Customs and Border Protection (CBP) installed a 5-foot barrier inside the underground tunnel that runs perpendicular to the border and connects Nogales, Sonora, and Nogales, Arizona. When the monsoon arrived that July, and the runoff from the heavy rain rushed downstream from Mexico toward the United States, the concrete barrier formed a bottleneck. Water pressure kept rising until a thousand feet of the tunnel collapsed, inundating the streets in Nogales, Sonora. Mexican authorities declared flooded part of the city a disaster zone, and cited damage to 578 homes and forty-five cars.[17] Two days after the flooding, US officials recovered two bodies from the wash, suspecting the dead were unauthorized migrants who were trying to get through the tunnel when the flood began. Despite calls for investigations and reparations, the federal government's only concession to the mayors of the split city was to grant permission to lower the concrete barrier by a foot and a half. Accidents like this reveal that topographical forms have political implications. We see how the materiality of terrain—its texture and volume—is weaponized to serve the ends of security.[18] We can discern the physics of terrain underlying the politics of wounding.

The Border Patrol uses the concept of "tactical infrastructure" to refer to the assemblage of materials and technologies that both impede and facilitate movement. It aims to stop trespassers while creating a smooth surface for enforcement operations. The agency calls it a "force multiplier." Infrastructure is "tactical" in both senses of the term: as relating to small-scale actions serving a larger purpose (in this case, national security), and as "being weapons or forces employed at the battlefront."[19] The question is therefore how space and law enmesh on the border to produce injury. Achille Mbembe suggests seeing space as "the raw material of sovereignty" and a vehicle of violence, underlying the "terror formation."[20] It is operationalized and molded into the practices of the security apparatus.[21] This move requires stripping off any competing discourses of territory and place, leaving its physical qualities exclusively meaningful for national politics. Writing about the sectarian conflict between Protestants and Catholics in Northern Ireland, Allen Feldman noted how attempts to transform the material fabric of the social order took the form of topographic violence because space in Belfast functioned "as a mnemonic artifact" for storing historical narratives.[22] Urban terrain was not merely the stage where violence was performed. Rather than a passive setting or the location, it was fundamental to the very performance of violence—the source precipitating action, the condition of its possibility, and its ultimate target. Technical language, commonly associated with war operations, allows the Border Patrol to detach terrain from additional layers of signification: if it is tactical, then it is not ecological or historical. Binational trajectories and communal practices sedimented into the built environment are irrelevant. The border does not even mark the perimeter of the tactical field—it is enclosed within it. Despite the government's attempts to portray the area as a zone of reversible violence, where the Border Patrol tries to outmaneuver the enemy—drug traffickers and human smugglers—it is almost exclusively unilateral. Tactical space does not have an interface outside of the state's imaginary.

Terrain acts as a mechanism of injury. Its form underlies the kinematics of trauma. When a human body collides with an object, such as when a border crosser falls off the wall—the transfer of energy upon contact produces injury that varies in severity depending on the height of the fall, the part of the body struck first, and the type of surface on which it lands.[23] Kinetic energy is a function of an object's mass and velocity ($E_k = 1/2 \ mv^2$). But this is more than physics. To understand how terrain is made tactical and deployed as a weapon I will use the frame of "field causality." Eyal Weizman proposed this term as a counterforensic technique, a method for interrogating the built environment to uncover state violence. Field causality traces linkages that he describes as "multidirectional and distributed over extended spaces and time durations."[24] Therefore, it can capture indirect, slow, and diffuse forms of violence, prescribed by policy, operating through laws, and carried out by human and nonhuman agents.[25] Field causality expands the ecological milieu to bring into focus the threads and relations that formal parameters of legal investigations preclude. It shows how built environments "actively— sometimes violently—shape incidents and events."[26] This approach requires abandoning the linear path between cause and effect: federal agents did not build the barrier inside the tunnel to flood the town and drown the border crossers. These emergencies resulted from a juncture of security policies, urban infrastructure, and natural forces. The field, Weizman writes, is "a thick fabric of lateral relations, associations, and chains of actions" that "connects different physical scales and scales of action."[27] Establishing field causalities entails acknowledging multiple agencies and feedback loops, including those factors that are ordinarily absent from public discussions of violence, such as kinetic energy, Newton's second law of motion (F=ma), and the force of gravity mobilized as instruments of extralegal punishment for trespass. Kinematics of trauma reveal political tactics disguised in the form of the material.

FIRST DUE TO THE BORDER

The task of mitigating threats to human life, whether accidental or deliberate, falls to emergency responders. Firefighters, also trained as EMTs or paramedics, have a pragmatic, hazard-oriented disposition toward the border region that many people know only from sensational and politicized media coverage.[28] Previously called "smoke eaters" and associated with untamed bravery, by the beginning of the twenty-first century firefighters had evolved into a highly skilled, all-hazards response task force—the embodiment of what Mark Tebeau described as "the melding of men and technology into an efficient, lifesaving machine."[29] Their performance hinges on competence— practical types of knowledge, an understanding of the city and the country, acquired through repeated encounters with the dangers presented by urban and natural landscape.[30] Rescuers are uniquely attuned to the characteristics of physical space and to the temporality of uncertainty.

But this focus on accidents, as unexpected events, and practical engagement with material surroundings obscures the politics and law that enable the use of the environment to perpetrate violence. Many emergencies along the US-Mexico border result from the state's attempt to impose a legal grid over the region's rebellious topography. Dispatched to correct the deleterious consequences of the narcoguerra in Mexico and immigration policies in the United States, Alex and his peers witness and experience the most palpable effects of border militarization. They rescue injured border crossers who fall off the fence and those who are hurt in the desert; they discover drug loads hidden in containers carrying hazardous materials; they fight wildland fires started by migrants in distress as well as those that are used as a diversion for smuggling.[31] More times than any of them would have liked, they were called to the overcrowded Nogales Border Patrol station to take undocumented minors with seizures, fever, or heat illness to the local hospital. But it is not only migrants and refugees that they are called to rescue. Though it happens less often, paramedics also help federal agents—when they get shot, bitten by a service dog, or crash an all-terrain vehicle. Last year, an off-duty Border Patrol agent engaged in recreational target practice started a wildfire that burned over 46,000 acres and required a crew of over six hundred firefighters to contain.[32]

Rescue operations—corrective practices that hide injurious consequences of violent state actions—reveal contradictions inherent in statecraft. Rather than being "accidents"—unanticipated occurrences that happen unintentionally and result in damage—emergencies on the border are deliberately caused by government policies. The adoption by the Border Patrol of the infamous "prevention through deterrence" strategy in 1994—which involved increasing the length and the height of the border fence in urban areas—significantly expanded the number of wounded migrants, while providing the government with a "moral alibi."[33] Along the US southern fringe, border-related trauma became so common that it no longer surprised anyone or made it to the news. It was evident that the shifting design of the border fence produced particular forms of injuries. The sharp edges on the top of the previous fence, made of corrugated sheet metal leftover from the Vietnam War, amputated limbs; the tall slatted steel wall we have today fractures legs and ankles. In Douglas, Arizona, fire department personnel have been dispatched to care for patients with orthopedic injuries—they call them "fence jumpers"—with such frequency that they began referring to the cement ledge abutting the international wall as "ankle alley."

The Border Patrol's plan correctly predicted that, as a direct consequence of border security buildup in Nogales, Douglas, and other border towns, "illegal traffic will be deterred, or forced over more hostile terrain, less suited for crossing and more suited for enforcement."[34] "Prevention through deterrence" purposefully pushed migrants further away from populated areas, rerouting them through remote rural corridors, where border crossers often need medical treatment for dehydration, kidney failure, or heatstroke. To bypass checkpoints permanently installed on all northbound roads, they walk across the vast expanse of the Sonoran Desert, where they become exposed to extreme environments. Firefighters and paramedics in southern Arizona have also responded to multiple deadly accidents involving pickup trucks and vans, sometimes carrying over a dozen unauthorized migrants, when these rolled over during pursuits by the Border Patrol on roads with dangerous curves, often at night. Migrants who walk along the Nogales Wash through the tunnels still get swept away by turbulent waters; every year somebody drowns. Joint Mexican and American rescue teams walk the entire length of the wash to search for their bodies. In 2015, they recovered five corpses.

These injuries do not work the same way as wounds linked to other histories and geographies of violence. When trauma happens abroad, especially in places governed by regimes accused of having a dubious human rights record, scars of torture and other bodily imprints of force become evidence of victimhood and vulnerability—a corporeal marker of persecution that entitles the individual to asylum.[35] But border wounds—whether a leg fracture or kidney failure—caused by policies of the same state that the injured was trying to reach, without permission, do not warrant mercy. On the contrary, their wounds, rather than making border crossers qualified to receive care and protection, are read as proof of crime. A broken ankle or an amputated finger serves as evidence of an illegal entry into the country, which US law classifies as a civil offense. In the court of public opinion, it alone may not be enough to justify condemning unauthorized migrants to harsh treatment. But in the popular imaginary this rather mild violation of the law—crossing the border through a clandestine passage—precedes and substitutes for a possibly more serious one: suspected trafficking, which would be a criminal offense. An injured border crosser is recast as a drug mule or a gang member, a violent subject and a security threat. When an accident, such as a fall from the fence or drowning in a flooded arroyo, is treated as a potential crime, the state assumes the right to exercise force against the survivor.[36] Therefore, instead of exposing their wounds the way asylum seekers do, border crossers must hide them. In the global economy of wounds, their injuries lack legitimacy and political value. In the eyes of the government, unauthorized migrants are always already implicated as criminals. They stand in for the narcos and the "murderers" and "rapists" that conjure up fear in the nationalist political rhetoric.[37] But wounds tell more than one story. Iraqi physician-turned-anthropologist Omar Dewachi calls them "the interstitial tissue of the social," which reveals shifting ecologies of violence and care.[38] On the US-Mexico border, the same injured body can be read as evidence of several layers of crime: it bears the scars of political violence committed by more than one state, marks of wounding left by multiple institutions and policies.

"We all have the same red blood," Chief Mario Novoa said the morning he invited me for a ride along "ankle alley" in Douglas. "We help everyone. It's human nature to want a better chance of life." A firefighter in Nogales made a similar comment: "We are not in the business of law enforcement or immigration enforcement. We are in the business of helping people." Yet the traumatic injuries they witness, read as evidence of a crime, made the blurring of emergency medical services and border policing possible. The erosion of legal and ethical boundaries between care and enforcement takes various forms. Most often, fire and rescue departments in small rural communities, struggling to make ends meet, are forced to report injured migrants to the Border Patrol in order to cover the costs for ambulance services. But there are times when 911 calls from migrants in distress never even reach local first responders because the sheriff's department transfers them to the Border Patrol. Their advantage of manpower and resources, including Black Hawk helicopters suited for the rugged mountain terrain, is bolstered by their claim to righteousness. Echoing the humanitarian turn in the European security regime, where the rescue of migrants in danger of drowning in the Mediterranean provides the moral and political grounds for interception, the Border Patrol expanded the scope of its work to include the prerogative of saving lives.[39] At first glance this seems like a reorientation of border enforcement toward the provision of care, but it is merely a humanitarian "bandage" that allows for bare survival.[40] In 2017, Tucson Sector had over two hundred Border Patrol agents trained as EMTs who were qualified to provide basic life-saving care.[41] Descriptions of spectacular rescue operations in remote canyons circulate in the press under headlines that hail their heroic efforts. The CBP agent, carrying both an M-4 assault rifle and an emergency first-aid kit, becomes a superhero in the border-turned-war zone.[42] Rebranding border enforcement officers as benevolent rescuers improves the agency's public image and deflects persistent criticism for mistreatment of migrants.[43] But this facelift obscures the causes of life-threatening trauma: the Border Patrol made the injuries that agents are now helping to stabilize.

This fusing of violence and aid should not be surprising. As a field of expertise, emergency medicine developed within the military.[44] It was none other than Baron Dominique Jean Larrey, chief surgeon of Napoleon's army, who invented a "flying" ambulance—a light horse-drawn carriage for evacuating wounded soldiers from the battleground to the field hospital. The Civil War in the United States prompted the introduction of forward first-aid stations to rapidly administer medical care to combat casualties, while medical personnel discharged from the military established the first civilian ambulance services. The history of EMS winds through the fault lines of twentieth-century conflicts: during World War I and World War II, enlisted men with first-aid training were assigned to companies on the frontlines, where they provided treatment to injured soldiers on site, controlling bleeding and splinting fractures right there in the trenches; Mobile Army Surgical Hospitals (MASH) were built in Korea before the US military used them in Vietnam and the Persian Gulf, reducing deaths from hemorrhage due to vascular injuries and limb amputations; wars in Afghanistan and Iraq allowed the military to improve tactical combat casualty care, using tourniquets and hypotensive resuscitation. In the early twenty-first century, EMS in the United States is a civilian practice shared between public and private providers, but its links with the armed forces have not been severed: even today, cutting-edge life-saving techniques such as the use of hemostatic agents to control bleeding or needle decompression in chest trauma are tested on the frontlines before they are adopted on the homefront. As knowledge moves from the battlefield to the street, so do people: after their deployment, combat medics often find work with ambulance companies. Or they join fire departments.

In their early days, fire departments in the United States were neighborhood associations staffed by volunteers from the community who knew how to "put the wet stuff on the red stuff," as the old-timers like to say. But over the last few decades the institution has undergone significant changes. Following the creation, in 1966, of the National Highway Traffic Safety Administration, and the adoption of the first federal standards for emergency medical services, large metropolitan areas started developing advanced field emergency medical care programs using firefighters. Today, many urban fire departments even in smaller towns like Nogales and Douglas, run their own ambulances and consider EMS to be an integral part of their work, a trend that is spreading to the rural districts, albeit at an uneven pace.[45] Also recently, these traditionally community-centered organizations began to be systematically incorporated into the operations of the federal state.[46] The process of folding local emergency services into the national security apparatus started in the latter half of the twentieth century, at first under the banner of civil defense and preparedness during the Cold War, but it rapidly accelerated after 9/11.[47] The role of firefighters in responding to the 9/11 attacks, when 343 of them died under the collapsing towers in New York City, solidified their symbolic status as national heroes in the "war on terror."[48] With the creation of DHS, fire and rescue departments across the US were swiftly absorbed into the political and administrative system of emergency management. Tasked with handling an evolving list of threats to national and global security, firefighters and paramedics are now prepared to respond to incidents involving "all threats and hazards": from industrial waste spills to terror attacks involving biological, chemical, radiological, and other WMDs to epidemic infectious disease. Not everyone in the municipal emergency service agrees with this expanded mission: some are nostalgic for the days when all they did was fight blazes. But, in concert with the evolution of new threats to public safety, strict building codes and other regulations have reduced the incidence of structure fires; in order to avoid becoming obsolete in matters of public safety, firefighters had to adjust.

BINATIONAL SECURITY

In the early twenty-first century, vectors of injury on the border have converged: new technologies and infrastructures of fencing meet changing environmental conditions, and intensification of violence related to drug trafficking in northern Mexico meets counterterrorist tactics on the American side. The range of possible event structures and scenarios that lead to unexpected and dangerous situations stretches beyond what emergency responders have ordinarily been trained to do. On the one hand, this happens because the clustering of politics, weather, infrastructures, legal regulations, economic projections, and terrain increases the chances of their collision at potentially lethal angles. On the other hand, however, more types of events are now coded as threats and thus fall into the domain of "risk management".

As parameters that define an emergency change, so does the meaning of security. In the borderlands, public safety cannot be contained within the contours of the state. Arizona is downstream, downwind, and downhill from Sonora.[49] "What happens in Vegas, stays in Vegas. What happens in Nogales, Sonora, doesn't stay there—it comes and affects us," says Louie Chaboya, former emergency manager and the coordinator of the EPA's Border 2020 program. I stopped counting how many times and on what diverse occasions he insisted: "When we are helping Mexico, we are helping ourselves." It's not only wildfires and flash floods that spread north into the United States, but also chemical spills involving the release of sulphuric acid from derailed Ferromex and Union Pacific trains. Government officials at federal, state, and local levels have long been aware of this situation. In 1983, to protect the environment in the border area, presidents Ronald Reagan and Miguel de la Madrid signed the La Paz Agreement, which obliges both countries to notify each other about emergencies that occur within a zone of 100 kilometers (about 62 miles) on either side of the international boundary. The US Forest Service and the National Forestry Commission in Mexico have an agreement allowing agencies to combine resources to fight wildland fires within 10 miles of the border: US helicopters do water drops in Sonora, while Mexican hand crews come to work in Arizona. In the early 2000s, split cities—Nogales/Nogales, Naco/Naco, Douglas/Agua Prieta, San Luis/San Luis Río Colorado—formalized municipal mutual aid agreements to assist each other in emergencies that threaten the public health, safety, and welfare of residents on either side of the international boundary.

Such cooperation makes sense. The bifurcated towns of the desert are the products of the border.[50] Since their founding in the late nineteenth century along the railroad that transported copper, silver, and cattle, binationalism has been embedded in the urban landscape of Ambos Nogales—"both Nogales," as the split city is called. Back then the boundary line between the two countries ran along the middle of a wide thoroughfare known as International Street (in Arizona) and Calle Internacional (in Mexico); today, the parallel streets are on opposite sides of the border wall. But the logistical infrastructure of Ambos Nogales is intermeshed, both on the surface and underground: the roads and train tracks link Arizona and Sonora, circulating commodities; the wash and the pipes cross the border south to north collecting runoff water and carrying raw sewage. There are talks of creating a joint electric grid. In a binational city built on contiguous terrain, trying to disentangle the two communities according to the jurisdictional boundary conflicts with the pragmatics of public utilities and with the operational logic of emergency response.

Municipal fire departments in Ambos Nogales have a long history of sharing resources. For one hundred years—or as long as the border fence has existed—firefighters have been crossing from one side to the other to help with structure fires, search and rescue operations, and, more recently, hazardous materials incidents. Since Nogales, Sonora, has few hydrants and its water pressure is low, firefighters in Nogales, Arizona, have for decades supplied their counterparts with water, sometimes by hooking hoses to hydrants on the US side and passing them through the gaps in the fence to their peers in Mexico. When the Hotel San Enrique, located steps away from the border in Nogales, Sonora, caught fire in 2012, firefighters in Nogales, Arizona, parked their brand-new fire truck on the American side and extended its 100-foot ladder over the fence into Mexico, directing a powerful water stream at the roof of the burning building down below; they didn't need to cross the international divide at surface level. At the request of emergency responders in southern Arizona, the United States government has helped train over thirty Mexican firefighters in Nogales, Sonora, as hazmat technicians, and many more in the region are now at least operational-level responders. NORTHCOM and EPA, working through local partners, provided them with equipment, such as hazmat kits and the fully encapsulated suits required to contain leaks during chemical and biological emergencies.

Security concerns in the border region, traditionally focused on disease, drug trafficking, and unauthorized migration, have expanded to include more diverse threats, such as fires, floods, and hazardous materials, but this shift has occurred unevenly across the branches of the state apparatus.[51] While city governments have long worked together, and the Forest Service and the EPA recently extended their mandates to areas south of the border, stretching emergency management into Mexican national space and downplaying the significance of the boundary between the two countries, other government units continue to build barriers and highlight territorial divisions. This work is not limited to adding reinforcements along the jurisdictional line; it entails the thickening of the border by creating zones of legal exception.[52] Within 100 miles of US external boundaries, federal regulations give CBP authority to conduct searches without warrants for "aliens" in "any vessel, [. . .] railcar, aircraft, conveyance, or vehicle."[53] This "Constitution-free zone" is wider than the 100-kilometer radius established by the La Paz Agreement, a detail that highlights how the DHS definition of security supplants the ecological perspective of threats underlying the priorities of the EPA. At this disjuncture, it is less surprising that the security infrastructure assembled on the US-Mexico border ends up further exacerbating the intrinsic natural hazards of the desert terrain, and local emergency responders are often the first to palpate the deleterious effects of these constructions.

Nogales exemplifies the misalignment of two security paradigms with different approaches to space. The first, enacted by the CBP, is territorial. It is based on the Westphalian system of sovereign nation-states codified in international law; it is anchored to a piece of land, endowed with nationalist imaginaries, and circumscribed by political boundaries; its operative principle is the defense of this enclosed space, hence the importance of fortifying the barrier—the border wall—as "tactical infrastructure" deployed to control undesirable flows. In recent decades, as the category of risk has expanded to "all threats and hazards," security tactics adapted to the logic of anticipation and preparedness, and adopted practices of pre-emption, including mitigating potential threats outside of the territorial boundaries. Yet this approach continues to rely on a purely legal definition of defensible space. A different paradigm, in this case represented by the EPA, works on scales both smaller and larger than sovereign states. It is anti-territorial, but not anti-spatial: it takes the materiality of terrain very seriously. Rather than considering it as a blank screen on which political aspirations are projected or a physical site of an emergency that randomly falls into one jurisdiction or another, this paradigm acknowledges that the environment, both built and natural, actively produces disastrous events, contingent not on national laws, but on such parameters as the density of particles in the atmosphere.

Emergency responders are caught up in this tension between two paradigms of security. On the one hand, fire and rescue departments across the United States have been integrated into the operations of the national security state, and absorbed into the political and administrative system of federal emergency management. On the other hand, however, their work requires pragmatic engagement with built and natural environment that depoliticizes space and allows for temporary erasure of legal boundaries. On the US-Mexico border, the jurisdictional line brings the disjuncture of these two security paradigms into focus. It is here that we must account for the role of law in deliberately modifying the environment to cause harm. Yet it is also here that we see how in emergency situations the politics of space can be suspended and supplanted by the ethics of rescue that hinge on the primacy of terrain.

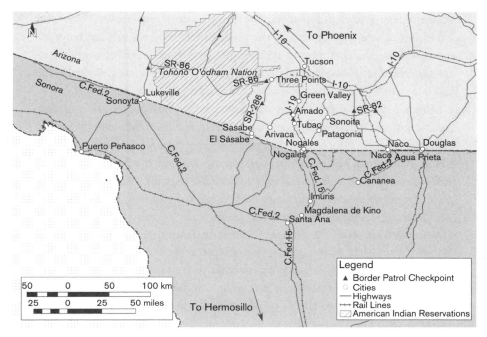

Southern Arizona and northern Sonora border region (by Bryce Davenport).

TOXIC STATECRAFT

Emergency responders work at the splintered space of what Pierre Bourdieu called the "bureaucratic field," where "the left hand" of the state is remediating the negative effects resulting from the actions of "the right hand."[54] They provide rescue services and prehospital health care under conditions of increasing border militarization, precipitated by the "war on drugs" and what has become a "war" on migration. In the borderlands tensions and informal compromises between official doctrines and vernacular cultural forms have always been acutely present.[55] But after September 11, 2001, as fire and emergency medical services became ever more tightly integrated into the national preparedness and homeland security apparatus and invested with political and symbolic functions of state authority, their professional and ethical mandates have been put further at odds. Today emergency responders find themselves caught between the imperative of the counterterror state, or "security logic," and their obligations of rescue and medicine, or the "humanitarian reason."[56] On the frontlines, where they operate at the point of friction between law enforcement and social-humanitarian policies, making choices between order and compassion, firefighters and paramedics simultaneously enact this duality of the state and lay bare the violent impulses at its foundation.

The state is a template. It is an institutional blueprint and a legal form that comes into being through practice, animated by its agents and the social effects of what they do. Max Weber proposed that, like other social collectivities, the state must be studied through "particular acts of individual persons" who orient their action based on the premise that it exists and that it is endowed with normative authority.[57] More recently, Didier Fassin suggested a similar approach to understanding the state as "what its agents do under multiple influences of the policies they implement, the habits they develop, the initiatives they take, and the responses they get from their publics."[58] Like other "street-level bureaucrats" mandated by municipalities to ensure basic public services, emergency responders interpret the letter of the law, fine-tuning the rules to the situation on the ground, and vice versa. "Shot through with the contradictions of the State," as Bourdieu phrased their predicament, they experience the tension between its two hands as "profoundly personal dramas."[59]

Many firefighters and paramedics in towns along Arizona's southern fringe, including Nogales, are Mexican Americans who are regularly profiled and questioned at interior Border Patrol checkpoints, sometimes by agents with Hispanic last names. In an incident in 2015, the police in Tucson followed two firefighters from Nogales, Arizona, suspecting that they had stolen the fire truck they were driving. "No wonder! One of you looks like Chapo Guzmán, the other—like Pablo Escobar," joked their colleagues, referencing two notorious drug traffickers. Their own fire chief used to tell these Spanish-speaking emergency responders that they were "just a bunch of overpaid tomato pickers." Although, as Josiah Heyman has shown, officers of Mexican or Mexican American descent who work for federal immigration agencies tend to see themselves and their relationship to immigrants through the prism of their US citizenship instead of experiencing solidarity along ethnic lines, Nogales firefighters, who are local to the binational border community, have a more nuanced position in the American social hierarchy.[60] They call their town, where 95 percent of the residents are Hispanic, "Nogales, Arizona, Mexico."

Their families are scattered across the territories of two countries, but now these firefighters rescue people who, just as they or their parents once did, are coming for the "American dream." Instead, these border crossers get to live their worst nightmare. Alex's Mexican father crossed the border to enlist in the Vietnam War and, in exchange for his service, became a legal US resident. Years later, surplus panels used as portable touchdown pads for military helicopters operating in that war were repurposed to erect a metal fence that new generations would scale in order to join their kin up north, and Alex had to bandage fingers amputated by its sharp edges. In the vernacular of Ambos Nogales, two popular colloquial phrases—"across the line" and *"al otro lado"* (on the other side)—refer either to the United States or to Mexico, depending on where the speaker is at the time. The sayings imply relativity and arbitrariness, and mark the border as the anchor for making meaning and value. They don't warn that one's position vis-à-vis this border can have fatal consequences.

Because emergency responders have such intimate knowledge and deep experience of the physical qualities of the landscape and the effects it has on human bodies, their perspectives are particularly helpful for exploring entanglements of statecraft and violence on topographies sliced up by political-legal boundaries. Firefighters and paramedics embody and wield the two hands of the state. Their routine work of saving lives requires them to transcend national jurisdictions as the outer limits of knowledge and action, and to overcome the notional contradictions between their ethical mandates as medical professionals and their political-symbolic functions as agents invested with government authority. Yet, from their position on the frontlines of the state, where they deal with its injurious effects, emergency responders also reproduce the dual modality of governance—the split between order and benevolence, or the optic of security and the ethics of rescue.

A threshold is a point of entry. In common usage, the term "threshold" refers to a sill, or a strip of wood, metal, or stone forming the bottom of a doorway crossed to get into a building. But in the past the word had a more nuanced meaning. In Old English "to thresh" was to separate the grains of cereal from the husks and straw by rubbing, shaking, trampling, or beating with a flail. It could also mean to "to beat by way of punishment," to flog with a stick or a whip.[61] As a noun, "threshold" was sometimes used to indicate an obstacle or a stumbling block.[62] The Spanish term *umbral* has a similar meaning, but it is derived from *lumbral,* a combination of Latin *limen* (entrance) and *lumen* (light), literally, an entrance through which light passes.[63] But its closeness to *umbra*—"shade," or "shadow"—is noteworthy.[64] Depending on where the source of light is positioned, the thick beam that holds the arch of the doorway—the *umbral*—also casts a shadow; *subumbrare* is to "to put on shade." Today, scientists talk about "threshold" or "umbral" as the magnitude or intensity that must be exceeded for a certain reaction, phenomenon, or condition to occur.[65] In hazardous materials manuals that emergency responders use, "threshold" refers to "the point where a physiological or toxicological effect begins to be produced by the smallest degree of stimulation"—the moment when exposure to carbon monoxide begins to cause symptoms of headache and nausea, or when nitric acid vapor burns the eyes.[66]

The border is a quintessential threshold of the state. It looks like a margin, both spatial and social, but, as anthropologists have shown, it acts as the core, where political authority is perpetually remade, its legitimacy renewed.[67] At the edges of polity, Begoña Aretxaga wrote, "power is experienced close to the skin."[68] Passport control at ports of entry, metal fences cutting through neighborhoods, x-ray machines above railroad tracks, surveillance cameras, and other minute practices of national governance, as well as its subversion—from tunnels to ultralight aircraft, from guns smuggled into Sonora to drugs trafficked to Arizona—form a mesh that makes the state, in its post-9/11 form, visible and palpable in Ambos Nogales. The border conscripts practices into security logic, pulling more and more actors and things into this all-encompassing project. It is here, as it starts producing noxious effects, that the state reaches its threshold: when the desert ceases being a landscape and becomes a killing field; when the fence stops being an infrastructure of protection and turns into an amputation machine; when an injured body is read as an index of trespass and a sign of potential crime; when rescuers hand their patients over to punitive immigration enforcement authorities.[69]

Threshold denotes the juncture between territory and terrain, when an otherwise innocuous constellation of policies and materials achieves the level of toxicity that is harmful to humans. Violence, Jacques Derrida argued, is "not an accident arriving from outside law."[70] The perspective of emergency responders brings this into light: it allows us to locate the moments the state shape-shifts, exposing violence as the central method by which its power operates. This shape shifting is never complete: biopolitics is not replaced by necropolitics. At the threshold, the state is teetering. Indetermination allows it to use both law and force as tools that coexist at its disposal. The state may still adhere to its normative ideologies of governance enshrined in the Constitution while simultaneously engaging in practices that negate those foundational principles. It both wounds and cares.

As if one state weren't enough, emergency responders on the US-Mexico border operate at the edges of two states, where their physical and legal contours are sharply defined and policed, yet where their social effects ooze across jurisdictional boundaries. They are at the very center of this splintered bureaucratic field, where the state's two hands are enmeshed in a struggle over the matter of public goods: who has the power to define what they are and who is worthy of receiving them. But theirs is a field inflected by the border, which distorts the balance of power even further. While the state's right hand wages wars, the left hand is tied behind its back. The security apparatus swells and sometimes reaches out across the territorial boundary, but national social-humanitarian functions abruptly end where rusted steel punctures the surface of the earth: the other side is somebody else's problem.

POLITICS OF WOUNDING AND OF RESCUE

As a paramedic intern at the Jacksonville Fire Rescue Department, I spent hundreds of hours on an ambulance that covered a poor, predominantly African American neighborhood bisected by the train tracks and I-95. It was 2013, when Duval County was called "the murder capital of Florida," and Jacksonville held some of the highest rates of reported rape and assault.[71] There, on one of city's busiest paramedic units, I learned how to identify arrhythmias, insert IVs, calculate drip rates, and place endotracheal tubes into the throats of patients who had stopped breathing. Injuries that I saw were physical as well as social.[72] There were shootings, car crashes, overdoses. There were people suffering from diabetes, asthma, and mental illness. We ran over a dozen calls a day and throughout the night, snacking on energy bars that hospital staff would leave for us to grab when we brought a new patient to the emergency room. Sometimes, on a rare quiet evening, when sirens paused, we would sit outside the fire station and smoke cigars. These moments of calm never lasted, which may be why I remember them better than the vehicle accidents and the strokes. By the time my internship ended, it had changed how I taught about violence and urban marginality in my anthropology classes. Death from a gunshot wound becomes less abstract once you try to stop the bleeding from a femoral artery.

This book bears the marks of the five years I volunteered as an emergency responder: first an EMT, then a paramedic and a wildland firefighter. Through training, I learned to embody an intimate, pragmatic approach to space and the environment, which changed my relationship with terrain. I remember how, in my early days, we practiced forcible entry on a metal prop, using axes and Halligan bars, and then walked up and down the neighborhood discussing techniques for breaking down different types of doors. When I joined the Micanopy Fire Rescue Department, I learned to drive a fire engine through the narrow streets that bore strange names from the Seminole past: the firehouse was on Cholokka Boulevard and by the end of your rookie period you had to know the fastest route to Wacahoota, Eestalustee, Tuskawilla, and Okehumkee. We learned our territory like a grid—by memorizing each street with two cross streets. Most shifts were slow in this quaint historic town, but a stretch of I-75 ran across the swamps and the prairie that belonged to our jurisdiction and Chief made us cut up a lot of cars to prepare for vehicle extrications on the highway. Cars were dropped off behind the station, and we practiced different ways to use hydraulic tools and hi-lift jacks, do cribbing and roll the dash. Pileups on the highway, especially those involving heavy semi-trucks, stalled traffic for hours.

Emergency responders are attentive to the materiality of terrain, aware of its role in creating emergencies. They listen to the weather forecast: temperature, precipitation, wind speed and direction alter the physical qualities of the landscape in which they work. Rain makes the surface of the road slippery, wind ignites fires and spreads flames, excessive heat strands helicopters on the ground because the air is not dense enough to allow liftoff. This concern for the material properties of the environment is also important for safety. On scene, emergency vehicles are always parked upwind and uphill from a potential hazardous materials incident. Looking at space through the lens of threats—both natural and manmade—is a perspective that I wanted to bring to this book.

But my experience as an emergency responder left another, more profound, mark on this narrative: the mode of storytelling inflected by the language I was taught. Through several revisions of the text, I eliminated unnecessary medical jargon and technical vocabulary, leaving just enough to give the reader a sense of how firefighters and EMTs talk about what they do. However, I could not change what may appear like a cold, detached tone: a methodical description, not soaked with anger or empathy.[73] I didn't do it to avoid sensationalizing trauma, though it serves this purpose well. Rather, it is a consequence of being familiar with the pragmatic approach that EMTs and paramedics need in order to work in emergencies. A life-threatening injury must be treated immediately, but—as in the case of internal bleeding or spinal fracture—it is not always evident. Therefore, the initial response is structured according to algorithms that guide action without the need to pause and think. It's automatic. It's also scripted. First come the ABCs: airway, breathing, circulation, sometimes preceded with an X for exsanguination. We check for DCAP-BTLS in rapid trauma assessment; we ask about OPQRST to evaluate pain; SLUDGE helps identify organophosphate and nerve gas poisoning.[74] Critical interventions in the field happen before emotions seep in. This systematic approach reduces errors in messy situations and provides vocabulary to describe the patient's condition in a way that everyone understands. It's supposed to be accurate and objective. Banished from the scene, emotions may not resurface until days or even years after the event. There is an acronym for that too: PTSD. Recent studies show that the prevalence of posttraumatic stress disorder among firefighters is comparable to that of combat veterans.[75]

It is not until later, when they tell stories about what happened, that emergency responders try to put it in their own words. I recall the evening, when standing around the kitchen counter at the station in Nogales, firefighters talked about the incidents that had made them cry. They remembered the New Year's Day when a ten-year-old girl who lived in a house near the border was shot in the head. The drive-by shooter was aiming at her father, but the bullet ricocheted and killed the sleeping child. They spoke tenderly about a little girl who was chasing after a packet of M&Ms when it rolled under a car—the driver didn't see her, backed up, and the wheel crushed the girl's skull. There was nothing they could do. I understood. I still can't forget the numbness I felt as a paramedic trainee the night we could not save a three-week-old baby who had stopped breathing. It was not sorrow or anger. I didn't cry. I couldn't feel anything, as if my nerves had been severed.

Recounting accidents and describing injuries in their graphic and gory details is the vernacular through which those on scene process their experiences. Sometimes, if you read between the lines, their stories begin to approach social critique. Emergency service espouses heroic sacrifice and an ethics of anti-politics. The Star of Life on their uniforms, like the red cross on medical tents in war zones, signals service to humankind and impartiality in conflicts. But every time they splint a fractured leg in "ankle alley" or run fluids to rehydrate a hypovolemic border crosser, emergency responders experience the disagreements between the state's two hands—the one that enforces order and the one that provides care—in the most immediate way possible, creating a dissonance that may produce moral injury.[76] They don't take sides in the struggle between powers vying to define and allocate public goods. Their anti-political stance is a matter of survival. Firefighters have to rely on each other; in emergency situations their lives are literally in the hands of their peers. Despite their leadership's historical entanglement with local elections and their current placement in a militarized zone, topics that could splinter the brotherhood are taboo. Politics is not discussed at the station. Nor, for that matter, is religion or race.[77] Thus, while these disturbing narratives about amputations and dehydration don't assign blame, they form a record that can be used to reconstruct the chain of events leading to the incident, framed as an accident. Sometimes the stories point to individual responsibility; other times they hint at policy failures.

This difference in how scholars and emergency responders approach violence and social suffering was an important motivation for why I decided to write this book. While the former outline structural forces, focusing on conflicts over politics and the economy and explaining how certain groups of people are marginalized and pushed into adopting criminalized and sometimes brutal survival strategies, the latter find themselves on the frontlines, where policies impact the human body and where action precedes analysis: on the US-Mexico border, they treat the wounded in what Timothy Dunn calls "a low-intensity conflict."[78] Their encounters are with individuals—always a singular, particular case. Yet through years of experience they have noticed patterns, accumulating knowledge of social trends that have had direct effects on the well-being of people in the communities they serve.

When it comes to politics, my goal in this book is twofold. First, I explain the depoliticized stance adopted by emergency responders as a precondition for rescue work. Then I question it. I follow emergency responders to the threshold, where anti-politics becomes unviable. How much trauma is too much? When does it exceed the level that those whose daily job it is to respond to heart attacks and drownings stop considering it "normal"? When do they start recognizing border infrastructure as a weapon? What is the threshold of politics in emergency response?

The structure of this book reflects the effort to capture this ever-fleeting threshold—almost there but not quite yet. A 911 call can be for anything: first responders don't know what they will find on scene. Sometimes, compounded by an unfortunate constellation of forces, emergencies are scaled up. Other times, the run is for nothing. The work of firefighters and paramedics consists of a practiced reaction to surprise. Configurations of events to which they respond are unlimited and they don't follow a logical sequence. A call for domestic violence may be followed by a fire alarm followed by an overdose followed by a quick stop to get teriyaki chicken followed by a bomb threat. The narrative, which stitches up episodes from my fieldwork, replicates this pattern of rescue work. If some stories are incomplete, it's because encounters are often abruptly cut off. Tidy storytelling would obscure the fragmentary nature of emergency work. It would also conceal the surprise element of events as they are experienced by those on the frontlines. The strange, unsettling, occasionally bizarre qualities of the situation do not register until after it's over. Or never at all. What would be an adequate explanation of the run to help a customs agent we found lying flat on a parking lot floor after he ingested crystal meth while scraping the ceiling of a trailer pulled over for inspection? Or another call, for a woman who broke both ankles when she fell off the border wall but asked the paramedic for her shoes? Some stories convey more when left in their raw form, unprocessed. Still others could not be included—it was impossible to do so without violating HIPAA—but nevertheless left their imprint on these pages.[79]

To do this research, I went back and forth between the United States and Mexico, sometimes crossing the border several times a day. I also spent many hours on the road, driving between Arivaca and Nogales, crossing the two Border Patrol checkpoints now permanently set up in Amado and Tubac, and regularly going to Tucson, Sonoita, Douglas, Sasabe, and other towns. The field of emergency expands and contracts depending on the site from which the events are experienced, yet—as my shifting perspective between these sites will show—they cannot be understood in isolation from one another. The threads that entangle these localities are central to rescue work. I begin in Nogales, Arizona, which remains my anchor point as I move across the line to Nogales, Sonora, and beyond the urban perimeter to remote, sparsely populated communities. The book is divided into three parts, held together by the narrative that continues through all of them. Part 1 focuses on tactical infrastructure on the border and the bodies caught up in its traps. It is about bisection. In contrast, Part 2 examines security, understood through a spatial and ecological lens, and the operational landscape of emergency response, which straddles the line. It is about entanglement. Finally, Part 3 looks at how terrain refracts laws and ethics, and their competing claims over vulnerable bodies. It is about survival.

In 2015, when I arrived at the border to start fieldwork, firefighters told me: "You are part of the family." My relationship with Mexican and American emergency responders began even before I met them, thousands of miles away, when I first put on a helmet and rolled hose, and this shared background has helped strengthen our bonds ever since. We shared spatial, hazard-oriented thinking and the habits of pragmatic, functional engagement with the human body and with the physical environment—dispositions acquired through coursework and training exercises as well as real emergency situations. As a member of the first responder community, I accepted my share of the duties. During my time in Arizona I volunteered at the Nogales Suburban Fire District, where, besides staying on shifts at the firehouse, I served as the instructor for medical training. I also accompanied the Tucson Samaritans to provide first aid at the Kino Border Initiative's migrant aid center, known as "el comedor," in Nogales, Sonora. Being there, wearing the navy-blue uniform with the insignia of a fire department and clutching a stethoscope, gave me a more nuanced view of what it was like to provide care on both sides of the line.

Though my experiences in fire and emergency medical services have left a mark on the narrative that unfolds in the following pages, the center stage in the story belongs to the firefighters in Arizona and in Sonora. *Threshold* is about them. They live on the frontlines, where my presence was temporary.

———

PART ONE

Ankle Alley

NOGALES, ARIZONA, MEXICO

"This is Nogales, Arizona, Mexico," Bojo told me when we met in early May 2015. His curly black hair was beginning to recede and, when he bent his head, a gold chain highlighted his thick neck. "The United States begins north of the checkpoint," he said, unsure how I would take it. We sat in the bay, next to the trucks. Bojo preferred it here, despite lingering smells of smoke, rubber, and diesel—the smells of a firehouse—seeping into our lungs. I recognized in him that deep respect for the engine—*his* engine—that is rare among the younger members of the department. "We can go across," he said, meaning Mexico. "But we can't open the fence and just throw lines." The fence is federal property. "But there is a way around it." For Bojo, who is a binational citizen, Ambos Nogales has always been one community, its two sides held together by strong family ties. For the government, this Spanish-speaking region was akin to a foreign country, which prompted setting up a Border Patrol checkpoint in Tubac.

Earlier that morning I sped past the checkpoint (there is no control on southbound lanes), then past a warning to drivers on I-19 South that weapons and ammunition were illegal in Mexico, and took a left-side exit ramp to get off the highway, entering the city from the north. The sign announced: "Nogales; Elevation 3,865 feet; Founded in 1859." Mechanic shops, motels, storage facilities, and supermarkets line both sides of Grand Avenue—the asphalt backbone of this desert town—and the streets that splinter from it to the east and to the west. There's a Walgreens, a Safeway, a Walmart, a JC Penney, a Home Depot; most vehicles in their parking lots display Sonoran plates. Vehicles with Sonoran plates also surround identical square buildings sprinkled all over the town. Announced by colorful signs, only their names distinguish one from another: Carl's Jr., Denny's, Panda Express, City Salads, IHOP, McDonald's.

Nogales has three ports of entry, which explains the proliferation of customs brokers, money exchange, and insurance offices; large signs advertising their services stand tall on the main road. Huge tractor-trailers and semis make wide turns as they descend from the highway to the warehouses, where they drop off or pick up their cargo. Up to 1,600 trucks, loaded with fresh fruits and vegetables from the fields in Sonora and Sinaloa—watermelons, squashes, tomatoes, cucumbers—pass through the Mariposa port of entry every day, accounting for more than a third of all US produce imports from Mexico.[1] Only a fraction of traffic can be inspected without bringing NAFTA-enabled commerce to a screeching halt, allowing licit and illicit businesses to seamlessly converge. CBP press releases cite examples of this symbiotic relationship: on April 21, 2016, customs officers made the third-largest pot bust in Arizona's history when they seized 14,800 pounds of marijuana, worth $7.4 million, comingled in a shipment of watermelons.[2] It happened only a month after a drug-sniffing dog alerted authorities to 240 bundles of pot, weighing 5,700 pounds, hidden in a trailer carrying Italian squash. It gets repetitive, though some captures are more peculiar than others; for example, when the authorities at the Morley gate arrested a woman carrying burritos filled with more than a pound of methamphetamine, or when some men tried to smuggle meth made to look like tamales and hidden in stacks of hollowed-out tortillas.[3]

The city's main street aligns with the train tracks. In 1882, Nogales became the site of one of the oldest railway connections between the US and Mexico—an important trade route between the Sonoran seaport in Guaymas and towns north of the border in Arizona. The construction took half a century because the sonorenses were suspicious of what they saw as an American encroachment on their soil.[4] But commerce interests triumphed over anxieties about national sovereignty. It wasn't just freight. In the 1960s, Ferrocarril Pacífico was inviting passengers into first-class Pullman cars for trips all the way to Mazatlán.[5] Today, Union Pacific trains pass through the city several times a day hauling tanks with propane gas and industrial chemicals, including sulphuric acid for the copper mines in Sonora. Northbound, the railway carries Ford cars from the company's manufacturing plant down in Hermosillo. Before the government stepped up security, undocumented migrants used to hide in brand new automobiles to get past US immigration control. With the gamma ray scanners now in place, it would be reckless to try that today.

Running parallel to the street and the railroad is the Nogales Wash, an intermittent stream that empties into the Santa Cruz River and serves as a major gravity drainage system for cities on both sides of the border. Most of the year, the channel is dry. Pieces of clothing, plastic bags, and other debris may still be clinging to the low branches of trees, lodged there during the previous monsoon. The wash connects Ambos Nogales: it begins uphill in Mexico, where streets were built on top of arroyos and turn into rivers with every rain; flows through a 3-mile-long tunnel in Nogales, Sonora; passes under the wall right beneath the Dennis DeConcini port of entry; and reemerges about a mile north of the border in Nogales, Arizona. Although both cities have made repeated efforts to control the flow of the water, buttressing the main drainage channel with concrete panels, the water digs under these reinforcements, causing cracks and eroding the bed of the Grand Tunnel.

The wash gathers so much water from the arroyos that the powerful current sweeps vehicles off the roads. Running at 30 miles an hour, it has carried away many people unaware of its potential force—visitors from out of town as well unauthorized migrants, who know that the gate inside the tunnel automatically lifts when the water level rises and pressure builds up, but underestimate its power. Bodies have been recovered miles north of the border: some are found without being lost—they remain, unidentified, in a drawer at the medical examiner's office in Tucson; others are lost but never found—volunteers still hike along the wash in hopes of discovering what's left of the missing. Firefighters in Nogales remember how once the arroyo carried away two adolescent girls and their mother. They were part of a group of seven border crossers who were trying to enter the United States through a storm drain that empties into the Nogales Wash.[6] Although it was not raining when they got inside, the wash quickly filled with water further south of the city. Police officers saw the girls first and got into the wash trying to catch them, but they were not properly equipped. "We first had to get the cops out, then the girls," one of the responders recalled. Then they pulled out the mother's body.

Perched on top of a hill overlooking the valley is the Santa Cruz County Complex. It houses the Office of Emergency Management and the Emergency Operations Center—three windowless rooms on the first floor, where cell phones have no signal. Once every three months, when the office hosts the meeting of the Local Emergency Planning Committee, representatives of fire and police departments, state public health services, CBP, and other US agencies sit down and talk together with the Mexican bomberos and delegates of protección civil from Nogales, Sonora. Here, planning for the next emergency unfolds on a binational scale. In 2015, the committee applauded Union Pacific for bringing a training car to teach firefighters from Arizona and Sonora how to secure loose or broken valves on nonpressurized liquid tanks. Railcars carrying hazardous materials have derailed, raising the alert for emergency managers on both sides of the border.

The larger part of the county complex is occupied by the Tony Estrada Law Enforcement Center, with a jail that can boast having the best views of the area. Estrada, who was born in Nogales, Sonora, and grew up a few blocks inside the United States, has been the county's sheriff since 1993. "Tony Estrada *is* the law here," a correspondent for *USA Today* described the situation.[7] In 2016, Estrada appeared in the news as one of several sheriffs vehemently opposed to Arizona governor Doug Ducey's Border Drug Strike Force. "You can't just come in here and do your thing," Estrada criticized the governor's top-down initiative, arguing that more funding should instead go to local counties, which better understand border issues.[8] When President Donald Trump began talking about building a wall with Mexico, Estrada was furious. He compared earlier fences to "iron curtains." "We've got to put up some resistance," said the seventy-three-year-old sheriff.[9] He took it personally when during his campaign Trump alleged that Mexicans were "murderers" and "rapists." "He insulted my people," he said.[10] Not everyone was as articulate as the sheriff, but many nogalenses agreed with him.

For a greater part of the past century, the Nogales Fire Department operated out of the historic building on Morley Avenue, steps away from the border fence. Their first hose cart and pumper, named "Able and Willing," which the volunteers acquired in 1895, is still displayed at the old firehouse, now converted into the Pimeria Alta Historical Society and Museum. Today the department covers an area of 20 square miles and employs forty-two shift workers, split between two stations: Station 1, the headquarters, is right next to the City Hall; you can see Station 2 on the right when you take exit 8 off the interstate. It's just past Villa's Market, which wraps excellent cuts of meat for carne asada in pink paper. In the backyard behind the station, Captain Lopez and his crew toss steaks onto an old, rusty grill over smoldering mesquite. Firefighters enjoy them with tortillas, guacamole, and refried beans.

Dividing Nogales, Arizona, from its namesake to the south, a dark metal fence crawls across the hilly terrain. The people who ordered this wall to be built have come to wield laws as weapons in hopes of protecting the illusion of the national economy and social order. The steel fence in Nogales is but a tiny piece of nearly 700 miles of barriers that have been built along the border between Mexico and the United States. They are not meant to be impermeable: rivers flow north and south; wildlife slips through; even undocumented migrants and drug mules get across. It's not an all-out war. It's about tactical advantage in the never-ending game.[11]

"That's just an extension of this city, and this is the extension of that city. It's just got a border in the middle of it," one fire captain told me. From the perspective of those working in the fire service, trying to disentangle the two communities by drawing jurisdictional boundaries does not make sense. Nogales, Arizona, has just over twenty thousand residents, most of them Hispanic or Latino, settled in one-story houses that climb up the hills on both sides of I-19, images of the Virgen de Guadalupe in their yards facing the street. At least ten and possibly twenty times as many people live in Nogales, Sonora. Hundreds go back and forth every day. Not everyone realizes that the dolares that foreign nationals spend at Home Depot or at Walmart, at Panda Express or at Denny's, fund the Nogales Fire Department. While the four fire districts—Tubac, Rio Rico, Nogales Suburban, Sonoita-Elgin—get a share of the county's property taxes, public services in Nogales, the only city in the Santa Cruz County, rely solely on revenues from the sales tax. Since Mexican shoppers are responsible for up to 80 percent of retail transactions in Nogales, having the streets full of vehicles with Sonoran license plates is a good sign for the local and state economy.[12] The Nogales Police Department doesn't even ticket foreign drivers with expired vehicle registrations, honoring Mexican laws that allow a three-month grace period in the beginning of each year.[13]

Firefighters have a unique relationship to the manmade and natural environment. Most residents take urban design as a given, and law enforcement—in this case, the Border Patrol—modify and use it to gain tactical advantage over unauthorized entrants and drug traffickers. Emergency responders, by contrast, look for "hot spots": they focus on the vulnerabilities and fissures of buildings and infrastructures; they identify the dangers inherent in the topography and material forms that can injure or kill those who use and inhabit them. They relate to landscape through risk. In the United States, where the Emergency Planning and Community Right-to-Know Act of 1986 mandates companies to submit inventory forms for hazardous substances that exceed set threshold values, fire departments have access to confidential information about facilities that store dangerous chemicals in their jurisdictions.[14] The threshold level for gasoline is 75,000 gallons, while for "extremely hazardous substances" (EHS), such as ammonia, chlorine, or sulphuric acid, it is only 500 pounds.[15] But firefighters must look beneath the surface of official paperwork and recognize dangers to life and health lurking beyond the veneer of urban infra/structures. For example, a 13,350-gallon capacity rail tank carrying only 500 pounds (around 33 gallons) of sulphuric acid through Nogales would be considered "empty," even though this residual amount of oily liquid would be enough to cause severe inhalation injury and corrosive burns.[16]

Seeing the city through this conceptual lens allows firefighters to detect structural weaknesses invisible to the naked eye. They have been trained to consider the possibility that every construction and container, given the right circumstances, may fail. Tunnels collapse. Assembly plants and warehouses catch fire. Tank cars leak. On a windy day, fire could use old furniture and appliances accumulated in the backyard as a trampoline to jump from one house to another, setting an entire city block ablaze. A person walking across unfamiliar terrain at night may fall into a long-abandoned mine shaft. The train may derail, spilling toxic chemicals into the wash and contaminating the county's groundwater supply. This last scenario has been popular in training drills and tabletop exercises held in preparation for a possible emergency.

But what actually happens in Nogales often surpasses the wildest imagination of emergency managers. The city's location has attracted the most peculiar infrastructural incidents. In 1999, a suspected drug tunnel was discovered downtown: it had both lighting and ventilation, was reinforced with plywood and cement, and was big enough for a person to crawl through.[17] But nobody knew where it led—searchers who descended into the tunnel bumped into a steel wall and could not advance any further. The fire department's special operations team placed a smoke machine at the tunnel's entrance in a private house and saw that the smoke emerged from under the altar in the Sacred Heart Church. Out of 183 illicit tunnels that have been discovered crossing the US-Mexico border since the mid-1990s, 107 have been found in Nogales.[18] Nowadays, to protect their agents, the Border Patrol sends small UAVs— unmanned aerial vehicles, or drones—to explore them.

Bundles of marijuana have also disrupted the flow of sewage through Nogales. In July 2015, the acting chief called NFD personnel on scene for something that he did not explain over the radio. The following morning local media reported that a cross-border sewer line, which in dry weather carries approximately 15 million gallons of raw sewage from Colonia Héroes in Nogales, Sonora, to the Nogales International Wastewater Treatment Plant in Rio Rico, Arizona, ruptured under Morley Avenue. Video footage from inside the International Outfall Interceptor (IOI) showed drug bundles blocking the pipe.[19] A house just south of the Nogales Medical Clinic was flooded by sewer water, which prompted the discovery of an illicit tunnel connecting it to the Nogales Wash. Officials suspected that the steel pipe was damaged during the process of digging the drug tunnel. Uncanny incidents like these tend to repeat. The IOI, which collects both stormwater and wastewater, runs next to the Morley Tunnel and approximately 3 feet below the concrete floor of the Nogales Wash, creating "three layers of nightmare," as one local public health specialist aptly put it.[20]

Firefighters have seen worse. People have been swept into the sewer, which ranges from 24 to 42 inches in diameter and in some places is big enough to walk nearly upright. A woman who fell into the IOI in Mexico was still alive when they pulled her out in Rio Rico, about 8.5 miles north of the border. "Her skin was badly damaged by the acids in the sewer, but she made it there," recalled Alex, who participated in the rescue operation. Another time two women and a man from Mexico descended into a manhole on Morley Avenue and Washington Street to hide from the Border Patrol. But the wastewater, which can rush at a speed of up to 14 cubic feet per second, swept them away. Rescuers pulled the women out two hours later and miles north, battered and bloody, but alive.[21] The man also survived.

Bojo carries an old photograph of his mother as the background on his smart phone, and has her light green eyes. He was born in Yuma, Arizona, a town where he never lived, and was raised across the line in Nogales, Sonora. His family calls it home. During the Mexican Revolution, his grandmother would walk to the Sacred Heart Church on the US side of the border and return with ammunition belts hidden under her clothing; a small duck lapel on the inside of the collar was a sign to the Mexican border guards to let her through. Growing up in Nogales, Sonora, Bojo played in the downtown area by the train tracks. In the mid-1960s the first maquiladoras opened their doors, and soon the city was full of them.[22] People from other regions who were looking for work eagerly joined the ranks of cheap non-unionized labor in the assembly plants manufacturing electrical appliances, hospital gowns, door knobs, and other products for the US market. The newcomers built precarious houses on the hillsides surrounding the centro. A lot of them were from Sinaloa, and they opened seafood diners in the landlocked desert town. Bojo particularly likes the breaded shrimp tacos served at El Galeno's—we still go there every time I visit.

In 1985, at the age of twenty, he joined the local fire department: Honorable Cuerpo de Bomberos Voluntarios "Gustavo L. Manriquez." A hundred years old, the department now has 120 service members and thirty emergency vehicles. Back then they didn't even have airpacks. "We were real smoke eaters," he recalls: You wet a handkerchief, cover your nose and mouth, and go in. The bomberos were not paid, so they had to take other jobs to support themselves and their families. Bojo worked for the water department across the line in Nogales, Arizona, as a meter reader. The intimate knowledge of the city's water system proved useful when in 1997 he was hired by the Nogales Fire Department and became the engineer in charge of running pump operations. At the station, in the hallway facing the captain's office, there is a large map with colored pins for each hydrant in the city: blue for those with the best flow capacity, red for those with the worst. An engineer knows that water resources dictate the approach to fire. "There are two ways to fight fires. One is aggressive and the other is passive," Bojo told me. In Nogales, Arizona, they take the passive approach because it's safer. US regulations require that hydrants be placed 500 feet from any house. In Nogales, Sonora, hydrants are few and far between. The bomberos have to fight fire aggressively, trying to extinguish the flames with the little water they have. After twelve years of being a volunteer firefighter in Mexico and earning the rank of lieutenant, Bojo was forced into the reserves: NFD did not want to be liable if he got hurt while working south of the border. But his ties with the department in Nogales, Sonora, remain strong.

One slow afternoon at the station he spread the old laminated maps on the table. The top sheet has a grid of black lines to indicate streets and a list of street names with alpha-numeric codes: A1, A2, A3 ... B1, B2, and so on. Once you know which of these close-up maps to look at, it is easy to find the street in question. There is also an atlas for Santa Cruz County maps, which can be used for mutual aid calls. The maps were printed many years ago—they were here when Bojo joined the department— and they are most often used by rookies learning territory for their exams. We looked up several locations where Engine 2 and Medic 2 were last called to an incident: intersection of Mariposa Road and Mastick Way for a motor vehicle collision; Valle Verde Place for a six-month-old with fever and vomiting; 1500 West La Quinta Road for high fever at 09:51, hyperventilation at 17:00, and a pregnant female having cramps at 21:54. West La Quinta Road is the address of the Nogales Border Patrol station. The federal agency owns the county's largest warehouse, but even those 200,000 square feet were not enough to house children who sought asylum in the United States during what President Obama called a "humanitarian crisis" in 2014.

The city of Nogales falls within the jurisdiction of the Border Patrol's Tucson Sector, which covers 262 miles from Yuma County in the west to New Mexico in the east. The sector continues to be a major route for northbound migrants and drug smugglers, even though in recent years more people coming from Central America have been crossing the border in Texas. In 2015, the Border Patrol's Tucson Sector reported apprehending 63,397 unauthorized border crossers and capturing 746,868 pounds of marijuana.[23] These numbers don't say much about anything. There's no hard formula to plug them in and calculate how many people and drugs get across. Yet this fact did not stop the federal agency from using statistics to justify projects that have converted southern Arizona into a testing ground for state-of-the-art security infrastructures and surveillance technologies.

Security buildup began in the mid-1990s with the new national strategy to secure the US southern border with Mexico. The paradigm was modeled on Operation Blockade—a bold and risky move initiated by El Paso Border Patrol chief Silvestre Reyes. In September 1993, heeding criticism of agents' abusive practices, Reyes withdrew the Border Patrol from the city's Mexican American neighborhoods and posted them directly on the Rio Grande, along the patched-up fence, facing Juárez.[24] The operation received much praise in El Paso, and despite their initial skepticism, federal authorities adapted its innovative approach to revise enforcement efforts in other parts of the border region. Launched a year later, in October 1994, when California was mired in intense debates over Proposition 187 (a ballot initiative that called for denying unauthorized migrants access to public services, including education and health care), Operation Gatekeeper proceeded to build 14-mile-long solid fence in San Diego, a statement by the Clinton administration that it was taking border enforcement seriously.[25] Shortly after, Doris Meissner, commissioner of the INS, traveled to Nogales to unveil Operation Safeguard, a plan that borrowed from the earlier experiments in Texas and California but tailored them to the characteristics of Arizona's southern border. Replicating the "line-watching strategy" pioneered in El Paso and utilized in San Diego, Meissner also announced that the Department of Defense would build over 4 miles of fencing east and west of downtown Nogales. "Beyond that the mountains and the desert become useful for us," the commissioner explained.[26] The terrain is "extremely inhospitable," she said, which should work to the Border Patrol's advantage.

Two months earlier Meissner signed a document outlining the new national border control strategy. It was built on the premise that "those attempting to illegally enter the United States in large numbers do so in part because of the weak controls we have exercised over the southwest land border in the recent past."[27] The centerpiece of the Border Patrol's 1994 Strategic Plan was a "prevention through deterrence" program calling for "bringing a decisive number of enforcement resources to bear in each major entry corridor."[28] These resources—an increased number of agents on the line, aided by landing mat fencing, ground sensors, high-intensity lighting, and night vision scopes (to take away "the cover of darkness," as Meissner explained)— were thought to raise the risk of apprehension to the point where many would "consider it futile to attempt illegal entry."[29] The plan predicted that, as a direct consequence of border security buildup in urban areas, "illegal traffic will be deterred, or forced over more hostile terrain, less suited for crossing and more suited for enforcement."[30] After the initial effort to "gain control" in San Diego and El Paso, the second phase focused on the Tucson Sector.

Twin cities, such as Ambos Nogales, which straddled the international boundary and were "sometimes separated by little more than a line in the dirt," were "the areas of greatest risk for illegal entry." The federal agency understood that border crossers "exploited" the urban environment, which allowed them to blend in with the local population, provided them with opportunities to hide in safe houses, and gave them access to roads and transportation. This placed federal agents "at a significant tactical disadvantage."[31] The new strategy had to change the odds in their favor by pushing border crossers further away from towns and onto "hostile" terrain. As one senior official said, "Mother nature has provided us with the barriers."[32] Compared to densely populated urban areas, rural roads "offer less anonymity and accessibility." This gives the Border Patrol tactical benefit. The plan also predicted that as traditional patterns of traffic shifted, smugglers would change methods, fees would increase, and there would be "more violence at attempted entries."

By 1995, the chain-link fence that divided Ambos Nogales for most of the last century had been replaced by 12-foot-high corrugated steel panels. The number of Border Patrol agents in the Tucson Sector had increased to 376; they had two Huey helicopters, five lookout cameras, and six infrared scopes.[33] Such enforcement efforts had mixed effects on crime. According to the Santa Cruz county attorney, there was a notable decrease in felonies in downtown Nogales as it became more difficult for thieves to cross illegally into the United States and run back to Mexico.[34] However, in its evaluation of the seven years of INS southwest border strategy, the GAO also noted an increase in crimes against border crossers pushed to travel through remote areas. "Cases are difficult to make and prove because assailants are seldom captured, crime scenes in remote areas are rarely located, and victims disappear."[35] Despite efforts to deter them, migrants attempted to cross through harsh terrain where the Border Patrol knew they were "in mortal danger."[36] The GAO acknowledges that the strategy "resulted in an increase in deaths from exposure to either heat or cold." By the time "prevention through deterrence" marked its fifteenth anniversary, over five thousand migrants had died crossing the US-Mexico border.[37]

The BP Strategic Plan includes a curious detail: among the indicators measuring whether the efforts at gaining control were successful is a "reduction of serious accidents involving aliens on trains, drowning, dehydration."[38] Border enforcement had to prevent injury and death. But, as with crime, it only changed the patterns. Even more curiously, migrant well-being—protecting them from potential accidents and injuries—became an argument for further hardening the border. During a congressional hearing on the construction and placement of fences, California representative Duncan Hunter noted that people coming across the border were walking through the Yuma testing range, where the US Air Force and Marines train in preparation for deployment to Iraq and Afghanistan. To avoid hurting migrants, the military had to pause their activities. Congressman Hunter called it "a health problem" and "an accident problem," arguing that the 37 miles where the testing range abutted the border should be fenced. "If that testing range was in the interior of the United States [. . .] and you had people wandering into the testing range. The first thing you do is what? You would fence it."[39] In the summer of 2006, when this hearing took place, only 75 miles of a

Pedestrian bollard-style fence gives way to Normandy vehicle barriers east of Nogales.

nearly 2,000-long US-Mexico boundary had some type of fence. Lawmakers agreed to a extend it tenfold.[40] The Secure Fence Act of 2006 mandated the secretary of Homeland Security to "achieve and maintain operational control" over US borders by means of "systematic surveillance" (including satellites, radars, and drones) and "physical infrastructure enhancements" (such as checkpoints and vehicle barriers).[41] With the exception of a short stretch of land near New Mexico, the entire border in Arizona had to be strengthened by two layers of reinforced fencing.

The federal government's approach to the border has since evolved. "The threat and terrain dictates the strategy and equipment [. . .]. There is not one single piece of equipment or technology or infrastructure that is a panacea to border security," explained Manuel Padilla, the former chief of the US Border Patrol's Tucson Sector.[42] In 2007, the Secure Fence Act was amended to allow for more flexibility with regard to terrain. In many areas, building two layers of reinforced fencing did not make sense. Today, CBP accepts that "the border is not merely a physical frontier." Rather, they claim, it is "a continuum of activities where the physical border is the last line of defense, not the first." Therefore, "effectively securing it requires attention to processes that begin outside US borders, occur at the border and continue to all interior regions of the U.S."[43] This approach has justified the spatial diffusion of immigration enforcement, both vertically and horizontally. Collapsing different layers of government and expanding into the interior of the US through 287(g) and Secure Communities programs, local and state police were deputized to act on behalf of federal agencies and arrest people suspected of being in the country without authorization.[44] There is no evidence that this expansion into new fields of surveillance and control has increased security along the border. Rather, what these government policies did succeed at was blurring the lines between previously fragmented forms of illegal activities—human smuggling and drug trafficking—thus further increasing risks to undocumented border crossers.[45]

Still, the show of force on the border that Chief Reyes began over two decades ago and nearly 300 miles away continues. The number of agents had increased fourfold by 2010 and doubled again by 2015, to 3991.[46] And that is not enough: CBP needs to hire many more, but they are having trouble drawing recruits to Arizona. The agency has had better luck with deploying surveillance. Replacing an earlier unsuccessful attempt to create a "virtual fence," in 2011 CBP inaugurated the Arizona Border Surveillance Technology Plan.[47] Expected to be fully operational by 2020, the plan consists of a combination of Integrated Fixed Towers, ground sensors that can detect a single person, and long-range night vision scopes mounted on mobile surveillance trucks. The program will give Border Patrol "ninety percent situational awareness."[48] Israel's giant private military manufacturer Elbit Systems won the government's bid.[49] Working through an American subsidiary, the defense firm will bring to southern Arizona the same security technologies used in Gaza and the West Bank. Integrated Fixed Towers will be equipped with cameras that provide agents with high-resolution video at a range of 5 and 7.5 miles during the day and at night, respectively, allowing them to see "whether someone is carrying a backpack or a long-arm weapon."[50] Seven such towers are already perched on the rolling hills around Nogales. Bojo pointed them out when, in 2015, he took me to see the fence for the first time. Construction of thirty-one others—in Douglas, Sonoita, Ajo, and Casa Grande stations—was still pending.

In Nogales, the paths of municipal firefighters and federal agents regularly cross: at the ports of entry, in the desert canyons, underneath the city. Whenever emergency responders go inside the tunnels, the Border Patrol comes along to provide security. Firefighters teach federal agents how to do confined space rescue. Agents train firefighters for active shooter scenarios. These days, however, they usually meet at the border fence, where NFD ambulances come to collect the injured in the "war" against "illegal aliens." "We don't call them that," firefighters were adamant to point out when they read the draft of this manuscript. But CBP refuses to call them anything but. "We do not recognize the term "unauthorized border crossers," wrote the officer handling my FOIA request. "Does the requester mean illegal aliens?" she asked.

FENCE JUMPERS

May 18, 2015. I pulled into the parking lot behind Station 2 minutes before 8 A.M., the start of the incoming shift. My first day of fieldwork with the Nogales Fire Department was slow to begin. Captain Lopez, Alex, Bojo, and Carlitos were at the dining table, sipping coffee and talking about the news. On Saturday morning two senior citizens from Michigan were killed in a side impact crash—we call it a T-bone collision—when their gray Volvo was hit by a semi-truck on State Route 82. Captain Lopez said he was about to go home when he overheard code "963" on the radio, which stands for "accident with fatalities."

Besides the long dining table, the pages of the *Arizona Daily Star* spread out over it, the station's day room has a flat screen TV, several worn leather recliners, a desk with a computer, a white board, and a stack of folding chairs and tables. The walls are decorated with city maps and posters containing information about Arizona's labor laws, notices on employee safety and health, and advertisements for the state fire school. Next to the announcements board, a bronze plaque surrounded by photographs commemorates firefighter Sterling Lytle; until his death in a hit-and-run incident in 2012, the twenty-five-year-old was part of Captain Lopez's crew. A BP cuff hangs above a small table by the door; once in a while, usually in the afternoons, residents come in to get their blood pressure checked. The kitchen is part of the common space and whoever is cooking or making coffee can participate in the conversations at the table. Three captains, one for each shift, share an office with windows looking out into the bay; the division chief has his own. Sleeping quarters, showers, and the dressing room are located in the back—that's where the rank-and-file retreat to when they want a reprieve from the eyes and ears of the officers.

Angel, the shift's regular paramedic, took a day off to study for a course he was taking at a community college, and asked Scott to cover for him.

Despite having worked for the department for several years, Scott did not speak Spanish, so, as soon as he walked in, the conversation at the table seamlessly switched to English. But we didn't talk for much longer: it was time to start station duties.

Out in the bay, the crew checked the supplies and restocked the ambulance. They then proceeded with engine inspections. Bojo worked on Engine 2, a 1999 Pierce that carries 1,000 gallons of water. "Mi Gorda," he calls it. His fat one. With all that water, it's the department's slowest truck. "But she is one of those sexy voluptuous babes," he added. Though the engine had been nicknamed "Apache," in honor of the Nogales High School football team, everybody now calls it "La Gorda." The guys are scheming to put a picture of a curvy woman on the inside of the doors. Alex took Ladder 2, the smaller of the two the department owned, out to the parking lot in the back and tested its controls; Carlitos started Brush 2, a Ford F550 wildland fire truck. Like Bojo, Carlitos had been a volunteer firefighter across the line before he joined NFD. Firefighting was in his blood, as they say; his father used to be the comandante of the bomberos. When Carlitos was on duty, his wife would often bring their two kids to visit the station; the boys' exuberant behavior earned them the nickname "los talibanes." They both had firefighter uniforms and plastic helmets, and particularly enjoyed playing with Alex.

When the station duties were completed, we got into the trucks and left for the headquarters. The fire department was hosting seventy school-children from Nogales, Sonora. On their day trip to Nogales, Arizona, the kids were scheduled to meet with firefighters and the police, then have lunch at McDonald's. We were all helping with the preparations: setting up chairs for guests from the city government, testing the sound system. Alex and Carlitos were sent to raise the flag behind the Santa Cruz County Honor Roll in front of City Hall. The Honor Roll lists names of soldiers killed in action during America's foreign wars—many men with identical last names; at least half or more are Hispanic.

The call came in around 10:45 A.M., just as the presentation by the Mexican students was about to begin. Over the loudspeaker, the city's 911 dispatcher instructed Medic 1 and Engine 3 to respond to the area west of the Mariposa port of entry for a thirty-year-old female with traumatic injuries from a fall. Firefighters on shift at Station 1 quickly got into the trucks. Although I was riding with Engine 2, Captain Ashcraft gave me permission to accompany his crew, so I jumped inside and buckled up in the rear-facing seat behind the officer. Lights and siren on, it took us only a few minutes to reach the scene of the emergency. Because of the rugged terrain near the border fence—la línea divisora—in this place rescue vehicles couldn't get close to the patient. We left Engine 3 parked on a hill and ran toward the wall.

Lying supine on the strip of concrete that stretches parallel to the rusty metal fence was a young woman, whom I will call Araceli. That's not her real name, but leaving her without one would erase what little was left of her dignity after the steel barrier maimed her body. She had climbed a ladder on the other side, but was unable to hold on to the structure and fell down from a height of approximately 24 feet. Araceli had bilateral open ankle fractures and complained of back pain. We were told that she had been lying there for two hours when a Border Patrol agent found her.

"Ay, mis piernas!" She shouted, grimacing from the pain in her legs.

The rescuers acted quickly. At the direction of JLo, an energetic bilingual paramedic, they removed her sneakers and cut off the bottom part of her jeans to expose the injuries; they cleaned Araceli's feet with normal saline, and bandaged and splinted them using cardboard and tape. A cervical collar was put around her neck to protect her spine from further injury. Araceli was dehydrated, so JLo started an IV to give her fluids. Next, he had to ease her pain. I noticed him struggling to administer morphine while one of his hands was occupied with the saline bag, and I offered to hold the IV set. Captain Ashcraft took pictures of the injured foot and sent them to the helicopter crew waiting on standby. "Quiero agua!" Araceli repeated several times, imploring her rescuers to give her water, but nobody responded to her plea. After her third or fourth attempt, JLo explained that their protocols did not allow them to give her anything by mouth, not even water.

All the while three Border Patrol agents clad in green stood and watched what the firefighters were doing. They had Anglo last names printed on their uniforms and it wasn't clear whether they could understand the conversation between the patient and the firefighters, which was in Spanish. Occasionally, the agents would peer through the fence to the other side, perhaps checking for threats. "Rocking"—the practice of pelting the agents with stones to distract them while smugglers snuck across—was less frequent since the new fence was built, with gaps that allowed agents to see into Mexico, but it was not outside the realm of possibility. Several firefighters now helping the injured woman have experienced what it was like to care for the patient with rocks aiming at them flying over the fence. But that did not happen this time.

Firefighters secured Araceli to the backboard, put her onto the gurney, and pushed her into the back of the ambulance. The mechanism of injury—falling from an estimated height of 24 feet—and bilateral leg fractures qualified the patient for trauma alert, which meant that she had to be flown directly to the University Medical Center in Tucson, the only Level I trauma facility in the region. The fire department could have asked the helicopter to land at the scene, but Holy Cross Hospital was close, so they decided to take Araceli to the helipad by ambulance. En route, Chuy took the patient's vital signs: heart rate in the 140s; she was not hypotensive; oxygen saturation at 95 percent on room air. JLo started a second IV line to administer more fluids. Araceli was still calling for water.

"Se trajeron mis zapatos?" she then asked. Did anyone bring her shoes?

She had broken both of her legs, and months would go by before she was able to walk again. But she was thinking about her shoes—a weapon of the weak, which migrants use against the state and its restrictive policies and against the treacherous desert ready to obliterate them: to walk under the light of the moon, to run from bandits who want to rob and hurt them, and from the Border Patrol agents who want to capture them and send them back to start all over again. Without her shoes, she doesn't stand another chance. Before we left the scene, one of the firefighters collected Araceli's blood-stained shoes and put them into a red biohazard bag. JLo reassured the patient that her belongings were in the ambulance. He then pulled out his cell phone and called in his medical report:

"She is alert and oriented, GCS of 15. She states her pain at level 5. She has two large-bore IVs in place. The patient has no allergies. She is not taking any medications. We are two minutes away from the helipad."

A Border Patrol vehicle was following us from the border fence to the helipad, but they had no more interactions with the emergency medical personnel. They didn't approach the patient again. As soon as we arrived at the hospital, the flight crew got inside. They placed the patient on their monitor. JLo informed the flight nurse of the patient's chief complaint, relayed her signs and symptoms, and described the treatment they had done. Together, they moved the patient to the helicopter and we watched it take off.

On our way back to the station I asked Chuy whether it was his first call to the border fence. It's been about two months since he started working for Nogales Fire, having previously been a volunteer with Nogales Suburban.

"No," the rookie said. "On my second shift I had three. And a structure fire."

By the time we rolled into the station, the dance performance was over. The kids were now getting a tour of the fire trucks. Later they poured into the bay and sat on the floor to hear Mayor Doyle's address. Speaking in fluent Spanish, the mayor of Nogales, Arizona, encouraged the children to stand up to injustice and poverty. "This fight begins in your community," he said. He spoke about the unity of the people on both sides of the border. Doyle's address was inspiring, meant to motivate the Mexican schoolchildren to study hard to achieve their dreams. They received gifts from the department—plastic water bottles. Then they had a few minutes to change their clothes and get their towels ready before they got sprayed with water: an end-of-the-school-year tradition in Nogales. Delighted, they ran under the hose set up as a shower on top of Ladder 1, and screamed.

"They are all wetbacks now," one of the firefighters said, looking at them.[51]

The contrast between the laughter of these Mexican kids and Araceli's cry at the border fence was jarring to me. I needed a pause to comprehend what had happened only a few miles and one hour apart. To the firefighters in Nogales it was just another day at work. They could even joke about it.

TACTICAL INFRASTRUCTURE

"Tactical infrastructure," as the Border Patrol defines it, is not limited to the fence.[52] It includes gates, roads and bridges, drainage structures and grates, observation zones, boat ramps, and lighting and ancillary power systems, as well as remote video surveillance, which together "allow CBP to provide persistent impedance, access, and visibility, by making illicit cross-border activities, such as the funneling of illegal immigrants, terrorists, and terrorist weapons into our Nation, more difficult and time-consuming."[53] Installed on the frontlines of the US government's converging "wars" on drugs, terror, crime, and migrants, tactical infrastructure harms the latter category—people—most. A 2009 report for Congress, using the terms "tactical," "operational," and "deployed," conveys the Border Patrol's mission through the language of combat:

> Border fencing is most effective for its *operational* purposes when *deployed* along urban areas. In these areas, individuals crossing the border have a short distance to cover before disappearing into neighborhoods; once they have entered neighborhoods it is much more difficult for USBP agents to identify and apprehend unauthorized aliens. Also, from populated areas it is relatively easy for unauthorized aliens to find transportation into the interior. For these reasons, all of the border fencing constructed by the USBP to date has been built in urban areas abutting the border, such as San Diego, Nogales, and El Paso. In rural areas, the USBP testified that it has a *tactical* advantage over border crossers because they must travel longer distances before reaching populated areas.[54]

To determine the placement of tactical infrastructure, DHS devised an algorithm called the "border calculus." It was part of the Secure Border Initiative (SBI), a multi-year, multi-billion-dollar program inaugurated in 2005 that combined the expansion of "tactical infrastructure" along more than 600 miles of the US-Mexico border with the creation of a "virtual fence"—a high-tech barrier consisting of surveillance towers that monitor activity and look for incursions using radar, sensors, and high-resolution cameras. Border calculus bolstered the program's credibility by making security appear like science, emphasizing both the spatial and temporal dimensions of enforcement. In the words of Gregory L. Giddens, who directed the Secure Border Initiative, the chart lays out "a very simple algorithm that our ability to respond to a border incursion needs to be much less than the time it takes an illegal alien to get to a vanishing point."[55] This is how he explained the meaning of the lines, dots, arrows, and circles in the chart:

> The middle of the chart has borders, barriers, and fences along the port of entry. If you think about a border town such as Nogales, the time that someone would get to that vanishing point is very short, so you would want to use technical infrastructure to slow them down and allow us to have more response time. This basic border calculus chart and its governing algorithm that we want to make sure we can respond well within the time it takes an illegal alien to get to that vanishing point is what is going to guide us in a very systematic, disciplined manner to lay out the solution in each part of the border by understanding that it will change as we go forward. As we go forward in secure areas, the coyotes and the smugglers are going to react to that, and they are going the use different routes and different parts, and we need to be able to be less bureaucratic and more nimble in our approach so we can be more responsive to that so we can try to predict some of that, so we can be ready.

Temporality adds an important new layer to the conventional mapping of border security. But the chart flattens space (and time) into a two-dimensional system. It fails to account for the height and depth—the volume—of terrain.[56] The fence is not a line on a map that separates two planes. Movements of smugglers and migrants are not limited to the surface of the earth. In a three-dimensional space, they can breach a barrier by passing under it through a subterranean tunnel or using a ladder to climb over it. Initially, the border calculus missed the significance of terrain's volume. But it took CBP only a few years to start embracing "the politics of verticality."[57] Today, agents in Nogales send handheld drones to scout the tunnels extending under the international border, while from Fort Huachuca military base southeast of Tucson, the agency operates unmanned aerial vehicles, including Predator B drones, equipped with radar and sophisticated sensors that can follow movement in real time and distinguish people from animals 25,000 feet below their flight path. Dubbed VADER (Vehicle and Dismount Exploitation Radar), these systems were developed for the US Army to detect enemy combatants planting roadside bombs in Afghanistan, but are now deployed to track men, women, and children who risk their lives for a chance to escape violence, reunite with their families, and join the exploited labor force.[58] Drones work in conjunction with checkpoints. Since 2007, a system of interior roadblocks has proliferated on all northbound roads in southern Arizona, providing visual testament to the extralegal powers that CBP claims within a zone that stretches 100 miles from the boundary of the United States.[59] Checkpoints link the horizontal and vertical axes of spatial border enforcement with temporality: they push unauthorized migrants off the main roads and into the desert, prolonging the "time to vanishing point" not by hours, but by days. "Vanishing" acquires a different meaning here: people disappear in the desert. Aerial surveillance—the eye in the sky—may detect those still moving against the clock on this pale canvas, before the bodily fluids that keep them alive run out. But others are gone without a trace. Vanished before they reach "vanishing point."

A few days after Araceli was airlifted from Nogales and flown to Tucson, I drove north in hopes of finding her in recovery at the hospital. Two rescue helicopters stationed closest to the border, LifeLine 3 and LifeNet 6, can deliver a patient to the regional trauma center in about twenty minutes. It takes over an hour to cover the 70-mile distance by car. All ground transportation halts at a massive Border Patrol checkpoint on I-19 north of Tubac. Since its appearance as a "temporary" roadblock in 2007, undocumented border crossers and long-term residents alike have been avoiding calling 911. Going north to Tucson, where all major hospitals are located, requires them to pass the cameras, dogs, and agents at the checkpoint. If they seek medical care, they may be detained and deported. Paramedics who live and work in border communities understand this fear. Sometimes they can take undocumented patients to Holy Cross Hospital in Nogales, but it provides only basic services. Other times, no matter what they tell patients about the risk of refusing to go the hospital—they tell them that they could die—they still won't risk going through the checkpoint.

Roadblocks annoy residents, who have to answer questions about their citizenship status whenever they leave their communities to go to a pharmacy or a grocery store. Outraged, they have staged demonstrations and monitored checkpoints on Sasabe Highway and on Arivaca Road.[60] Those who protest include liberal activists, ranchers, and libertarians, most of them white American citizens who feel secure to take a stand against practices that impinge on their freedoms and constitutional rights. However, the brunt of profiling falls on Mexicans and Mexican Americans. Alex explained how the checkpoint reinscribes ethnic hierarchies:

> My sister's boyfriend is a typical white guy: he's big, he's tall, he's got white hair, he's bold, he's got a beard. You see him and you think you are looking at Santa Claus—typical white guy. He drove up to the checkpoint and they asked him if he had anything to declare. He said: "Yeah, I've got three hand-guns in the back and my shotgun." And the agent started laughing at him. He goes: "No, it's true. That's what I have." He opened the trunk and the agent looked inside and said: "OK, sir. Have a good day. 'Bye." He never asked him: "Are they yours? Why do you have them in there?" Nothing. "OK. 'Bye." That's all. When I go up there, they usually ask a bunch of questions: "Where are you from? What are you doing? Where are you going?" Sometimes they will send me to the secondary to wait there. And they'll bring the dog. Now even when I drive with the firefighter plates on they'll do that.

I rarely traveled with other people in the car, but, when I did, it was with firefighters from across the line. One time I accompanied three bomberos to pick up donated bunker gear and other supplies in Phoenix. We were riding in the command truck, a red Ford Expedition with "Nogales Bomberos" signs and a Mexican flag. As soon as we approached the checkpoint and started slowing down, the guys took their Border Crossing Cards out of their wallets and were ready to present them for inspection.[61] The agent greeted us. He didn't ask whether we were citizens—probably Mexican plate numbers on an official vehicle made it clear. He only asked whether we had anything in the trailer that we were hauling behind. "Nothing, empty," Pablo, who was sitting with me in the back, said in English. "OK, have a good day," said the agent. Only later, when we made our first stop for gas, did I notice that the vehicle looked different that day: emergency lights on the roof were wrapped in a black cloth. Apparently, the CBP agent at the port of entry instructed the bomberos to cover up the lights so that Americans wouldn't confuse them for a "real" emergency vehicle. There are no official regulations that require Mexican rescue trucks to hide their lights when in US territory, but some agents like to show who is in charge on the border.

As you approach the checkpoint, the speed limit gradually goes down from 75 to 15 . . . Signs command attention: "All vehicles must stop ahead." "Use low-beam lights." "K-9 on duty. Restrain your pets." The agent waved me off before I could utter a greeting.

Beyond Tubac, the snaking highway straightens up, stretching out from Amado to Green Valley to Sahuarita. Vehicle crashes are frequent here—drivers become sleepy as they speed through the desert landscape, which looks the same, mile after mile. A vast crust of dry earth frying in the sun. Tall saguaros. Fanning ocotillos. Dust devils. Sometimes you can see smoke clouds rise from the Santa Rita Mountains. We were still in wildfire season, which starts in spring and ends with the first monsoon rains around the Fourth of July.

Dr. Hann met me in his office at the University of Arizona's Department of Surgery, located on the hospital's fifth floor. The border wall looms large in the emergency room where he works. "Most commonly we see people who are trying to cross the border by trying to climb the wall. In certain areas, the fence is up to 20 to 30 feet high. A fall from that height can be pretty serious. Very frequently we see patients with orthopedic injuries. Ankle fractures are very common, tib-fib—or lower extremity—fractures, and spinal fractures," he said, listing the most common injuries caused by the barrier. "It's a pattern of injury," the surgeon explained. "When someone falls and lands on their feet, the energy is transferred from the feet all the way to the spine. We've had quite a few head injuries as well. With good outcomes. We've also had patients that had devastating head injuries who did not have good outcomes." Dr. Hann has seen the limits of surgical intervention to saving lives on the frontlines—not just on the US-Mexico border; he experienced it in Haiti immediately after the earthquake in January 2010.

"You don't know who is legal and who is illegal. You just treat them," he told me. As trauma surgeons who work in a facility less than a hundred miles from Mexico, he and his colleagues get critically injured patients from both sides of the border as well as on both sides of the law. Undocumented border crossers are not the only ones receiving care here. There are Border Patrol agents who wreck their vehicles on the rugged desert terrain. There have been high-profile criminals from Mexico, including a woman who sustained a bad injury when she was shot in the head. Her recovery was difficult, remembers

Dr. Hann, but despite her family's protests she was repatriated to Mexico. The UMC Trauma Center got even more public exposure in December 2010, following an altercation between three Border Patrol agents and a group of heavily armed men—a "rip crew"—that robbed migrants and drug smugglers crossing through the canyons west of Rio Rico. Agent Brian Terry was wounded in the exchange of gunfire and died while his colleagues were rushing him to the hospital.[62] On shift that day, Dr. Hann treated one of Terry's assailants, who was shot during the confrontation. "I think it was his liver, colon, and stomach ... suffice to say, he had quite a few injuries." The man lived and, after pleading guilty to first-degree murder, is serving a thirty-year sentence. Trauma surgeons don't always know the legal circumstances surrounding their patient's critical condition. They focus on what needs to be done to save a person's life: suturing arteries to stop the bleeding, lowering intracranial pressure to prevent brain herniation. "We don't care where they are from and what their nationality is, how much money they have. None of us cares about that. We just take care of them."

The Emergency Medical Treatment and Active Labor Act of 1986 (EMTALA) requires ambulances and hospitals receiving Medicare funds to triage, treat, and stabilize any patient who seeks emergency services regardless of ability to pay or legal status. But injury and illness are not distributed evenly across the national territory, and neither are the costs of treatment. The deployment of tactical infrastructure on the US-Mexico border, which injures those who are undeterred by the government's security policies, has placed a considerable burden on health care providers in southern Arizona. Under Section 1011 of the Medicare Prescription Drug, Improvement, and Modernization Act of 2003, the federal government designated funds to compensate ambulance companies and hospitals for emergency care of undocumented migrants, but the reimbursement program ended in 2008.[63] However, the Border Patrol continues to bring about fifty patients with fall injuries to UMC every year.[64] UMC treats anyone who needs care, but most of the costs incurred by undocumented patients are written off because few are able to pay. Financial concerns have pushed the administration to seek ways of sending stabilized patients back to their country of origin. The hospital has an international patient services coordinator who works as a liaison with foreign consulates and helps locate adequate options abroad. Because so many of their patients have been from Mexico, over the years UMC has built relationships with health care providers in Sonora. Preparing a discharge plan for an unauthorized border crosser from Mexico is thus easier than sending patients back to Honduras, El Salvador, or other countries that don't have established ties with Tucson-area hospitals. Dr. Hann:

> From my standpoint, the frustrating thing is . . . you know with absolute certainty that the care that they get here is as good as anyone else's. The ones that go back to Mexico, you really wonder what's gonna happen to them. For example, patients with spinal fractures who need rehabilitation, they can hardly move. Once they go back to Mexico . . . I'm assuming most of these people who were trying to climb walls to get to the States don't have a lot of financial resources to begin with. Now they go back to Mexico in an even worse physical condition, having suffered pretty significant injury. What's gonna happen to them in terms of their ability to survive in their environment? What's their follow-up going to be? If there is a surgical complication, what's gonna happen to them? They are not gonna come back to the States to get treated. Say there's a hardware infection, what happens? I don't know. These are things that are unsettling, but at the same time it's . . . it's reality. Where does our care end?

I didn't find Araceli at the hospital. A woman at the information desk referred me to another woman in the administration who kindly agreed to look for her in the admissions log. But she was not there. Patients who arrive at the hospital through the Border Patrol are not registered under their real names. They stay at UMC for a few days and then they are taken to the Border Patrol station for processing. Some are detained and others are transferred to Nogales, Arizona, for immediate deportation. Mexican migration authorities meet them at the port of entry and transport those who need medical treatment to the Hospital General Nogales, where they stay until they are well enough to travel back to their hometown. Araceli could be anywhere now.

In 2015, the Mexican Consulate registered 59 Mexican nationals hospitalized in Tucson.[65] May was the busiest month: 11 cases. In 2016, they counted 66 people, 12 of them in March, 10 in July. Most of these were fractures caused by falling off the "muro fronterizo"—even the consulate calls it a "border wall," not a fence. Other common reasons for hospitalization included dehydration, injuries to the feet (blisters, cuts), and GI problems from drinking contaminated water. The consulate also registered bites by poisonous animals, spontaneous abortions due to severe dehydration, drowning in the arroyo during the rains, sexual abuse by human traffickers, and ingestion of cactus. The numbers may seem low, but that is because the consulate only learns about a patient when either the Border Patrol or the hospital lets them know. On the other side of the border, Juan Bosco migrant shelter in Nogales, Sonora, accepted thirty injured people in June 2015 alone. That year the consulate and the migrant shelter both reported an increase in serious injuries along the fence.[66] Ricardo Pineda, the Mexican consul in Tucson, said that they were seeing more migrants in need of medical attention from falling off the border wall than from crossing the desert. Most of them were women with fractures to their feet, ankles, or legs. Gilda Felix, the director of Juan Bosco shelter, told the press: "They think it's easier than walking for days in the desert but it's not. [. . .] It's the same crossing through the wall or through the desert, both difficult and dangerous."[67]

Several weeks went by before I saw JLo, the paramedic who treated Araceli, again. He heard that a woman in Nogales, Sonora, complained on the radio about the ill treatment by the Border Patrol. She said that when she fell off the fence, she was left lying there for hours. She said she saw Border Patrol agents passing through, but they didn't stop to help her. JLo was sure it was Araceli. "It seems she has been just deported back to Mexico," he told me. Shortly afterward, news media in Arizona circulated a story about a thirty-one-year-old woman from Oaxaca who spent twenty days recovering from injuries to her legs and spine at Juan Bosco shelter for migrants in Nogales, Sonora.[68] She told the reporters that she paid smugglers $13 to climb a ladder propped against the fence, but once she reached the top, she didn't know how to get down and slipped. A Border Patrol agent spotted her two hours later. She broke both of her legs and her spine. With the assistance of the Mexican Consulate she was being flown back to Oaxaca, where she was looking at a six-month recovery before she could walk again. Her injuries meant that she could no longer work to pay for the needed therapy and continued medical care, the newspaper noted matter-of-factly.

It may or may not have been Araceli. Hers is but one among many painful stories echoing back and forth across a militarized border.

In the middle of the nineteenth century what is now the steel wall separating Mexico and the United States in Nogales was just a small pile of rocks, "a pyramidal monument of dressed stone."[69] It was put in place by the Joint United States and Mexican Boundary Commission, sent to survey and map the region following the US-Mexican War. Lieutenant of Topographical Engineers Nathaniel Michler described "the pretty little valley of Los Nogales [. . .] clothed with rich green verdure," contrasting it with "the bleached barrenness of the Colorado and Gila" that they encountered to the west. In the 1890s, when the

US-Mexico boundary commission sent the Corps of Engineers back to the line, the pyramid of stones left in Nogales during the first survey was replaced by a 6-foot tall four-sided obelisk and renamed Boundary Monument 122.[70]

The origins of the fence that divide Nogales, Arizona, from Nogales, Sonora, may surprise many. The historical record shows that it was first proposed to protect Mexicans. Due to their strategic location, during the Mexican Revolution border towns became battlefields. Stray bullets that crossed the boundary line killed a handful of Americans. Rising anxieties about security, amplified by refugees seeking shelter in the United States, warranted the placement of National Guard troops on the border. There was no physical barrier between the two sides: the bodies of armed soldiers walking along the boundary enacted the division that was otherwise unmarked. According to historian Rachel St John, the idea to construct a 6-foot wire fence was first raised by the presidente municipal of Nogales, Sonora.[71] Mexican authorities hoped that it would prevent US soldiers from accidentally shooting Mexican people. The mayor didn't survive the Third Battle of Nogales, but the US government followed through with his plan and extended a single strand of barbed wire separating the two cities. In 1929, it was swapped for a 6-foot chain-link fence, which was later doubled in height downtown. This fence remained the material form of the border for most of the twentieth century. Still today, residents nostalgically remember the so-called "picket fence" between neighbors.[72] It served as a marker of the international boundary for legal purposes, but it let the sights and sounds get through. The fence was easily disassembled during parades on official American and Mexican holidays, allowing ties between the communities to be maintained.

William Sanchez, assistant chief of the Nogales Fire Department, remembers that unauthorized crossing was very common. "When it used to be the old fence, people would cross, go in and out. Not a big thing." Many of those who worked in the fire service were local, and over the years they experienced changes to border infrastructure as residents of these towns. "When we were kids, we used to cut through the fence and go buy bread and stuff over there [in Mexico] and then come back," another firefighter told me. Another reminisced about a man on a bicycle who would bring lemons and cheese from Nogales, Sonora, to sell them at the fire station in Nogales, Arizona. The fence was there, but it didn't mean much to anybody.

However, in the mid-1990s, Operation Safeguard brought to Nogales the Border Patrol's "prevention through deterrence" strategy. The new metal wall separating Mexican and American urban spaces was made from surplus steel planks that the US military used as portable pads for landing Hercules cargo planes and Huey helicopters during the Vietnam War.[73] Even the US Army Corps of Engineers, who designed the M8A1-style solid corrugated steel panels, acknowledged the flaws of their construction: the landing pads had rough edges that frequently ripped the tires of heavy aircraft. By the end of the war the military had replaced them with aluminum mats, relegating M8A1s to taxiways and parking lots.[74] After Vietnam, landing mats were easily repurposed for other ends. Measuring 12 feet long, 20 inches wide, and a quarter-inch thick, and weighing 147 pounds, the panels became free "army surplus" and were redeployed to the US southwest border.[75] Each mile of fence required 3,080 metal sheets.[76] By 2006, they were used to build over 60 miles of border fence in California, Arizona, and Texas. In Nogales, the new rusty steel barrier was first erected in 1994. In the beginning, it stretched for nearly a mile, but was soon extended to 2.8 miles. Depending on the location, the landing mat fence was 8 to 12 feet high, and it was "enhanced" with features to make climbing over it more difficult. The community didn't like it, as even Commissioner Meissner admitted. "We would love to build more aesthetic looking fences," she said, but it would be "extraordinarily more expensive."[77] Despite their initial enthusiasm with free construction materials, the Border Patrol soon noticed the drawbacks too. "The landing mat fence, it is opaque," Chief Kevin Stevens said in a congressional hearing.[78] The solid texture provides border crossers with tactical advantage. "They have time. They have time sitting on the foreign side to be able to attempt to defeat it."

In 2011, the landing mat wall was removed to build a sturdier and taller bollard-style barrier, made of rectangular steel tubes reinforced with concrete, with metal plates on top. Extending up to 20 feet above the ground and 10 feet below the surface, this wall was designed to act as a more effective deterrent against climbing over or digging under.[79] See-through fence was also safer for the Border Patrol: officers could anticipate "rocking" and, a year after the fence was completed, assaults on agents were down by over 60 percent.[80] Even residents were reportedly happier with the face-lift: 4-inch gaps between bars allowed them to hear mariachi music, watch neighborhood movement, and chat with their neighbors.[81] At least that's what was celebrated in the press.

If you talk to the locals, not many would say they like the barrier. On the Mexican side, it went from being known as *el cerco* (the fence) to *el muro* (the wall).[82] In October 2015, Tijuana artist Ana Teresa Fernández enlisted bystanders to help her paint a stretch of the fence west of the Dennis DeConcini port of entry in Nogales, Sonora. In her performance, rusty dark brown bars turned blue, merging with the color of the sky and becoming "invisible." The project was called "Borrando la frontera"—erasing the border. One of the men who picked up a brush, dipped it into a bucket of blue paint, and worked alongside Fernández was a deportee separated from his family in the United States; another was a Mexican police officer.[83] Dozens of volunteers joined the effort to create the optical illusion that the wall had "disappeared." But the art project didn't change anything. A Nogales resident told a news reporter: "I wish it was magic like that, but you can't just erase it."[84]

"When they first built the fence, I worked for Nogales Fire and we had a lot of people jumping the fence and breaking their ankles," remembers a former city paramedic who is now a captain in a district further north of the border. The same sharp edges that damaged the tires of the military fleet in Vietnam caused large gashes, limb amputations, and degloving injuries to the people who were scaling the barrier separating them from jobs at construction sites, hotel kitchens, and vegetable fields in the north.[85] "When they were climbing down, [border crossers] would slip and their hands would get stuck up there, so they would get their fingers cut off," is how Alex described it.

The border sliced those who challenged it, cruelly mutilating the bodies of men—it was mostly men back then—who were coming to find work. "They would land on this side, and the finger parts would land on the other side, usually; or they would get lost between the plates, so we could never get them out," Alex recalls. They had to tell the injured people that their fingers were gone. "I don't know how many times we searched and searched and searched and never found the fingers." He continued: "In some places they used to have openings at the bottom [of the fence] with grates on them for the water to go through. You could still see across and you could see the fingers [. . .] on the other side of the border, and the people were over here. Sometimes we would reach over and grab the body part, [. . .] and put it on ice." Other times people on the other side would pick up the fingers and hand them over the fence. "We would use trauma dressings, 4x4s, and lots of ice packs."

The Border Patrol knew about this. Chief Stevens, who oversaw the Nogales station in the early 2000s, mentioned the injuries when he spoke to the US Congress:

> People were climbing over the top of the landing mat fence depending on the height of it or, in some cases, they would put ladders up against it and come

over the top. One of the things I experienced when I was in Nogales was people who were not really physically capable of climbing the fence on their own, they would get assistance to climb the fence and then not be able to handle their own weight when they came over the top of the fence and we would have people losing fingers on the fence, we would have people breaking ankles coming to the ground with compound fractures. That was among the things that we were faced [with] that prompted us to place an additional structure on top of the fence that even with assistance, somebody who was not physically strong would not be able to negotiate the fence. It stopped those people from even trying and significantly delayed even the most able.[86]

"I thought it was just inhumane," Alex said about those dispatches to the border fence. "One time we went to a call where the guy cut off his finger. I think it was his index finger or his pinkie . . . I can't remember which finger it was. One guy was stabilizing him and the other guys were looking for the finger. And we saw a piece of his finger being carried away by ants. The ants went into Mexico and they went into the ant hole with a piece of his finger."

I was warned not to take stories like these for granted. In a conference room in Washington, DC, where I gave a presentation about the tactics of security and the gory details of trauma to an audience of anthropologists, colleagues criticized me for believing these narratives, which they said were exaggerated. Firefighters always boast about their calls, they told me. I knew that rescue stories can become heroic tales, with each repetition further removed from reality. Back on the border later that spring, Alex and Bojo, who responded to that call when the ants carried a piece of a finger into an ant hole in Mexico, shrugged their shoulders, and said: "But that's what happened." They reached a consensus that it was the pinkie. The genre of everyday life on the line was best described as magical realism. It didn't have to sound reasonable to be true.

In Douglas, about two hours east of Nogales, paramedics have also treated numerous trauma patients. "We are not seeing just closed fractures. You see the bone sticking out," said Gerardo, who became a Cruz Roja volunteer in Agua Prieta at the age of fourteen and has been working for Douglas Fire since 2009. His colleague Jorge, who also began in the Cruz Roja in Mexico and later joined the fire department on the US side of the border, said it was actually worse "before they built the big fence." But wounds didn't stop when the new barrier came up: "We had a lot of falls from the fence. We had head traumas, back injuries, pelvic fractures." They often ended up going to "ankle alley" two or three times a day.

Over the years, the changing design of the barrier has produced different types of wounds. While the earlier version, made of corrugated sheet metal, caused gashes and amputations, the present border wall is difficult to hold on to and results in multi-system trauma. Most commonly, these are ankle, tib-fib, or femur fractures. Once, when Nogales Fire Department was tied up working a structure fire, two paramedics from Rio Rico came to provide mutual aid in the city: "We went to the border. A lady had paid to go up a ladder. She decided she didn't want to jump, and, whoever she paid pushed her off the fence," one of the paramedics told me. "There's a good 10 feet of jagged rocks near the fence. When she fell, her ankle was so severely broken it was almost amputated from her foot. She had tib-fib fracture, possible femur fracture, and her foot was literally separated. She couldn't even feel it. When I put my hand to palpate, I could almost put my fingers through, I could see my bloody glove."

Calls to help the injured along the border fence could be dangerous. While the Rio Rico paramedics were trying to stabilize the injured woman—start an IV and splint her foot—they heard something hit the steel barrier. At first, they thought it was gunshots, but it turned out somebody was throwing rocks. Border Patrol agents who were with the paramedics ran to hide behind their vehicles. "It's almost like a war zone. You have the good and bad fighting against each other, but you are literally in the middle, trying to take care of the patient. And we did," the paramedic said. Such incidents were not frequent, but they did happen. "We secured her foot as best we could with a pillow splint because it was about to fall off her body. We did our C-spine precautions because she was pushed over 20 feet." When they took the patient to Holy Cross, she was immediately airlifted to the regional trauma center.

Few knew these dangers better than JLo. As a paramedic, he is regularly dispatched to help people at the fence. He looks petite in the company of his peers and punctuates his sentences with "neta" and "güey." JLo is careful and attentive to detail—during downtime between calls he sits at the dining table with a tiny screwdriver replacing damaged iPhone parts, a side job to help pay the bills. When on scene, he acts fast. Once we were called to a residential apartment community to check on a woman who complained of high blood pressure. As we were rushing to wrap the cuff around her arm and take her vitals, Frank jumped and shouted: "Un ratón!" There was a mouse. JLo immediately turned to the patient: "Is it your pet, señora?" When she shook her head, he straightforwardly asked: "Do you want us to kill it for you?" She didn't seem to object and JLo crushed the mouse with his boot. It was not the first time this happened. In the firehouse, the guys used to call him Percy, after a character from the movie *The Green Mile,* the one who killed the pet rodent Mr. Jingles in the prison.

JLo didn't plan on becoming a firefighter. He wanted to join Border Patrol. With a criminal justice degree from Pima Community College in Tucson, his chances of being hired by the federal agency were fair. But when the twenty-one-year-old went in for a medical exam, he was told he had poor vision and needed surgery. "I was really disappointed," he remembers. Thinking that he was too young to undergo vision correction, JLo accepted an invitation from his brother-in-law to volunteer at the Nogales Suburban Fire District. He became an EMT, started at the fire academy in Tubac, and two months before he got his certificates, JLo was offered a job at the Nogales Fire Department. It was 2002. Six years later he finished paramedic school and, after a brief period working in Tucson, decided to return and stay in the border town.

Some stretches of the wall are more perilous than others. In downtown Nogales, there is an offset landing with cement and rocks, where most dramatic injuries occur. "That's probably about a 4- to 5-foot area, like a sidewalk, but with rocks sticking out from it," JLo said. We were having chilaquiles and menudo for breakfast at El Zarape, a Mexican restaurant right in front of the fire department headquarters. "What other reason are these there for?" Bojo chimed in, referring to the rocks near the fence. "They are there to injure people so that they couldn't run from the Border Patrol," he said. The firefighters knew this from experience, having responded to help numerous patients with orthopedic, spinal, and head trauma on that small piece of land right next to the CBP parking lot.

"We had people that landed on their head and died," one of them said. In February 2012, a forty-four-year-old man from Oaxaca, Mexico, died on the west side of town when he sustained head and neck injuries. Two years later, in March 2014, a forty-one-year-old man from El Salvador died from head trauma after falling from the border fence near the end of Short Street.[87] In 2016, the Nogales Police Department was investigating the death of a thirty-two-year-old woman from Juchitepec in the state of Mexico whose body was found near the border wall east of Nogales. She, too, had fatal injuries after possibly falling off the fence, the police said. Security buildup on the border was largely based on weaponizing the already difficult physical terrain. To emergency responders the causation was obvious: they did not hesitate to implicate the agency in deliberately altering the landscape to cause

A strip of asphalt with rocks along the border fence in Nogales, Arizona.

serious injuries to those who did not have the required documents to cross through the designated port of entry.

The fence constitutes what EMTs call an MOI, "mechanism of injury": the forces that act on the body to cause damage. Protocols regulating prehospital medical services list the conditions under which emergency responders must transport patients to a major trauma center, often by air.[88] It includes anatomic and physiologic criteria, such as penetrating injury, amputation of a hand or a leg, fractures of two or more long bones, or a Glasgow Coma Scale of less than 14. But even when these signs and symptoms are not evident, falls from heights greater than 20 feet for adults and two times their height for children—that is, any falls from the border wall in Nogales—are severe enough to raise the index of suspicion for life-threatening blunt trauma: skull fracture, tension pneumothorax, internal bleeding. This mechanism of injury alone warrants immediately transporting the patient to a hospital with a surgical unit. Such patients are placed in a helicopter that passes above the checkpoints and lands in Tucson less than half an hour later. The Border Patrol and the Mexican Consulate decide what happens when they are stable and can be released. From the medical perspective, the current bollard wall in Nogales is thus worse than the previous corrugated steel fence: finger amputations did not trigger trauma alert. Those wounds were bandaged at the local hospital, and an hour or two later the ambulance would return the injured to the line.

POR OTRO LADO

In Nogales, Sonora, a few blocks west of the port of entry on Calle Internacional, there is a building covered with bullet holes. They date from the night of October 10, 2012, when Border Patrol agent Lonnie Swartz, standing on the US soil, aimed his gun through a gap in the fence and shot sixteen-year-old José Antonio Elena Rodríguez. The Border Patrol accused José Antonio of throwing rocks at the agents and police officers who responded to a call about suspected smuggling. The autopsy showed that ten gunshot wounds were angled from the back to the front: the teenage boy was hit from behind. A federal grand jury indicted Swartz in 2015, but the trial has been delayed several times.[89] Since the shooting happened through the fence, with the Border Patrol agent standing in one country and the victim in another, the case presents a legal limbo. In a similar cross-border shooting in

The street corner in Nogales, Sonora, where Border Patrol agent Lonnie Swartz killed Mexican teenager José Antonio Elena Rodríguez.

Texas in 2010, when Border Patrol agent Jesus Mesa Jr. shot and killed fifteen-year-old Sergio Adrián Hernández Güereca, who was also accused of throwing rocks across the Rio Grande from Ciudad Juárez, the court ruled that Hernández's family had no grounds for a lawsuit because at the time of his death he was a Mexican citizen standing on Mexican soil. These cases raise a question of whether, in binational border towns, constitutional rights should apply extraterritorially.

When Bojo showed me the place where José Antonio died, he waited until I took pictures of the bullet-pierced wall, a small colored poster with the boy's face, and a simple white metal cross below, decorated with flowers. Then he told me to look around: the rusted brown fence, 20 feet tall, was looming high on a rocky cliff, at least 25 feet above the street. "Do you think they could throw rocks up there?" he asked. I said it seemed impossible. James Tomsheck, the former head of CBP's internal affairs, had the same impression when he visited the site: "There was no potential for José Antonio to have thrown any projectile from where he stood when he was shot that could cause injury on the US side of the border, not even if he were a major-league baseball pitcher."[90]

The border conduces injury and emergency care materially as well as legally. The physical barrier produces trauma directly, when individuals fall from the top, and indirectly, by creating situations that raise the level of violence and the potential for wounding, such as when migrants suffer assault or dehydration in the desert. Or, as in José Antonio's case, when the fence provides impunity for those launching rocks and bullets across the jurisdictional line. But its permeability also applies to emergency care. Sometimes the border saves lives.

NFD call records show that in 2015 there were 337 occasions when emergency responders provided medical services at ports of entry.[91] They are often dispatched to transfer patients brought to the border by Mexican ambulances, sometimes from as far away as Guaymas or San Carlos in the western part of the state. Some of them are American citizens or legal residents who get critically ill or injured while on vacation in Sonora or who live there because of cheaper medications and affordable health care services, and return to the United States only when their medical condition seriously deteriorates. Given that in northern Mexico the closest hospital with trauma surgery capabilities is in the state capital, about 200 kilometers south of Nogales, critical patients have better chances of survival if taken to Tucson. If they have no passport or visa to enter the United States, the port director has the authority to provide humanitarian parole, which allows them to cross the border to seek medical assistance that is not available in Mexico.[92] CBP has no hard rules regarding this practice. Officers at the border crossing use discretionary powers to issue humanitarian parole. Joe Agosttini, then the assistant port director in Nogales, who had worked for the agency for over thirty years, told me in 2015 that this only happens "on a case-by-case basis and depending on the circumstances." Once in a while CBP refuses to grant entry to sick or injured people or accompanying family members who can't present proper documents. Nogales firefighters have returned without patients they were called to pick up because the agents would not let them through. In those situations, Bojo said, "we feel like shit."

The arrangement wasn't always like this. Until the mid-1990s Mexican ambulances regularly crossed the border to take patients to Holy Cross Hospital in Nogales and further north. Officials at the port of entry did not even ask Cruz Roja volunteers for their visas. But this practice has been discontinued. Agosttini said it was because they were concerned about allowing the entry of emergency vehicles that may not meet safety requirements: "If they get involved in an accident, if the person suffers beyond the injury that they already have—it's all about liability, insurance, lawsuits. You know how it is in the United States: they sue you for anything." He explained that the state of Arizona and the federal government have firm guidelines for ambulances, which must be covered by insurance and meet strict regulations and safety standards. Emergency responders, however, say that the Cruz Roja stopped coming north after a few instances when US authorities busted Mexican ambulances loaded with drugs.

There are exceptions to the rule. In "life-and-death situations," for example, when a Mexican ambulance is carrying a baby in an incubator, or if a patient is intubated and needs to be on a ventilator, agents use discretion. Transferring patients in such critical conditions is very difficult, so the paramedic talks to the agents at the port and they usually give them permission to go through. They form a convoy: the NFD ambulance goes first, the Mexican ambulance follows, and the CBP vehicle trails behind. Once the patient is transferred to hospital personnel, NFD and CBP escort the Mexican ambulance back to the line.

Emergency responders have seen how such exceptions work. In July 2007, firefighters in Nogales, Sonora, heard a report about an accident on a highway looping around the city and three of them rushed to the scene. "It was typical Nogales," Victor recalled. "There was so much water that you couldn't see anything. When they were going downslope, the [fire] truck lost traction, it yawed and, when it turned, it hit a post. The impact was strong enough to break the windows." One firefighter was ejected and run over by a passing vehicle. The rain continued and the arroyos flooded the roads, preventing the ambulance from reaching the location of the accident. The injured bombero was loaded into the bed of a police pickup truck and taken to the closest clinic. But he could only get first aid there, so they soon decided to transfer him to a bigger hospital. "I got inside with him. I remember his body bouncing around. The doctor began working. We took off his shirt and everything. They began intubating him," Victor remembers. At the hospital, they learned that his condition was critical. "They were telling us that he needed a head surgery because his brain was swelling. There were two options: either take him to Hermosillo or to Tucson." It was a three-hour drive to Hermosillo, while Tucson was less than an hour away by helicopter. "Por otro lado?" they asked. And we said yes, por otro lado." The bomberos decided to rush the injured firefighter to the other side. "When we get to la línea, NFD ambulance was waiting there, but to avoid moving the patient the Americans let our ambulance cross into the United States." After about ten days in Tucson, where the surgeons had to open the skull and remove a piece of the cranium to reduce pressure from the swollen brain, the injured firefighter was transferred to Hermosillo, where he underwent more surgeries and therapy. "The bill was sky-high," Victor said. But the doctors didn't charge for their work, so the bomberos ended up paying reduced hospital expenses.

The border also becomes rather flexible in emergencies that involve small children. After the June 2009 fire in the ABC Day Care Center in Hermosillo, where forty-nine children died, twelve infants and toddlers, with burns covering from 17 to 80 percent of their body surface, were treated at Shriners Hospitals for Children in Sacramento and Cincinnati.[93] More recently, on June 30, 2015, nine-year-old Michel Tapia and her younger brother were playing by a pool in a ranch near Cibuta, a popular place for city dwellers to spend weekends located about 20 miles south of Nogales, Sonora, when the girl was hit by lightning. Her family immediately pulled the unconscious child out of the pool and called EMS. Two bomberos on duty at the station in La Mesa met them at a checkpoint on the federal highway about 13 miles south of Nogales.[94] A police officer drove the ambulance while they performed CPR all the way to the hospital. Once they reached the emergency room, the girl regained pulse, but remained in critical condition. Michel was then taken to the port of entry, where an NFD ambulance picked her up and took her to Holy Cross Hospital in Nogales, Arizona. The next day she was transported to the intensive care unit at the University Medical Center in Tucson, where, despite binational rescue efforts, she died.

The international boundary regulates emergency care in ways that may appear straightforward. The fence marks on the map and on the ground where Mexican jurisdiction ends and US jurisdiction begins. It divides the two sovereign domains. But boundary treaties and other formal agreements are a claim to sovereignty, a performative act, rather than a description of an existing social reality.[95] The threshold of the state is a space of discretion. Those who enforce the línea divisora, drawing their authority from the law and displaying it as insignia on their uniforms, and those who undermine it work together in negotiating the meaning of the border and the extent of its social effects. The legal membrane and the material barrier that separate

Mexico and the United States are simultaneously rigid and flexible. They allow some to get through, while they stop others.

One summer afternoon about a decade ago a man crawled under the landing mat fence south of the Morley gate, but did not succeed at what the US law designates an "illegal entry"; he was trapped. Emergency responders from both sides of the border were dispatched to the scene, where they found the man wedged halfway under the metal sheets: his upper body was in Nogales, Arizona, but his legs remained in Nogales, Sonora. He pleaded with the bomberos, who got out their hydraulic tools, to pull him back into Mexico; he didn't want to end up in the United States, where the Border Patrol was waiting to take him into custody. The bomberos tried, but without success. "We couldn't get him out here. We had to push him over there," Temo told me. The man was injured and NFD took him to the hospital in Nogales, Arizona. They don't know what happened to him next. Temo remembered an unusual detail about the unlucky border crosser: he was barefoot. Before the bomberos arrived the man shouted at passersby to help him out, hoping that one of them would pull him back into Mexico. Instead, somebody stole his sneakers. "Que chiste!" What a joke! Temo laughed, telling me about this incident, just one of the many he witnessed during his career as an emergency responder on the US-Mexico border.

A locksmith by occupation, Temo spent fourteen years volunteering for the Cruz Roja before he joined the bomberos. His passion has always been rescue—confined space rescue, high-altitude rope rescue, water rescue. He left the Cruz Roja because of what he described as dire shortages and mismanagement of the organization. It was so bad, he told me, that once when they were transporting a patient experiencing a heart attack, the ambulance broke down. "Except it didn't break down. Later, when we checked, we realized it had no fuel," he remembered. After a couple more similar mishaps, Temo left. At the fire department, he became a hazmat technician and participated in special operations, which included search and rescue.

In April 2015, Temo was on the team sent to find a lost Ecuadoran migrant. She called C4 and said that she had run away from the guías because they tried to assault her.[96] However, she couldn't tell them where she was. Unable to trace the position of callers who use cell phones, operators are trained to ask lost migrants what they see and use "points of reference" to determine their approximate location. "I saw a water tank" or "I saw the Virgen de

Guadalupe" become the coordinates with which they work. The woman said she saw green trees. Because the desert west of Nogales is dry and flat, the bomberos thought she must be on the east side. "We walked approximately 8 kilometers, for five or six hours, until dawn," Temo recalled. C4 also sent the police and Grupo Beta on this call—the Betas, which are part of Instituto Nacional de Migración (INM), provide services to migrants and often know what trails polleros use to take them to the US. Sometimes, C4 also coordinates the rescue mission with the Border Patrol, since by the time the lost person calls for help, he or she may already be in Arizona. It seems that's what happened to the ecuatoriana: they found a woman's footsteps and followed them until they crossed into the United States. The Border Patrol reported the next day that they captured her north of the line. "She was dehydrated, very tired. But she was alive," Temo said.

Temo was assigned to estación central, the closest firehouse to the border. The old three-floor building has an antenna and a siren on the rooftop. The latter is rarely used these days: there are shift workers on duty 24/7 and volunteers who are not present when the tones go off hear the call on their radios. A spacious event hall on the second level has wooden floors and large portraits of men in formal uniforms, honoring the founders of the department. A balcony upstairs is made up of pillars shaped like nozzles, and holds the city's first hand-drawn hose cart, which the bomberos bought (together with 400 feet of hose, two oil lamps, an axe, and rope) from the firefighters in Nogales, Arizona. Founded in 1917, of the Honorable Cuerpo de Bomberos Voluntarios "Gustavo L. Manriquez" is the country's third oldest fire department after Veracruz and Mexico City.

The station is pegged to the ayuntamiento, a historic white building that houses the offices of the municipal government. Despite their proximity, the fire department is not legally bound to the local administration. Article 22 of Ley 161 de Protección Civil establishes that city administrations in Sonora are in charge of providing fire service to the community, but it leaves the authorities with a range of options to accomplish this, from having the municipal government itself render these services to using organizations formed by social groups and the private sector.[97] While Hermosillo, Ciudad Obregón, and some other Sonoran towns have municipal firefighters, bomberos in Nogales are autonomous. They are a private nonprofit organization: the statutes, adopted in 1945, define the fire department as an institución de beneficiencia privada, formed by a group of Nogales residents for humanitarian and philanthropic purposes and functioning "in perfect harmony" with municipal, state, and federal authorities.[98] The local government now pays wages to thirty-four bomberos, who work in shifts; the rest—in 2017 there were seventy-five—are volunteers. The ayuntamiento also buys fuel for their trucks. This arrangement costs city authorities less than if they ran their own department. "We are paid by the government, but we don't depend on the government," is how one of the bomberos put it. "We have nothing to do with politics. We work thanks to citizen support," the comandante of the department, Manuel Hernández, explained. Unlike in the United States, there are no federal or statewide standards regulating fire service in Mexico. There are no national EMT or paramedic certifications. There is no OSHA.[99] Emergency responders work under the Good Samaritan law and their services are free.

Built on the rugged terrain of a steep watershed, Nogales, Sonora, has been subject to destructive flooding. Efforts to control the washes began in the 1930s and 1940s, when the International Boundary and Water Commission constructed approximately 5 kilometers of covered channel and 2.1 kilometers of open channel on both sides of the border.[100] In the 1960s, the task of completing the four-sided cement encasing known as the embovedado fell under PRONAF, a national urban development program spearheaded by Mexican president Adolfo López Mateos.[101] Although the plan was to extend the covered channel to the city limit, the works stopped short of it. In the 1980s, a private company picked up where the government had left off, but the haphazard urban development throughout the twentieth century outpaced the improvements to the drainage system.

One of the major tributaries of the Nogales Wash is Arroyo Chimeneas, which spills over from the same-name reservoir created to contain it, rushes down Avenida Tecnológico, enters the embovedado, and continues through the Morley Tunnel into the United States. During the rains, the powerful current of the runoff used to sweep vehicles into the tunnel, compelling the authorities to install metal bars along the edges of the street. Chimeneas is not the only wash that causes trouble in Nogales. The Cemetery Wash, which has a tributary inlet at Calle Reforma, turns east when it reaches the border, runs parallel to the fence under Calle Internacional, and then bends north again, passing under the Dennis DeConcini port of entry. This is where people, not cars, get carried away. The bomberos once rescued an undocumented migrant who was holding onto the grate bars of the storm drain a few yards from the wall: they used "jaws of life" to cut the bars and pulled her out. Another time, when several border crossers were stuck inside the embovedado, shouting for help, the bomberos told them to go across into the US:

"There is a gate on the Mexican side, but at that time we didn't have the key," Victor explained. Now the storm drain along the fence is covered with new metal bars that are too thick even for the hydraulic tools.

To avoid such situations, every time the forecast predicts significant rain, the bomberos and protección civil warn residents to avoid certain parts of the city. But it is not the locals they should be concerned about. "The American dream does not belong to Mexicans," one firefighter told me. "Here, in Nogales, we have people that came from South America. There are people that travel on the train and spend twenty-five days to get here with a hope of reaching the United States." These newcomers don't know how the water behaves in northern Sonora. "We don't know of any people from here, from Nogales, who were involved in an accident in an arroyo. Es siempre gente de afuera," he said.

Between 2008 and 2015, eighteen people were killed on the streets that turn into washes in Nogales.[102] Among them was a forty-three-year-old woman who was traveling in an SUV with her husband and her son when the floodwater hit the vehicle, sweeping her into the arroyo.[103] Firefighters formed mixed Mexican and American teams and walked the wash on both sides of the border. The bomberos could not use any of their detectors to monitor oxygen levels inside the embovedado since they had run out of the gas used to calibrate them, so they borrowed equipment from the firefighters in Nogales, Arizona. But their search in the tunnel did not yield any results. The helicopter spotted a body miles north of the border in Arizona, and the family went there to identify the victim. When they asked the Mexican Consulate in Nogales how many of those carried away by the arroyo remained unidentified, the officials couldn't give them an exact number. They only said that there were many. Rescues are rare.

Emergencies related to the washes serve as a poignant example of how the built and the natural environments of the binational city have converged, with harmful consequences. Even the bomberos sometimes find it difficult to navigate the faulty juncture between natural topography and urban infrastructure. In September 2012, five firefighters were dispatched to rescue a woman reportedly caught by the arroyo. When they left the station, the bomberos made a left turn to go up the street, against the direction of traffic on Avenida Tecnológico. In this part of town, the right and left lanes are separated by a cement barrier, and the left lane is lower than the right. As they continued to go up the road, hoping to intercept the woman floating downstream, they saw a cascade of water rushing toward them. They panicked and

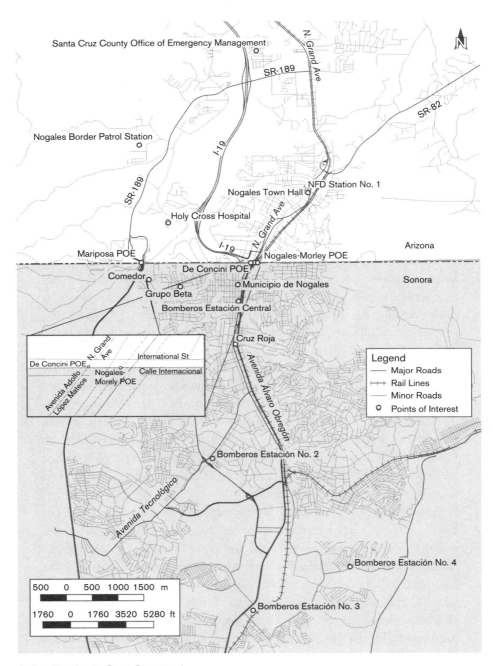

Ambos Nogales (by Bryce Davenport).

tried to turn around, but got stuck. Afraid of drowning, the bomberos sought shelter on the roof of the engine. It was a wrong move—four of them were swept away by the current; the fifth person, who stayed inside the cabin, called "Mayday" on the radio. Further down the street, where the wash widens and becomes shallower, they managed to get out. But the light green engine, trapped in the muddy waters of the arroyo, was no longer good for service.

The legally interstitial space between Mexico and the United States—the no-man's-land outside either country's customs and immigration control—has also been the site of emergencies. Sanchez was a rookie firefighter when one day in the 1980s he was called to the border for an injured person. He remembered that the incident involved two brothers riding a truck loaded with contraband. They approached a Mexican police checkpoint, and something happened; Sanchez was not sure of the details. Whatever it was, the driver turned around, the police officer shot at them, and the passenger was hit in the head. "The kid tried to make it all the way back to the United States, but the truck stalled 10 feet before they reached the port of entry. The driver got out, ran this way, all full of blood, and surrendered to customs." By that time, the Mexican police who had been chasing the vehicle also got to the port. Everybody pulled out their guns.

> We show up there and there's people pointing guns at each other. We are here saying: "Oh my God, what is going on here?" You have everybody—customs, police, DPS—pointing guns that way and Mexican law is out there. We go see the guy that's being detained—he's all full of blood. We say: "Man, where are your cuts, what's wrong with you?" "No," he says. "It's not me! It's my brother! They shot him!" "Where's your brother?" we ask. "He's still in the truck."

"The US boundary is about 30 or 40 feet before you reach the customs building," Sanchez explained. "By law, the truck was in the United States, but they [the Mexican authorities] wanted it. They thought it was in Mexico. They wanted the truck because it had money and everything." Sanchez was assigned to go and check whether the person in the truck was still alive. "So I'm walking there, with my stethoscope like a white flag. I'm looking—everybody is pointing their gun. Man, we're gonna have a shootout here at the port, I'm thinking. It would take one knucklehead [to] go buy a firecracker in a store and you're gonna have people shooting." When he reached the stalled vehicle and looked inside, Sanchez didn't doubt that the man was dead. "He had the whole side of his head blown off," he recalled. "It took almost an hour before everybody put their guns away and started talking to each other: "No, no, here's the line and this is the United States." The situation deescalated. "Sure enough, the guy had so much money and all that contraband in the truck. No wonder they didn't want to let them advance." Sanchez said he felt lucky that nothing happened. "It was the one time when I asked myself: my God, what the heck am I doing here in the middle of everything?!"

Not every standoff ends the same way. As a thirty-year veteran in the department, Captain Beyerle, whom everyone called Billy Bob, was one of the city's first paramedics. He has seen his fair share of bad injuries, close to and far from the line, yet whenever I saw him at the firehouse, he always wore a smile under his white mustache; on his days off he paired it with a cowboy hat and a large silver buckle on his leather belt. Billy Bob told me about one time he went to pick up a patient from the port of entry:

> There were Americans with their rifles and there were Mexicans with rifles. He was a high cartel guy. He got into a gun battle and he headed for the border and they shot him in the leg. They had a line right there: if he's on this side, he's on the American side; if he's on that side—he's on the Mexican side. He fell on our side of the line. He had a gunshot to his leg, so we were going to transport him to the hospital; that's our protocol. But the Mexican police came up to that line, and said: "No, you are not going to take him. We're gonna take him." "OK, he's a Mexican citizen. He's yours. Take him." They weren't about to let that son of a gun get out of their eyesight, so they dragged him back—literally, dragged him back—onto the Mexican side.

Billy Bob laughed when he told me the story. "What are you gonna do? You're not gonna fight over a patient with people with guns!"

In the 1990s, the Nogales Fire Department had a policy that required emergency responders to wear bulletproof vests when they were called to an incident near the border. This was primarily a measure of protection against rocks and potential bullets launched at Border Patrol agents from the Mexican side of the fence. Firefighters were easily confused with law enforcement, so the mandate extended to them. But they didn't like wearing bulletproof vests, which were strapped to the seats of the ambulances. "The vests were very, very heavy. You couldn't work with them," Captain Lopez remembered. So they didn't use them.

Nogales was not impervious to the violence unleashed in Mexico when, in the aftermath of the 2006 election, President Felipe Calderón deployed the military to the frontlines of the drug war. It was nothing compared to Michoacán or Ciudad Juárez. But in 2009, following a split between two formerly allied organizations—the Sinaloa and the Beltrán-Leyva cartels—the groups started competing for the plazas on the northern border and the situation in Sonora deteriorated.[104] In those days the bomberos also carried bulletproof vests on their rigs. On his smart phone, Victor showed me photos of an SUV in a ditch: in 2009, a group of sicarios who didn't know the local topography crashed their vehicle in Nogales. Several died. When the bomberos came to extricate the victims, they saw weapons and grenades in the car. The scene wasn't safe. "By the order of the comandante we couldn't go and do our job until the area was secured by the police. If the scene wasn't safe, we would not go in." The police had no other choice but to remove the bodies themselves.

"Violence became normal," Canizales said about those years, when, besides holding the rank of a lieutenant at the fire department, he headed the city's civil protection office. "As a first responder, you began to see rising levels of violence, executions. Here we are talking and there . . . rat-at-at-at-at-at . . ." In one incident, a shootout broke out between the federal and the state police and the cartel men. At some point, bullets perforated a gas tank and the house where the alleged criminals took shelter caught fire. "One of the police agents got shot and he was lying there, flames licking his face. The police wanted to get him out of there, so they called the bomberos." Canizales continued: "They asked for our ambulance. They trusted us more [than Cruz Roja]." Victor agreed: "People respect the bomberos. Even los malos have respect for the firefighters." But the scene wasn't safe. "There were bullets flying everywhere," they recalled. The bomberos didn't go in. Instead, they showed one police officer how to charge the hose, so he could drive the fire truck to the burning building and drag his injured colleague out.

When violent crime in Sonora escalated, Arizona feared a potential spillover. "It got pretty bad across the line," Captain Lopez said. "But it didn't trickle to this side . . . We did expect it was going to happen. We got prepared for it. We already had an incident action plan in place." But they didn't need to use it. The Sinaloa Cartel retook control of the Nogales plaza and the smuggling routes in the area, and by 2012 the violence had abated. "We prepared for the worst, but it never came. It just left a black eye on the city's image."

What came instead was something nobody had thought of preparing for.

OVERPAID TOMATO PICKERS

June 20, 2015. The dispatch announced over the loudspeakers:

"1500 La Quinta Road, Border Patrol Station. Female having a seizure. Medic 2 and Engine 2 respond."

We headed south, then west, under the I-19 overpass, and south again, upslope toward the commercial port of entry. Before reaching customs, we made a right turn and after a short drive up the hill we were facing the gate to the fenced-in grounds of the Nogales Border Patrol station. The gate was closed and a sign with a CBP logo declared:

> WARNING
>
> NO TRESPASSING
>
> RESTRICTED AREA
>
> KEEP OUT
>
> AUTHORIZED
>
> PERSONNEL ONLY

A Border Patrol vehicle approached us in less than a minute. The agent got out and opened the gate. We went inside, the ambulance first, then the engine, passing a large parking lot with an impressive fleet of Ford Excursions and other types of trucks, all white with green stripes. Many of them had cages mounted on the bed; that's where they carried detained UDAs, "undocumented aliens," when they picked them up along the border fence downtown or out in the canyons. On the radio, "UDAs" sounded more technical and discreet than "illegals." The cages into which they were shoved were not tall, and during those rough rides to the station, even when seated, UDAs would bang their heads on the roof.

"Look at that!" Carlitos exclaimed, pointing to the horse stables.

"I haven't seen those before," said Alex.

"This is where the taxpayer money goes," Bojo chimed in. With no captain on duty, he was the acting officer for the day. He sat in front, next to the driver. I was in the back with Alex. Steve and Frank were in the ambulance.

As soon as we approached the entrance to the facility, we got off and hurried down the hallway, which ended at locked metal doors.

Last year this large warehouse was full. Steel-fenced cages with rolls of barbed wire on top were full of children. "Kids were cramped inside como animalitos," Bojo told me. Like little animals. The Nogales Fire Department sent an ambulance up here several times a day, making rounds between the Border Patrol station and Holy Cross Hospital. Children had asthma attacks. They fainted. One had chickenpox. Another had a 104°F fever. A seventeen-year-old pregnant girl was taken to the hospital for labor pains and nausea.[105] "If that don't break your heart, nothing will," Billy Bob told me about those runs. "I'm a cowboy type of guy. I've seen cattle being herded just like that: put all your bulls over here, put all your cows over here. And here it's: put all the Guatemalans over here, put all the Hondurans over here." Thousands of unaccompanied minors detained along the US-Mexico border, many in South Texas, were brought to Nogales for processing. In June 2014, the station housed around nine hundred children, just a handful of over sixty-eight thousand minors apprehended along the southwest border that fiscal year.[106] "There's a lot of desperate people in this world. Enough to go home and just kiss your kids and say, 'Thank God I was born on this side of the border'," Billy Bob said. "As sad as it sounds."

I had been to the Border Patrol station before.

My first call was "in reference to a 17-year-old male juvenile with fever." That time Captain Lopez told me to ride in the ambulance with Scott and Frank. Once inside the building we passed shelves lined with water jugs, supplies, and belongings taken from the detainees, all placed inside transparent plastic bags. On the right and on the left were cells with numbers: some of them were full, others marked as empty. Several Border Patrol agents stood behind a counter in the main hall, with monitors hanging above their heads—not unlike a check-in desk at an airport. There were several signs in Spanish warning that crossing the border is dangerous. "No cruces el desierto" was written on a red poster attached above the door to cell no. 1. Emphasis was put on the words "muerte" and "peligro." Some adolescent boys pressed their faces against the dark glass of the cell, watching what was happening. On the opposite side of the hall, a cell with a sign that said "FEMALE" was occupied by young women and girls. Agents seemed to be busy. Three detainees from cell no. 1 were taken to collect their belongings—the small plastic bags from the shelves. A female detainee was called by her name, and an agent escorted her from the cell to the counter for processing. The facility had no windows; it was hard to tell the time of day.

The adolescent boy, whom I will call José Luis, was sitting on a bench outside of cell no. 1. He was wearing a white T-shirt with "Cozumel, Mexico" written on the front. Did he used to work there, serving American tourists? Has he been there on vacation with his family? Was the shirt a donation he picked up at one of the shelters along the migrant trail during his trip to El Norte? Questions swirled in my head as I pictured the contrast between the tropical beach resort and his present surroundings.

A representative of the Mexican Consulate, dressed in a black uniform, told the paramedics that the boy had been complaining of fever: 99°F, according to the Border Patrol. Scott asked Frank to check it again with their own thermometer: it recorded 102°F. The agent at the counter told us that José Luis was apprehended around seven o'clock in the morning, after walking in the desert for eight or nine hours. He didn't drink any fluids while he was walking, the agent relayed, but they gave him food and water at the station. When he talked to the boy, Scott needed help from Frank to translate for him. Via Frank, José Luis said that he had recently taken a Naproxen pill, an anti-inflammatory drug used for reducing pain and fever, which he carried in a hidden pocket.

"A secret pocket?" asked one of the agents, when he overheard the boy's confession, sounding surprised but nonjudgmental.

Frank took the rest of the boy's vital signs and ran an ECG. José Luis was slightly tachycardic, which was a normal response to fever and dehydration. Scott asked the Border Patrol agents whether they wanted the boy to be taken to the hospital. One of them replied that if José Luis wanted to go, then he should go. But when Frank translated for the boy, José Luis said he would be fine. "No, no es necesario," he said. Scott then asked the agent whether their protocols allowed them to start IVs, and got an affirmative answer. He said if they took the boy to the hospital he would be given IV fluids and medication to reduce fever. That's all. Since he was probably just dehydrated, Scott reasoned, he could receive fluid treatment right there in the facility. "I would give him two bags of fluids," he said.

"How about fever meds?" he then asked.

The agent explained that their protocols did not allow Border Patrol to administer medications to reduce fever, although the detainee could take a pill if he already had one with him. That's where those secret pockets become handy! According to the fire department's protocols, Scott and Frank could not administer NSAIDs either. Seeing the absurdity of the situation, I said that I had some ibuprofen in my shoulder bag and that I could give it to José Luis. This was not in anybody's protocols, but there were no objections. I located two red Advil caplets and handed them over to the agent, who glanced at them briefly and gave the medications to the boy. José Luis put the pills inside the pocket of his pants and thanked us.

We walked back to the ambulance in silence. "Public assist. Medic 2 is available," Scott notified the dispatch.

There were two other calls for medical emergencies at the Border Patrol station later that same afternoon. May was the busiest month; in 2015, eight out of nineteen times NFD responded to the Border Patrol station were in May.[107]

But June didn't seem much different.

A Border Patrol agent who was monitoring the camera at the metal door buzzed Bojo and the crew in. We walked past two or three rows of young men sitting on the cement floor. In front of each—a plastic bag containing their possessions. They were either being prepared to be transferred to a detention center or to be deported. The officers who were watching over the youths looked up at the firefighters.

"The whole crew!" one of them said, appearing surprised. Nobody reacted to the agent's remark. Instead, addressing the detainees in Spanish, Bojo asked: "Como están? Están bien?" Some of them returned a barely audible "bien."

Ana, our patient, was sitting on the bench in front of the women's cell, supported by another female detainee. She was in her late twenties. Steve asked two Border Patrol agents what had happened, and they said they had brought her in earlier this morning. She was picked up in town. They reported that she had been shaking as if she was having a seizure. Ana had told the agents that she had a history of seizures, but she didn't say much more. She kept her eyes closed and would only give short answers to Steve's questions. She complained of nausea and we were told that she had thrown up before we arrived.

The firefighters took Ana to the ambulance, where Steve started an IV and administered medications to relieve nausea. Bojo told me to ride to the hospital in the back of the unit, which they always asked me to do when the patient was a female—for the comfort of the patient as well as the paramedic. In this case, I could also help to translate since Steve spoke limited Spanish. The ride was short and uneventful. By the time Steve finished giving the medical report to the base hospital, we were at the emergency room.

We ran other calls: there was an incident with a dog locked inside a vehicle the owner had left in the sun outside of Walmart; a run to the elder care facility for a woman who had altered mental status and had to be taken to the hospital for a checkup; a call from a young man living in an apartment overlooking the valley who complained about bees making a nest under the roof of his balcony. By the time Engine 2 finally returned to the station, the crew was hungry. Food was taken seriously in this firehouse. Three large refrigerators—one for each shift—had locks on them. Even the kitchen cabinets were locked. Only those who worked together had the keys to what was theirs—no "borrowing" of milk or sugar from other crews. At least not officially; lock picking was the last resort. It was entertaining to watch when it came down to that.

But today they were too tired to cook. After some deliberation, a consensus emerged: tacos dorados. These were not ordinary tacos, but the street tacos from across the line. Mexican tacos. Bojo offered to pick them up and I volunteered to go with him. "It's not big deal," he said, though I still had doubts about how we'd be able to buy tacos from Mexico. We couldn't cross the border, not while on duty.

Bojo drove to the end of Morley Avenue and parked in a spot designated for law enforcement. From there, we could see a train slowly crossing the border: railcars passing through a scanner located on one side of the tracks, and CBP agents observing it from the other side. We walked to the fence, which in this part of town was made of metal sheets with small round holes, and spotted a taco vendor on the street corner on the other side.

"Taquero!" Bojo shouted. We waved. He shouted again: "Oye, taquero!"

Finally, the taco vendor saw us and approached the fence. Bojo counted the pesos and dollars that he had in his hand:

"We want tacos for 384 pesos." That should get us fifty-four tacos, he calculated.

Bojo instructed the taquero to put salsa in a separate container so that the tacos wouldn't get soaked while we drove back to the station.

"We'll meet you at the entrance."

The man walked back to his stand, and we headed to the pedestrian gate at the Morley port of entry, its old wooden building now encapsulated by the modern, more expansive infrastructure of border inspections. Three CBP officers were checking people's IDs—most of them young women— coming across through a rotating metal door. Bojo told the agents that we had ordered tacos from across the line and asked them whether we could wait there. They didn't object, though they did not seem enthusiastic about the request. We stood under the roof of the port, where cool air provided relief from the triple-digit temperature.

About ten or fifteen minutes later the taquero approached the turnstiles. Over the metal barrier Bojo handed him the pesos and took two white plastic bags containing tacos dorados. He walked straight up to the CBP officers and lifted the bags he was holding in his hands:

"Do you guys want to check it?"

The agent at the middle station smiled at Bojo. He didn't look inside the bags and he didn't say anything, just shook his head.

"Do you want to try some tacos?" Bojo then asked.

"No, thank you." It was the only time the agents said anything to us.

We walked back to the brush truck, content that "Operation Tacos Dorados" had gone smoothly.

Back at the station we had a feast. Once the tacos were gone, we pulled the recliners together, forming a semicircle around the TV and watched *McFarland, USA*. The film began with a white American family moving into a predominantly Mexican neighborhood in California. Bojo, Alex, and Carlitos laughed when Mr. White, or "Blanco," played by Kevin Costner, took his wife and two daughters to a restaurant. They were looking for a burger, but were told to choose from a menu consisting of tacos, burritos, enchiladas, and other types of Mexican food. "Tacos. We'll take the tacos, thank you," Mr. White decided for his family. When the waitress asked him what kind of meat they wanted for their tacos (asada, al pastor, chorizo, cabeza, lengua, jamón), my compañeros unanimously shouted—"cabeza!"—showing their preference for the meat cuts from a roasted cow's head.

They found another parallel between the movie and their own reality when the film's characters were derogatorily called "pickers." As children of immigrant farmworkers, the boys were expected to follow their parents to the fields of almonds and avocados instead of doing cross-country running, which was not seen as a realistic pursuit for immigrant youth in San Joaquin Valley.

"A former chief once told us: 'You are just a bunch of overpaid tomato pickers!'" one of them said.

ACCIDENTAL VIOLENCE

In some ways Mexican American firefighters in Nogales share more with migrant farmworkers in California's Central Valley than with white emergency responders in fire departments further north of the border. They are US citizens and long-term residents of a binational town cut in half by the fence, which makes them different from unauthorized migrants coming across the border from faraway regions in central and southern Mexico or beyond; yet they belong to a racially profiled, discriminated segment of American society. Being "documented" gives them more rights and privileges, including access to public service employment, but once in a while they are reminded that they don't belong. Border Patrol officers at the checkpoint send Alex for secondary inspection. A white male resident in Tubac refuses to let a female paramedic with a Mexican last name treat him, expressing doubts about her credentials. The former fire chief makes racist remarks about his crew. Emergency responders who work in Nogales and nearby communities along the border are not in Mexico—many have in fact never lived in Mexico—but they are not quite in the United States either. They are in the part of Arizona that the government considers as an extension of Sonora, where constitutional rights can be suspended to uphold social order. As Bojo said, the United States begins north of the checkpoint. Confinement to this legally interstitial space, where their ethnic background alone suffices as reason to question their commitment to the national security state, prevents local emergency responders from fully embracing its mandate. This incomplete identification or distance from federal policies also enables them to notice how the government uses terrain to shape the kinematics of trauma in order to make violence look like an accident.

In September 1966, the National Academy of Sciences published a paper that revolutionized prehospital management of injury in the US. The document, which laid the foundation of emergency medical services, was called *Accidental Death and Disability: The Neglected Disease of Modern Society.*[108] The report claimed that trauma-related deaths are an "epidemic," lamenting that "the general public is insensitive to the magnitude of the problem." It continued: "The human suffering and financial loss from preventable accidental death constitute a public health problem second only to the ravages of ancient plagues or world wars." The document emphasized the "accidental" nature of trauma-related injuries and deaths. An "accident" is an unfortunate eventuality, an incident that happens unexpectedly and unintentionally, resulting in damage. In Aristotelian thought, it signifies a property or quality that is not essential to a substance or object.[109] But, as Paul Virilio argues: "WHAT CROPS UP (*accidens*) is a sort of analysis, a technoanalysis of WHAT IS BENEATH (*substare*) any knowledge."[110] To invent the ship is to invent the shipwreck; to invent the train is to invent the derailment; to invent the automobile is to produce the pileup on the highway. In his critique of new technologies and scientific progress, Virilio revisits Aristotle's ideas and writes that "the accident reveals the substance." Accidents are programmed into the products of modernity. We can see this in forensic accident investigations, which challenge the fortuitous nature of vehicle collisions and airplane crashes. Scientific discovery of the incident's chain of causation allows moral and legal responsibility to be assigned, and "the accident as such ceases to be."[111]

The injuries on the US-Mexico border have never been accidental; they are not chance occurrences or contingencies. But unlike shipwrecks or automobile pileups, which happen without an intended cause, border trauma is deliberate. It is calculated and produced by those who deploy the security apparatus as the means of enacting the policy of "prevention through deterrence." The Border Patrol explicitly calls the fence part of its "tactical infrastructure" to give them advantage over those who disregard the blunt message "No trespassing." The steel barrier amputates fingers and fractures legs. Since the injured can't get far, the agents don't rush to help them. There is time for the pain to set in. The fence is designed to perform what Mbembe calls "demiurgic surgery," severing the limbs of those who try to scale it, keeping them alive in the state of injury.[112] The security assemblage is made up of parts that include elements of both natural and manmade environment. Jason de León refers to them as "the hybrid collectif" of both human and nonhuman actors—poisonous reptiles, flash floods, heat—that do the dirty work of enforcing the border.[113] Shifts in temperature dehydrate the migrant's body and make it vulnerable to heatstroke; this too provides the Border Patrol with tactical advantage over "UDAs." In the Sonoran Desert, the four states of matter—earth, water, air, and fire—play key roles in structuring "accidents" that injure and kill the unarmed.

Emergency is routine on the border, but not due to an error—the malfunctioning of the security assemblage's operating system, of which the border fence is but one part. On the contrary, migrant injuries are its intended outcomes. Newton's first law of motion states that a body at rest will remain at rest and a body in motion will remain in motion unless acted on by an outside force. What is this outside force? The higher the border fence, the more kinetic energy generated by a falling body, the more severe damage upon impact with the surface. Tactical infrastructure implicates those who commission and design the barrier in the act of wounding. Traumatic falls, like structure fires, car rollovers, or toxic spills, are programmed into the built environment.[114] Firefighters follow the cracks in urban infra/structures that threaten life and rescue those who trip and fall, in predictable—because intentional, therefore preventable—patterns. Rescue is a quintessentially spatial task, unfolding on landscapes that cripple trespassing bodies in ways that may hinder their survival: deplete them of oxygen, puncture their blood vessels, cut their spinal cords. Emergency responders know about the relationship between spatial forms—physical terrain, logistical landscapes, buildings—and the types of incidents and injuries they produce. Familiar with the kinematics of trauma, they use hydraulic tools to extricate bodies from mangled vehicles on the highway, apply foam to the spills of flammable liquids, and secure patients with potential back and neck injuries to the backboard before lifting them into the ambulance.

The approach to the US-Mexico border wall as tactical infrastructure encompasses more than the steel-and-concrete barrier—its most physical form and an essential element in the security assemblage. It includes the emergency services—cell phone towers and coverage areas, 911 operators, department jurisdictions, ambulances, and hospitals—and it extends across racially variegated landscapes to private detention centers and deportation courts in the north, as well as to the US-owned maquiladoras manufacturing medical supplies—cervical collars, nitrile gloves, IV tubing—across the border in Mexico. Seeing the wall only as a weapon obscures other types of infrastructures, or logistical landscapes, that underlie the resilience of border communities: water, sewage, and electricity flow under and over the steel barrier, forming binational socioeconomic knots that cannot be untied. Likewise, the work of those charged with mitigating the risks that arise from such deep entanglements of the built environment and natural ecosystems cannot be consigned to only one side of a politically engineered division. They are always crossing the line.

PART TWO

Downwind, Downhill, Downstream

PLATE 1. View of the border fence east of Nogales, Arizona.

PLATE 2. Emergency responders help an injured woman who fell off the border fence in Nogales, Arizona.

PLATE 3. Firefighters taking a break during an event welcoming Mexican schoolchildren to their station in Nogales, Arizona.

PLATE 4. Ladder from Nogales Fire Department in Arizona is helping to extinguish a hotel fire across the border in Nogales, Sonora (photo by Manuel C. Coppola, *Nogales International*, 2012).

PLATE 5. Downtime at the fire station in Nogales, Arizona.

PLATE 6. Firefighter Alex Flores.

PLATE 7. Border fence in Nogales, Sonora.

PLATE 8. Bunker gear at the fire station in Nogales, Arizona.

PLATE 9. Fighting a brush fire on the outskirts of Nogales, Sonora.

PLATE 10. Lieutenant Victor Garay and firefighter Daniel Osuna at the fire station in Nogales, Sonora.

PLATE 11. Helmets for new recruits at the fire station in Nogales, Sonora.

PLATE 12. A Mexican volunteer firefighter at the Revolution Day parade in Nogales, Sonora.

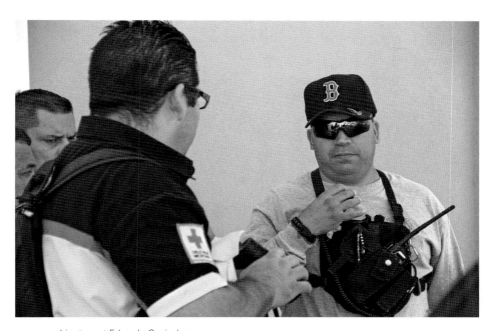

PLATE 13. Lieutenant Eduardo Canizales.

PLATE 14. American firefighter on the invisible boundary separating the US and Mexico during an emergency drill at the Agua Prieta/Douglas port of entry, July 2015.

PLATE 15. Mexican volunteer firefighters taking off hazmat suits during an emergency drill at the Agua Prieta/Douglas port of entry, July 2015.

PLATE 16. The bishop of Nogales, Sonora, at the fire station on the Day of the Virgin of Guadalupe.

BROTHERHOOD

The fence tears the social fabric of Ambos Nogales, but it does not become a barrier in the operational landscape of global capital. Nor, for that matter, does it split the infrastructures of public utilities. Extending from northern Sonora to southern Arizona, the railway, the highway, even the sewage pipeline facilitate dense ties between the two sides of the border. It becomes impossible to disentangle one town's everyday logistics from the other's. Emergency responders in Ambos Nogales know about the underlying material connections between the communities that, if severed, would have untoward effects. Over the years, they have drawn on bonds between families and friends to develop a plan for providing cross-border mutual aid wherever it's needed. They share knowledge and resources—water, manpower, thermal imaging cameras. The border can be a vulnerability that fire departments must consider as they assess urban space for risks, but it is also a conduit through which support flows in either direction. "La línea divisora has never been an obstacle," said Victor. Based on more than two decades of experience at the fire department in Nogales, Sonora, he told me that for firefighters the border doesn't exist: "The line is there, but when there is an emergency, it's as if it weren't."

Stories about structure fires that were fought by joint teams of Mexicans and Americans, scurrying back and forth across the border, go back as far as the beginning of the twentieth century.[1] When in 1915 the Hotel Escoboza caught fire, the only firehouse in the area was in the United States, so the Americans crossed into Mexico to extinguish the flames in the burning building, just a block away from the borderline. The incident prompted the creation, in 1917, of a volunteer fire department in Nogales, Sonora. The binational brotherhood is over a hundred years old now, with many examples of cross-border cooperation on the record. The veterans of fire departments on both sides grew up witnessing this. They still talk about the Father's Day Sunday in 1975 when lightning hit a palm tree and burning embers started falling on the wooden roof of a two-story house that belonged to the brother of Mayor Doyle. Four firefighters on duty at the old fire station on Morley rolled hoses from Grand Avenue all the way up the road to the house on Crawford. But they could not stop the fire, which started burning underneath the shingles, until Mexican firefighters crossed the border to help.

Many also remember a series of large fires that swept through Valenzuela Hermanos (VH) supermarket in Nogales, Sonora. The first one was on May 5, 1991. It started in the storage area on the top floor of a three-story building. Bojo, then a volunteer with the bomberos, said that the fire jumped faster than the firefighters, who had to cut through partitions between storage units, could advance. They had to evacuate the building. Chief Parra saw the smoke from across the line. The bomberos asked for assistance, and Nogales Suburban Fire District sent a fire engine and a tender carrying water. Arrangements with customs allowed the NSFD crew to go back and forth shuttling water from a hydrant on the US side to the fire in Mexico. Nogales Fire Department also sent help—a brush truck and a unit to refill the breathing apparatus. A thick cement ceiling prevented the fire from spreading downstairs, where the store and the garage were located, but the third floor was lost. For many firefighters on both sides of the border, this was the first big fire in which they remember seeing Mexico and the United States work together. In May 2005, another fire broke out in the same building, caused by a gasoline leak in the underground garage. Comandante Velez Ríos contacted NFD, and seven firefighters went across the line to provide mutual aid. NFD also attached a hose to a hydrant on Grand Avenue in Nogales, Arizona, and supplied Mexican fire trucks with water. It took three hours to extinguish the fire, which destroyed eighty-three vehicles in the parking garage.[2] In 2011, VH supermarket burned for the third time, and there was yet another fire in the same building in 2014.

But two recent fires have been etched into the living memory of Ambos Nogales deeper than any other. The first, named after the street where it started, became known as Ellis Fire. One thing everybody remembers about it is the wind. "The wind was whipping so hard," one firefighter told me. "The winds were shifting around," recalled another. "If you think last week was

Mexican-firefighter marching band at the Independence Day parade in Nogales, Arizona, July 4, 2015.

very windy, this was even worse," said a third, referring to repeated closures of a section of I-10 due to dust storms and gusts of wind so strong that driving south on I-19 toward Nogales that week in 2016 I felt the car swerving right and left. Six years earlier, on April 13, 2010, at 12:35 P.M., central dispatch paged Engine 1, Ladder 1, and Medic 4 to 164 W. Ellis Street, "reference to a structure fire." "Flames and heavy smoke showing," the first unit reported as they got closer to a pink single-family dwelling.[3] Backup from Station 2 was on their way. Flames engulfed the adobe, block, and wood structure and extended to the junkyard east of the house, where the owner stored tires and domestic appliances, a lawnmower, a propane tank, and two old vehicles. The blaze was intense, spreading rapidly due to the speed and force of the wind, with gusts up to 20 mph. It came from the south, but changed direction, helping the fire jump to adjacent buildings. "We tried every tactic in the book to fight the fire," Chief Robles told the local newspaper.[4] But too many things worked against the firefighters: the structures were made of wood, there was a lot of debris, and the houses were very close to each other, which provided limited access for emergency vehicles. NFD called for mutual aid from nearby departments: Rio Rico, Nogales Suburban, Tubac. Fearing structure collapse, the incident commander ordered two firefighters doing a search inside a house to pull out.

Meanwhile, the bomberos could see the big column of smoke from across the line. "We could tell that they didn't have control of the fire. The smoke was black," remembers Canizales. Like others who were there that day, he heard C4 alert about a large fire that involved multiple houses and asked for personnel with visas to cross into the United States. The last time the Americans had requested assistance from the bomberos was half a century earlier. Usually, when it came to help, Mexicans were on the receiving end. Now, gathered at the central station on Avenida Obregón, bomberos watched the smoke. They knew that their peers needed manpower, but they were waiting for the official invitation. "We had to go because it was the first time that the gringos asked us for help. We had to show up in force," César said, explaining their eagerness. Only half of those who came to the station had their Border Crossing Cards. The rest knew they would not be allowed to enter the United States because, as Pablo put it, "They did not have a piece of plastic with their photo."[5] They showed up nevertheless.

Some say the official mutual aid request never came, but the bomberos decided to respond anyway. They got into their trucks and headed for the border. Some say that when the federal agents at the port of entry asked them where they were going, they pointed to the smoke engulfing the entire neighborhood not too far from where they were. They say the port director jokingly asked: "What took you so long?!" What happened next surprised them. "Does everyone have a visa?" the agents inquired. "Yes," the bomberos replied, and as they were passing through, they raised their Border Crossing Cards. It took only four minutes for the first truck to cross onto American soil. But then Lieutenant Saavedra, who was driving the engine, suddenly realized he'd left his wallet back at the station. He was nervous. An agent asked him to step out of the vehicle. "He was all red," Canizales said. "He thought he was being arrested." But instead, CBP took down his information on a piece of paper and instructed him to present it to them on his way back to Mexico. Then—every story about the Ellis Fire I heard emphasizes this—they gave him a lift: US immigration and customs officials drove the Mexican lieutenant to the fire in one of their own trucks.

Following the same protocol used for Mexican ambulances, the bomberos were escorted to the scene—one police and one CBP vehicle in front and one CBP unit behind the fire trucks. "They showed up with thirty guys," Captain Lopez recalled. He was off duty that day. But he saw a large plume of black smoke from the window of his office and rushed to the scene, where he first assumed command and was later designated the safety officer. "All you had to do was put them to work. They knew exactly what needed to be done. They were there till we put out the last ember," he said about the bomberos. Having trained together, firefighters from both sides knew about the Incident Command System. "It was not easy to adapt," Pablo recalled. In Sonora, they are used to attacking fires aggressively, but in Arizona the bomberos were only allowed to do defensive operations.

They were impressed by what it was like working in the United States. "I will never forget the experience and satisfaction not having to worry about water supply, about how many tenders we had available." They used SCBAs (self-contained breathing apparatuses) donated by fire departments north of the border that no longer complied with NFPA safety norms, but they did not face the same shortages that they were used to in Sonora. They say they did not want to rest until the fire was out. "At some point there was not a single US firefighter working, except for the captains, who were directing the attack," one of them told me. "There was almost only puro bombero mexicano, working, working, working." César put it this way: "We arrived, the Americans went to rest, per chief's order. Y los mexicanos, chinganse cabrones, apagar el incendio." Temo compared jointly fighting fire to a party: "All the time, Nogales, Arizona, and Nogales, Sonora, worked well together. Many of us know each other. The relationship is very good. Es una pachanga, es una fiesta trabajar juntos."

At last, approximately five hours after the bomberos came to help, the crews gained access to the basement and extinguished the smoldering fire. The four-alarm incident, the biggest in recent Nogales history, was finally over. It destroyed three houses. "I think without them [the bomberos] we would have probably lost more homes. We were overwhelmed from the get-go," Captain Lopez recalls. "Had the bomberos not arrived to provide manpower, the Mexican Consulate and Pizza Hut could have burned down as well," the former county emergency manager told me. "It was historic." Though as volunteers they received no compensation for the hours they spent working at the fire, the bomberos were content: "They brought us food. Oh, we were happy!" Temo described it as "a bad but a very good day." Bad because the fire destroyed several houses. But good because it showed unity between firefighters on both sides of the border. As Victor put it: "We always say that Nogales, Sonora, and Nogales, Arizona, is Nogales—it is Nogales, Mexico."

Two years later, on May 10, 2012, which was Mother's Day in Mexico, a fire broke out in the Hotel San Enrique, located just a couple dozen feet from the border. The building, an old two-story structure on the corner of Calle Elias and Calle Internacional in Nogales, Sonora, had been abandoned for years, at least officially. Unofficially, it was used by homeless people who found comfort sleeping on the furniture still left inside. It was rumored that at one time the vacant hotel was a stash house for migrants waiting to cross illegally into the United States. People also talked about a suspected drug tunnel that led from the hotel to the US side of the border. "The entire structure was completely engulfed from all four points," Comandante Hernández said. "The roof was very old wood. We tried to contain it so that it wouldn't run to other buildings, which were also very old. Our operation was primarily defensive to prevent the fire escaping to other structures." But the bomberos needed water. The comandante called Bojo, who, as a reserve officer with the Nogales bomberos, was his first contact in the United States. "What we needed in that fire was water because the hydrant on the Mexican side did not have any." By that time NFD had received several phone calls alerting them of a large fire across the line near the Morley port of entry. Ladder 1 and Engine 1 went to investigate and, on arrival, found the building "fully involved with flames and smoke showing."[6] There were two fire hydrants on International Street, which runs parallel to the fence. American firefighters connected three supply lines to the hydrants on the US side, sending water through the gate to feed the Mexican fire trucks.

With hose lines running through, Morley port of entry was closed to the public. CBP left only one lane open, exclusively for firefighters, who were crossing back and forth. "Without a need to show a visa, without a need to show any document, all of those who were dressed up as firefighters could move from one country to another. CBP agents were there, you walked up to them and asked: "Can I cross?" "You don't have to ask," they said. Like that," Vicente remembers. Tubac Fire, responding to the call for mutual aid, brought an air compressor unit and parked it as close to the port of entry as they could. Bomberos walked across to the US to refill SCBAs and then returned to Mexico to fight the fire.

They were used to such arrangements. Mutual aid is deeply engrained in the binational infrastructure of public utilities: the first hydrant built on the Mexican side was connected to the water supply in the United States, while the iconic Fray Marcos Hotel, the tallest building in downtown Nogales, Sonora, still receives water from Arizona. The water pressure in Nogales,

Arizona, has always been better than in Nogales, Sonora, but some areas, including the vicinity of the Morley port of entry, had no functioning water hydrants on the Mexican side at all. So, even as the design of the fence has changed over the years, American firefighters have been ingenious at finding ways to help the bomberos by connecting Mexican hoses to US hydrants. This practice dates to at least the 1980s, when the Nogales Fire Department first started having issues with insurance and, instead of crossing, began staging next to the fence and passing hoses across the border. As Joe de la Ossa, who was the chief of the Nogales Fire Department in the late 1970s and 1980s, explained to the *L.A. Times* back in 1986, "If the fire is within 1,000 feet of the border, Mexican firefighters use the US hoses to fight the blaze. If the fire is more distant, water from American fire trucks is pumped into Mexican tank trucks and rushed to the scene."[7] Such arrangements were not limited to Nogales. In Douglas, Arizona, firefighters have also supplied their peers in Agua Prieta, Sonora, with water by setting up ladders against the fence and pulling the hose over them. Ladders protected the hoses from being torn by the sharp edges of the steel barrier.

"We had two beautiful hydrants right there," said Billy Bob, who was the first American officer on scene during the Hotel San Enrique Fire. "The call came in as: 'Can you come over and pump water to our trucks?' So we went in, we set one truck up and we started pumping water over there. And then we realized: You know what, our ladder truck will reach it!" This was the inaugural fire for their Rosenbauer Cobra with a 101-foot aerial ladder, which was originally purchased to take on warehouse fires. The department spent close to a million dollars to acquire it in 2010.[8] The truck was staged on International Street and the ladder extended up and over the border wall into Mexico. But they had to wait; there were high-voltage power lines traversing the front of the building. It took about half an hour for the utility company to cut off the electricity to the area, and the firefighters received the all-clear signal. The powerful stream from Ladder 1 poured down on the building below. Through its 5-inch hose it could pump water at up to 2,000 gallons per minute. "We killed the fire," Bojo said proudly. According to the incident report, approximately 100,000 gallons of water were supplied to the Mexican trucks. The US firefighter who stood in the bucket directing the aerial attack was technically inside Mexican territory. For the longest time after that his peers called him a "mojadito."

Five days after the fire, Manuel Coppola, the editor and publisher of *Nogales International*—who took the iconic photograph of Ladder 1 reaching over the border into Mexico—wrote an article about the binational efforts of the firefighters: "Some like to say that no matter how high the fence is between Nogales, Sonora and Nogales, Ariz., nothing can truly separate our border community. The reality is that the fence presents many obstacles. Still, it historically has not restrained the spirit of cooperation among border firefighters, who find ways to penetrate the barrier when it comes to helping each other battle blazes."[9]

Although government officials and the media have used the case of the Hotel San Enrique Fire to show the relevance of the binational plan, those who were on scene say that it was never activated. There was no need for it. "It was a collaboration between two departments," said Assistant Chief Sanchez. "We didn't call protección civil. We didn't call to the north." Authorities in Nogales did not inform state or federal government. "It was something between two fire departments that know each other and work together." Sanchez noted that US Customs did not assert its muscle as a federal agency. "Could they have been an obstacle? They could have said: 'Hey, you guys are playing in my sandbox!' But no. They saw the emergency and said: 'What do you guys need?' 'We need to cross some hoses here.' 'Go ahead.' We had their permission. Everything went like it was planned. And it was planned at the level of the people that do the actual work." Sanchez is unapologetic about how NFD handled it: "If I would have had to call the port director and the port director needs to get permission from the president, well, guess what would have happened with that hotel?"[10]

RED TAPE

"Do wildfires have a passport? Does the water stop at the border?" Louie asked me rhetorically when we met for an early lunch at a Mexican restaurant in Tubac, where he was immediately recognized. He brought his computer and, while we waited for our orders of carne con chile and tortillas, placed it on the table. It contained photographs that Louie wanted me to see—of train accidents, fires, floods—proof of the binational alliance forged between emergency responders on both sides of the border. "In Nogales," he said, "we are not associates. We are not business partners. We are not even friends. We are family."

Louie started his career in public service with the Highway Patrol. Born and raised in Tucson, he took the assignment in Nogales as a way to gain some independence while remaining within an hour's drive from home. Work in narcotics investigations came with risks. In 1991, his sergeant, Manny Tapia, died during an operation when he pulled over a drug runner on North Grand Avenue; a monument in his memory stands in the green patch of land between the street and the train tracks. It was the one time he did not wear the bulletproof vest. Louie remembers that the sergeant always told them to "wear the damn vests." Chasing traffickers on southern Arizona roads, Louie was shot at too, but he was never hurt. Not many who work with him now know that he held the rank of major in the National Guard, artillery.

Today his name is synonymous with binational plans—agreements between sister cities, counties, and states in Mexico and the US to provide each other mutual aid in emergencies. From 2000 to 2007, he served as the director of emergency services for Santa Cruz County, followed by five more years in emergency management for the Tubac Fire District. Although "semi-retired," as he puts it, which allows him to wear blue jeans and a checkered shirt instead of a uniform, Louie can't shake off the commitment he took on over a decade ago. If something happens in Mexico, his phone is the first to ring. Not surprisingly, he was offered the job of administering the US-Mexico Border 2020 program, the latest iteration in a series of binational frameworks dating back to the 1983 La Paz Agreement. The new Border 2020 program emphasized the EPA's commitment to "regional, bottom-up approaches for decision-making, priority setting and project implementation to address environmental and public health problems in the border region."[11] Together with Mike Evans, former Cochise County emergency services coordinator, and Les Caid, who from 2011 to 2017 was the chief of the Rio Rico Fire District, Louie also works for 5th Phase Training & Consulting LLC, a private company that the EPA contracted to teach hazmat and Incident Command System courses to first responders in northern Mexico. Though he hired Spanish-speaking firefighters from Nogales and Douglas to serve as instructors in Sonora and, more recently, his health has required him to limit his involvement, Louie Chaboya remains the *éminence grise* who pulls the strings behind the scenes to makes things happen. Binational plans are full of his fingerprints.

The mutual aid agreement in Ambos Nogales, like those in over a dozen other sister cities along the entire inland border, from San Diego and Tijuana to Brownsville and Matamoros, is modeled on the Mexico–United States Joint Contingency Plan, signed by the US EPA and by Mexico's PROFEPA and Coordinación General de Protección Civil.[12] The "border area" to which the plan applies extends 100 kilometers on either side of the international boundary, as noted in the La Paz Agreement.[13] US and Mexican governments must notify each other in the event of any fire, natural disaster, or release of hazardous substance that is likely to affect the other country. The protocols that outline the procedures in each pair of neighboring jurisdictions—who does what and when—already use a standardized script and, Louie hopes, will become even more uniform when binational plans are updated. But this top-down framework downplays the importance of place: it blurs the varied terrain along the border into abstract space and fails to recognize the history of communities, where cooperation has always first and foremost been a local affair.

Sanchez says that as long as he can remember, "If they [bomberos] had a structure fire, the guys from here would run over there and help them out. The same if there was an emergency this way." He joined the Nogales Fire Department in 1985 and, were it not for the city's nepotism law, he could have been the chief. For Sanchez's family, firefighting is a tradition that spans generations: His grandfather and uncle were firefighters in Nogales, Sonora, and his son works with him, continuing the tradition in Nogales, Arizona, which was only possible because Sanchez refused the top leadership position. He seems content with his decision to remain assistant chief. While department chiefs come and go, he stays. Sanchez was here when they first came up with a binational agreement, in 1995. The mayors of both cities were on board, he said. They had support from the state. Five years later, following the release of the Joint Contingency Plan at the federal level, Nogales, Arizona, and Nogales, Sonora, signed the Binational Prevention and Emergency Response Plan. In language adapted from the EPA, it promised to "ensure a full and effective utilization of resources and manpower essential to protect the public health, safety, and environment" in the border area "in the event of a disaster of serious proportions that may require a great deal of coordination and cooperation." Such incidents included the release of hazardous substances, fires, natural disasters, and "events involving weapons of mass destruction."[14] US and Mexican governments had to provide security for the personnel entering their territory "in pursuance of authorized emergency response activities."[15] It worked well at first. Sanchez recalls:

> When we were crossing into Mexico, we had a police escort. They would wait for us at the border and we had four units, lights and siren, protecting our trucks all the way to the scene. Once we got to the emergency, the Mexican

military were there, assigned as security perimeter for us, providing protection for the personnel and for our equipment. We would help them and then we would get another escort back into the United States. We were very comfortable going to Mexico. Bomberos would just call up the Mexican *aduana* [customs] and say, "We have an emergency, these guys want to cross this equipment." And everything was beautiful.

For years firefighters crossed between Nogales, Arizona, and Nogales, Sonora, without encountering any problems on the border. Since emergencies in sister cities unfolded on a contiguous physical terrain and across social space that extended from Mexico to the United States, rescues often required binational effort. "If I see a barricade, I will find a way to go over it or around it," Sanchez told me. The border fence did not stop mutual aid. The plans only formalized a practice that had existed in Ambos Nogales long before these documents were signed. "You have my back and I have your back" is how Sanchez described the trust between emergency responders on both sides of the line. "From 1995 to about 2010 we were able to do all that without any headaches," he said. Then they came up against an obstacle that firefighter training and tools could not defeat: a bureaucratic wall.

"Here the binational plan between the cities works because of the relationship between the people," a firefighter in Nogales, Sonora, told me. "Camaraderie works. Brotherhood between the firefighters works." But recently they got entangled in red tape. While the Mexican bomberos can come across to help NFD with an emergency on the US side of the border, American firefighters can no longer provide assistance in Mexico: first, because US insurance does not cover emergency responders or their equipment operating in Mexico, and second, because there are no laws that protect them from liability. If a driver hits a pedestrian on the way to the fire, he could be thrown into jail. If the aduana decides to impound a fire truck, they might not get it back. If emergency responders get injured, they would not receive workers' compensation. Chief Caid of Rio Rico stressed the significance of mutual aid during the Ellis Fire: "The bomberos came without hesitation. They are never concerned. They're gonna show up, even when they are not getting paid." But when it comes to US fire departments: "We were limited because our firefighters, if they go across the border and they get hurt, they don't get workers' comp . . . It drives me crazy!" Chief Caid said. "How can I send a firefighter over there, if they get injured and they no longer have their livelihood, their family can come back and sue the fire district. Because of the litigious society we live in, we end up limiting what we can actually do."

Sanchez explained:

> We respond to the emergency knowing that there are hazards there. But that's our job—to mitigate that emergency. In our hearts we want to mitigate whatever is happening in Mexico before it comes this way and does more harm. That's the way we look at this as firefighters. [...] They put the big title [on the plan]—"binational"—because it's international. It's between two different countries. We see it as Nogales and Nogales, Ambos Nogales. We know that the fence is a big issue. We know that crossing back and forth is a big issue. [...] Why can the United States send rescue teams to Chile or Japan, and we cannot get something that will cover us to go somewhere within crawling distance to prevent a big emergency?

The binational plan started between firefighters on both sides of Nogales as what Sanchez calls "a gentlemen's agreement." But he is concerned about what happens when it becomes political and gets scaled up. "The bigger the plan got, the more people put their hands in what here we call 'la masa,' the dough. Everybody has an opinion on it," Sanchez said. He later explained the same idea by using a different metaphor: "I can put a little pinch of salt in the pot of soup and you can say: 'No, no, it needs garlic salt!' 'No, no, it needs pepper!' Then everybody is putting their little bits and the soup that everybody loves is no longer palatable to the people." The more the plan is scaled up and the more government officials get involved, the less useful it is. "It looks really good on the shelf," Sanchez says. But it's not practical anymore.

Though firefighters from the two countries can work side by side in smaller incidents, which don't even require them to activate the binational plan, it is not clear what would happen if an emergency in Nogales escalated. "Previously it was very easy to open the gates at the customs so that the US firefighters could come or we go assist them in the United States," said Vicente, who is a lawyer by profession and who has been a volunteer firefighter in Nogales, Sonora, since 1989. "Now there are more laws, more regulation, more politics, more issues of firefighter insurance that put some barriers." Fire officials in southern Arizona have been appealing to the state and federal government, urging them to create a mechanism through which municipal first responders, when they cross the border to help Mexicans, would immediately become state or federal employees and could be compensated as such. It makes sense, they say: FEMA's urban search and rescue teams and the US Forest Service already operate under similar arrangements. But thus far their efforts have been futile.

At present, the only fire department in Arizona that sends firefighters across the border to Mexico is in Douglas. Chief Novoa did not even need the state or federal government to step in: his was a local arrangement with the city council. Novoa is proud to be the first Hispanic fire chief in the town where back in 1951 his dad's cousin became the first Hispanic firefighter. Two sheets of paper hang on the door to his office: one has a quote from Douglas Adams: "I love deadlines. I like the whooshing sound they make as they fly by"; the other contains colorful images of Squad 51 from the 1970s television show *Emergency!* Besides his job in fire service, Novoa is an active member of the Douglas Historical Society, and no other topic animates him as much as his town's past. During the Mexican Revolution people would watch Pancho Villa fight the government troops from the upper floors of the house he later grew up in. Being local makes things easier for Chief Novoa. He knows the authorities who control the border on a first-name basis. Some, like the cousin who is the director of the Douglas port of entry, are his family. "Decisions have to be made on the local level," he insists. According to the 2001 sister city agreement, the mayor of Agua Prieta has to call the mayor of Douglas to activate the binational plan, but Novoa wants to change it to make it chief to chief.

"We convinced the city council to insure our vehicles," he said—something the departments further west have been unable to do. They started with authorizing one fire engine and one pickup truck. In 2016, city management approved Chief Novoa's request to purchase insurance for five vehicles, and all personnel can now cross into Agua Prieta.[16] They go to provide support and advice, not to do the actual work of fighting the fire, Chief Novoa explained. But even that is significant. "We have to mitigate what happens over there before it becomes a threat for us," he said, justifying the additional line in the city's budget. Over the past few years, the Douglas Fire Department has responded to several calls for help with large structure fires across the border—a proof that binational plans can work.

On October 28, 2015, Assistant Chief Sanchez stood next to his counterpart, Comandante Hernández, at the city council meeting in Nogales, Arizona, when Mayor Doyle announced the donation of two ambulances and thirty-nine handheld radios to the bomberos in Nogales, Sonora. The council approved the order unanimously. Mayor Doyle told both chiefs that they had set the foundation for the relationship between the two cities. Sanchez was the first of the two to speak: "I've been here thirty years and we've always worked with Nogales, Sonora. Now we have a binational plan, we have sister city plans, but back in the old days it was just a phone call to the mayor, and the mayor would give us the green light to go help them out. We have built that bridge with bomberos from across the line. We see them as our brothers, as colleagues, as coworkers." Comandante Hernández echoed Sanchez: "We are the same city and one community divided by a fence. We're all one family." He, too, spoke about the times before the plans were written, when all they had was a telephone line. These political speeches were performative acts asserting the enduring mutual commitment of the two cities and their fire departments.

Two weeks later at the station, JLo, Alex, Bojo, and the rest of the crew were preparing the donated ambulances to be taken to Mexico. The rescue vehicles still had NFD logos and city government license plates. Nogales fire-fighters knew that the bomberos would be able to use anything they, on this side of the line, could spare: they cleaned several long backboards and put them inside; they went through the medical supplies—4x4 bandages, some needles, syringes, glucose tubes; they threw in an old but still functional AED. There were two bulletproof vests, in military-style green camouflage, which they strapped behind the driver's and the medic's seats. More supplies for the bomberos, including brand-new air bottles for the SCBAs, still packed in cardboard boxes, filled up the outside compartments. The plan was to deliver the ambulances in time for their official reception during the ninety-eighth anniversary of the Nogales bomberos at the end of the month. Yet, days went by and the ambulances remained where they were. Weeks passed. At some point, they were moved from the fire station to a warehouse nearby. The ambulances were still there two years later, when, in November 2017, the Nogales, Sonora, fire department celebrated its one-hundredth anniversary.

The bomberos blamed the aduana, but the reasons for the delay were not so straightforward. More often than not they could find a way to take the equipment across the border. Only a year earlier, in 2014, they successfully brought a ladder purchased at an auction from a fire department in Payson, Arizona. "A monster," César called the truck. He described the journey when they went to pick it up "an odyssey." The vehicle was heavy and it kept overheating as they climbed the hill toward Phoenix. They spent seven or eight hours—twice as long as usual—getting from Payson back to Nogales. "We couldn't immediately cross. We had to leave the truck in the United States and do the paperwork here in Mexico to legalize this vehicle," César told me. The process took almost a month and cost over a thousand dollars. But it was done. "This vehicle is Mexican now," César said proudly. The serial number has been erased from the databases in the United States. It was important for the bomberos to have this truck for fires in the maquiladoras. Made in 1994, with a 100-foot ladder, it was almost identical to the one NFD parked at the border fence during the Hotel San Enrique Fire. "Ojalá, we never use it. Ojalá!"

Fire departments in Sonora get most of their supplies, either discounted or donated, from the United States. In May 2016, I accompanied the bomberos to Phoenix to pick up used gear and tools from the city's fire department. We emptied the storage unit: old bunker gear—jackets, pants, boots, some helmets, gloves—all went into the trailer. It didn't matter whether the boots matched, whether jackets were torn. They gave the firefighter who received them a bottle of tequila, and he let them take several extension ladders and threw in a few rolls of old dirty hose. Back in Nogales the bomberos counted 87 jackets and 107 bunker pants, plus helmets, hoods, and gloves. It cost the department 1,001 pesos (equivalent to about $55 in May 2016) in taxes to take it across the border to Mexico. All cross-border donations of emergency tools and supplies were so tied up in the Mexican customs laws that it was easier to buy equipment in the United States and pay taxes than treat it as gifts.

But this was only possible because it was fire equipment; medical supplies were subject to even harsher tariff restrictions, which sometimes seemed absurd. Back in the day, Bojo used to collect worn cervical collars from the hospital in Nogales, Arizona, wash them, and take them across the line to Nogales, Sonora, where he handed them over to the Cruz Roja. He brought them boxes full of cervical collars. He also brought backboards. Until one day an agent at the Mexican aduana didn't allow him through, explaining that C-spine collars were medical supplies and, as such, they required custom clearance. Bojo tried to reason with the officers: if you get into an accident in Nogales, Sonora, you want the Cruz Roja to have this equipment. But the agent said he had no way of knowing whether Bojo was telling the truth and ordered him to stop taking the collars across.

At the fire station in Douglas I once saw several boxes of supplies lying against the wall in the corridor—donations for the Cruz Roja in Mexico. When I picked up one box of brand new cervical collars, the label said that they were made in Mexico. Gerardo saw the irony. "They were probably made in Agua Prieta," he said. The scheme seemed like a farce: maquiladoras in Sonora manufactured medical supplies, among them C-spine collars, which could not go directly to the Cruz Roja in the same town; first they had to be taken across the border to Arizona and then, through concerted efforts, back to Mexico. As in Nogales, firefighters in Douglas were not allowed to bring donated supplies across the border themselves. The fire department had to ask for help from the Mexican Consulate or do it during a binational meeting through the Border 2020 program.

Proximity to the border presented the Cruz Roja with other challenges. When they transfer immobilized patients to American ambulances at the ports of entry, Mexican emergency responders don't take them off backboards because moving them could cause further injury. Thus, dozens of Mexican backboards end up at Tucson hospitals, and the Cruz Roja can't go to pick them up. Alberto Ruiz, who in 2015 was the president of the Cruz Roja delegation in Agua Prieta, said that they lose three or four backboards each month. Backboards and straps are not cheap. Unable to get theirs back, Cruz Roja volunteers become reluctant to immobilize patients unless it is absolutely necessary. "Property of Cruz Roja," they started writing on the boards. They asked hospitals to hand them over to the ambulance crews from fire departments along the border, such as Douglas, so that they could bring them back to the port of entry. But it wasn't working.

I found it difficult to understand why donations of ambulances and medical equipment entailed layers of authorizations so complex that they stretched from the local customs office in Nogales, Sonora, all the way to the federal administration in Mexico City. Comandante Hernández, who, besides being the fire chief, owns an import business and knows the details of customs laws, explained it to me this way:

> Article 61 of the [Mexican] customs law talks about donations. Any kind of donations: [. . .] donations for the military, donations for hospitals. And everything is treated the same way. It doesn't matter whether it's a war plane or a fire truck. [. . .] The receiving entity in Mexico has to be authorized by the government to receive donations. But we are not just talking about tax barriers. We are talking about other permits. There are tariff restrictions that apply to most merchandize. Ambulances, for example, need a permit from the federal Secretaría de Economía. Firefighter gear, as textiles, need another type of permit. Boots, as footwear, require still another permit. There are many restrictions, not just taxes. That's where it becomes difficult. It is possible to receive donations and cross them legally into Mexico, but these trámites [procedures] take very long and are very complicated.

At the closing of one Border 2020 meeting in Nogales, Sonora, Chief Novoa, who was the new co-chair of the binational program, announced that Douglas

Fire Department would give forty sets of airpacks to the bomberos in Mexico. "The airpacks that we have are fifteen years old," he said. "They are like new, all the lights work, the heads-up display shows how much air is left. We are taking good care of our equipment because we know that we can't buy it every year." However, NFPA requires US fire departments to regularly replace SCBAs. Instead of throwing the old ones away, they decided to donate them. But Chief Novoa complained that Mexican customs was stalling their efforts. "Why are there taxes for something that helps people?" he asked. "I can't understand this." He said he would talk to customs again. "But, in any case," he added, "we already know how to cross them." Scattered laughs in the audience signaled approval of what the chief was referring to. "It's something we have to do. Are we doing any damage? No, we are doing it for the health and benefit of all." Loud applause followed Chief Novoa's speech. As frustrating as it was to encounter a legal and bureaucratic wall that obstructed binational agreements and mutual aid between fire departments, there were other ways of doing things at the border—ways that bypassed higher levels of government and red tape.

The inflexibility of the Mexican aduana limits cross-border initiatives and puts pressure on emergency responders to find ways of sidestepping the laws in the name of the greater good. The car seat program, through which the Arizona Department of Health Services, Tucson Medical Center, and several fire departments have been collecting used car seats and donating them to Mexican families, is a poignant example. Less than one-fifth of families with babies and small children in Sonora have car seats.[17] By the end of 2015, with the help of Rio Rico Fire, over 1,500 car seats had been taken across the border. "They are certified, they are in working condition, they are clean, and they will save lives," Chief Caid said of the initiative. "Those car seats, which cost a month's wages in Mexico, they are so expensive, are being put to good use." For Chief Caid it was common sense. But even this program occasionally stalls because of red tape, and emergency responders have had to take donated car seats across the border in their personal vehicles, one or two at a time. "If they ask me at the aduana," one Arizona official told me, "I say these are my grandchildren's."

MAQUILADORA

"Taxi, lady?" "Cuban cigars?" "Painkillers?" "Mexican boyfriend?" I heard men shouting their offers as soon as I emerged through the gate on the Mexican side of the border. The distance between my apartment on Potrero

Avenue in Nogales, Arizona, and the central fire station on Avenida Obregón in Nogales, Sonora, could be covered in half an hour on foot. There are no hurdles getting into Mexico: pass through the metal turnstiles, press a button, and, if the light is green, proceed; if it's red, open your bags and show them to the agent, provided there is one at the aduana desk. Nobody asks for your name, your passport, or the reason for your visit. Fewer Americans now come across than a decade or two ago—shoppers were scared away by graphic media coverage of violence in Mexico; students and army brats were discouraged by law enforcement officers waiting for their return on northbound roads, ready to charge them for underage drinking and driving under the influence. Those who are not deterred—mainly medical tourists—find familiar signs welcoming them to Sonora: "Discount Pharmacy," "Nogales Root Canal," "Dental Bliss." A dental appointment here is considerably cheaper than in the US. There are restaurants, too, where those who come to see a doctor can have a bountiful meal of carne asada before they head back north. Souvenir shops, known as "curios," crowd the sidewalks with ceramic pots and rusty metal sculptures of plants and animals. Further on, pharmacies, doctor's offices, restaurants, and curios thin out and give way to clothes and shoe stores frequented by Mexican shoppers.

I had been waiting in front of the station for a few minutes when I saw Victor emerge from a side street. He walked briskly, dressed in uniform: light blue shirt, navy pants, a zipper jacket; it was a chilly morning in early December 2015. He carried a bottle of water: by the break of dawn he'd already completed his daily run up and down the steep slopes of his native Nogales. Victor still lived close to where he grew up, with nine siblings, in a neighborhood of narrow winding streets and petite cement houses perched high above downtown. We got inside the command truck and headed out. The bomberos had been invited to attend a course on cyanide emergencies to be held at one of the maquiladoras in the city's industrial zone.

Victor joined the bomberos in 1990. Two of his brothers, Reynaldo and Mario, followed suit. All three Garays were volunteers, working elsewhere to earn a living. But when in 2010 Victor lost his job as a salesman for a pharmaceutical company, he was offered a paid position with the department. The job entailed administrative work, which he was good at. The department survives on voluntary contributions from city residents. Every year when nogalenses renew their license plates, they are asked to give 30 pesos to support the bomberos. In addition, every household can have 1 peso added to their monthly water bill. In 2015, 12 pesos per year was less than a dollar.

Businesses such as small stores and pharmacies pay 2 pesos per month; industrial companies pay 3 pesos. All of these contributions are voluntary. But even though this money typically makes up just a tiny portion of the municipal budget, various Sonoran towns chronically delay giving the bomberos what the residents contribute. Some years, when departments run out of funds to buy fuel, the bomberos stage protests. To avoid this happening in Nogales, when payments are overdue, Victor goes to the ayuntamiento and to the city's water authority. It still takes weeks of daily visits, all handshakes and smiles, before he gets the check. In addition to collecting money from the reluctant hands of government officials and paying the department's bills, he maintains the personnel roster, assigns shifts, and runs errands around town. If a thermal imaging camera shows blurry pictures, he takes it to be fixed. If a chainsaw needs a part replaced, he goes to the company that donated it and asks for help. Victor is always on the move, and often on the phone: "Échale! OK. Allí voy. Sale pues." "Ándale pues. Gracias. Bye." In the truck with him, I only hear his end of the conversation.

Victor's primary responsibility was negotiating with the maquiladoras. This sector operates more than one hundred plants in the city, manufacturing everything from apparel and paper products to parts for the aerospace industry.[18] Sonoran law stipulates that every company with over fifty employees must have brigadas de protección civil, or civil defense brigades. It also mandates that 10 percent of the company's employees be certified in first aid, search and rescue, evacuation, and the use of fire extinguishers. The bomberos offered them safety training and, in exchange, asked for support. Victor describes it as a win-win situation: on the one hand, if there is an accident, the firefighters can rely on trained maquiladora employees; on the other hand, these arrangements provide much-needed resources for the fire department, thus contributing to the safety of all nogalenses. I saw how it works when I accompanied Victor and two other firefighters to a safety week (semana de seguridad) event at a maquiladora that makes surgical gowns, gastric tubes, and other hospital supplies. They staged a competition between the factory's civil defense brigades and taught the children of factory workers about "stop, drop, and roll." In exchange for their participation, the company gave the bomberos two bottles of compressed gases—one containing carbon monoxide, hydrogen sulfide, methane, oxygen, and nitrogen, and the other filled with isobutylene—needed to calibrate gas monitors.[19] These can cost hundreds of dollars, which "may be nothing for the gringos," says Victor, but is more than the bomberos can afford.

That December morning we faced heavy traffic heading toward zona industrial, but we arrived at the Baldwin and Weiser Lock factory in time for the 8:00 A.M. training on cyanide emergencies. This maquiladora used cyanide, in its liquid form, to apply copper and paint to locks. A security guard took our IDs and gave us visitor badges and safety glasses. We put them on as we walked through the factory floor and up a metal staircase to the room where the training would be held. Company employees and workers from other maquiladoras were lining up for coffee and cookies. Canizales, Porfirio, Daniel, and César showed up in their duty uniforms. I noticed representatives from protección civil, newly appointed to the office following the election, sitting together in the back of the room.

Nogales firefighters have had uneven results when responding to hazardous materials emergencies at the city's industrial sites. One of the more serious incidents was at MOLEX, an assembly plant that manufactured electrical connectors, at the end of September 2001. Corrosive material used for cleaning was inadvertently transferred into an incompatible aluminum tanker, resulting in a dangerous chemical reaction. "Sodium hydroxide is caustic; its pH is 14, so it is a base," Canizales explained to me as he showed pictures of a white tanker with blotches of black. "They used it to wash the pipes in the factory and then poured it into a nonpressurized metal tanker. It began to buckle; the liquid inside was eating the metal." The bomberos advised the factory administration to evacuate workers, but the latter were reluctant to stop production. The Cruz Roja was there, and the military showed up. The bomberos called the Nogales Fire Department, which sent a hazmat team with equipment to test the samples. It turned out that sodium hydroxide was mixed with some other chemicals. The aluminum container started deforming and posed a risk of explosion, so they had to transfer 20,000 liters of the hazardous liquid to a tanker that would be compatible with the material. Southwest Hazard Control, a private company based in Phoenix, brought such a tanker down to Nogales. "Since they [US hazmat techs] were gringos, the gringo owners of the factory paid more attention to them," Canizales said. They finally agreed to close the factory and evacuate thousands of people. The MOLEX story served as an example of why cooperation between the industrial sector and the fire department was important.

The organizer of the course on cyanide, for which we had gathered, was an old-timer in the maquiladora industry who worked for a hazmat cleanup company in Hermosillo, but he knew Victor and Canizales from years back when they met on the scene of several industrial emergencies in Nogales.

He explained that in Sonora, cyanide is primarily used in the mining industry to extract gold, the same way that sulphuric acid is used in copper production. He told us about an incident when a tanker overturned and liquid
cyanide leaked into the river. The driver was trapped in the truck and
died from poisoning. Next, the instructor showed us two videos. One was
more recent and produced in Mexico; the other was a 1995 film made
by DuPont in America, dubbed in Spanish. Other than providing basic
first-aid guidelines for cyanide poisoning, they were not very informative.
The videos described antidote kits containing amyl nitrite ampules, which
must be crushed into a piece of gauze before being applied to the patient, and
sodium nitrite and sodium thiosulfate solutions administered via injection.
An antidote kit from the factory's own inventory was sent around the room,
and we inspected it carefully. The instructions of dosages on the inside cover
of the box were in English, so I translated. We noticed that gauze was
missing.

Firefighters are routinely exposed to cyanide when they work in burning
buildings: it is a byproduct of combusting materials, especially plastics and
synthetics used for insulation, but also wool, silk, and paper. Toxic smoke,
which also contains carbon monoxide, can make one feel lightheaded, nauseous, and tachycardic performing fireground operations. We are warned not
to take our SCBAs off during overhaul—not to let our guard down once the
fire is out, because it is then that we risk breathing in toxic gases. Recent
research suggests that repeated inhalation of hydrogen cyanide may be playing a more significant role in injuries and deaths of firefighters and civilians
than once thought.[20] In the United Nations hazmat placard system, cyanides
fall under Hazard Class 6.1, "POISON." They enter the bloodstream and
impair the process through which cells use oxygen to produce energy, resulting in metabolic acidosis, or chemical asphyxiation. First comes dizziness and
vomiting; then gasping, seizures, coma, and cardiac arrest.

We went over the MSDS on sodium cyanide ($NaCN$) and paged through
the ERG, a pocket guidebook first responders use during the initial phase of
a transportation incident involving dangerous materials. The ERG lists
sodium cyanide as UN 1689. Also known as sodium salt of hydrocyanic acid,
it is described as "a white crystalline solid, lump solid or powder." The guide
warns that this material is "super toxic; probably oral lethal dose in humans
is less than 5mg/kg or a taste (less than 7 drops) for a 70 kg (150 lb.) person.
Sodium cyanide is poisonous and may be fatal if inhaled, swallowed or
absorbed through the skin. Contact with sodium cyanide may cause burns

to skin and eyes."[21] Company workers explained that the maquiladora receives wooden boxes containing bags with cyanide briquettes. Only technicians are allowed in the area where they are stored. They go in pairs, dressed up in Tychem suits and accompanied by a nurse. They have never had any incidents.

We had not been warned that the company planned an emergency exercise for the afternoon. While Victor had to run other errands, the rest of us finished lunch early and rushed back to Station 3, which had jurisdiction over the industrial zone and would be the first to respond to an incident at Baldwin and Weiser Lock. Attentively listening to the radio, waiting for the dispatch to call them, the bomberos made a plan: Canizales and Porfirio would dress up in level A suits as hazmat technicians; Daniel and I were assigned to the ambulance; the rest of the crew at the station would go as firefighters; they were already putting on bunker gear and checking their SCBAs. Everything unfolded as the bomberos had expected: once the call from C4 came in, we got in the trucks and, fighting traffic, rushed to the factory.

I was anxious, even though I knew that training exercises are always programmed to fail. During the operations-level hazmat class I took in Boston, we only dressed up in level B suits—Tyvec coveralls, duct tape around wrists and ankles, and an SCBA. We played with Geiger counters and were allowed to handle small radioactive particles. But we were caught off guard when, undressing a patient for decontamination, we found explosives strapped to his chest. In paramedic school in Jacksonville, our instructor failed us on a hazmat scenario because we did not do a proper scene size-up to make sure it was safe before rushing to the rescue: the alleged patients had white powder on their clothes. Drills made first responders internalize both their duty to act and the inevitable failure to save all lives. I had never trained with cyanide in a building that stored large quantities of it, which seemed to raise the stakes of the impending defeat.

It turned out that there were only two patients. We were still struggling with the gurney when Cruz Roja volunteers carried the first patient, strapped to the backboard, to their ambulance. I noticed, too late, that our ambulance was not well stocked: in the rush, we did not realize that we left the medical bag at the station. All we had was the cardiac monitor, an oxygen tank, and a bag-valve-mask, but, considering that the emergency would be cyanide exposure and the company has antidote kits, oxygen and a defibrillator were our most important tools. We got to the entrance just as a group of people were helping to lift the second patient, already secured to the backboard. The company nurse said that he was conscious and breathing; she was administering the second amyl nitrite ampule by holding gauze to his nose. On our way back to the ambulance, I talked to the patient to evaluate his orientation to person, place, time, and event. He was alert and oriented to all four— A&Ox4, GCS 15. We should have asked whether the injured had been decontaminated prior to being placed on the backboards, but we arrived too late, when the role-play patients were already being taken away from the scene, accompanied by nurses who wore no personal protective equipment.

After we simulated placing the patient in the back of the ambulance, we returned to the scene. Canizales and Porfirio were already putting on level A suits, and we had no time to take their vitals before they went in. These fully encapsulated suits protect their wearers from vapors, liquid splashes, and dangerous particulate materials in exchange for misery: because the body cannot cool off by letting the sweat evaporate, core temperature rises and can result in heat-related illness.[22] Therefore, medical personnel must monitor the vital signs of emergency responders both before they put the suits on and after they take them off. If their heart rate or blood pressure is too high, technicians are not allowed to work. Since our ambulance did not even have blood pressure cuffs, I approached the Cruz Roja and asked them to at least evaluate the bomberos once they got out. The two volunteers were very helpful: they repositioned the ambulance closer to the scene and, as soon as Canizales and Porfirio returned from the site, they measured their pulse and blood pressure, and listened to their lungs.

The Cruz Roja got a larger share of contributions from residents renewing their license plates, so I wasn't surprised that their ambulance was better stocked than ours. The bomberos were torn about whether they should be providing emergency medical services at all. They have the ambulances in case one of their own gets injured; they don't trust the Cruz Roja to be there on time. But they have since started running general calls. Unlike in the US, where EMS has become a financial lifeline to fire departments, bomberos don't charge for ambulance rides and receive no payments from the residents or the government to replace IV catheters, cervical collars, or other supplies they use for patient care. Only one fire station in Nogales, Sonora, in the residential La Mesa neighborhood, can dispatch an ambulance. In 2015, it responded to 350 emergencies, leaving a significant dent in the department's budget.[23] Though the unit is equipped with a cardiac monitor, bomberos can't interpret ECGs or give cardiac medications, and, despite "paramedic" written on their shirt, the training most receive is equivalent to that of EMTs. Most volunteers with the Cruz Roja have the same skills.

Back in the classroom we went over the after-action review. The instructor said that it was very expensive for companies to buy their employees personal protective equipment and that they should take good care of the PPE they had. He said that some manufacturers had already left Nogales, hinting at the rising costs of maintaining safety. Somebody in the room made the point that the company's employees who work with hazardous materials in the US are paid more than others, but in Nogales, Sonora, they are not. The instructor didn't want to get involved in the company's internal politics and went over response and evacuation times instead. "All very good," he said. The company seemed to be well prepared for a contingency like this—a conclusion I had never heard at trainings and drills organized by public services.

For the bomberos, the knowledge about how this maquiladora handled cyanide—how often it was received, who had access to it, whether there were antidote kits in the building, and who was trained to use them—was particularly important considering that Mexico did not have a law equivalent to the Emergency Planning and Community Right-to-Know Act in the United States. Industrial use of hazardous materials falls under the purview of PROFEPA, but the agency doesn't have personnel to monitor compliance, so the task of performing inspections has been delegated to protección civil. In Sonora, Ley 161 posits that maquiladoras have to submit "a risk map" (*átlas de riesgo*) to the local office of protección civil. But the law is not enforced. Owners of maquiladoras that violated one law or another did not find it hard to pay off temporary political appointees. "Because this is a border area, we see how US firefighters work and how we have to do it in Mexico," Comandante Hernández told me once. "In the US, they work following the norms set by the NFPA. In Mexico, we are trying to follow these steps, but it's very difficult. For example, we arrive to a hydrant and it has no water. Or we get to a building that does not follow safety codes. Or we get to an industrial site and we are denied access." That used to happen a lot: during fires and other emergencies maquiladoras routinely barred the bomberos from entering, out of fear that they would cause further damage to the property or steal what they could get their hands on.

Therefore, to learn about the places of risk on the city's "topografía accidentada," as the bomberos call it—rugged topography—the fire department had to find their way out of the closed circuit in the law. They did this through collaboration with private industry, a slow process of building trust.

Since they had no legal authority to receive information from the companies about the hazardous materials they used, stored, and transported through Nogales, the bomberos had to be proactive, participating in planning and prevention, which is what this cyanide exercise was all about. The urban terrain was their jurisdiction a posteriori, only after the fact, once the incident had happened, when the emergency was unfolding, threatening lives, health, property, and the environment. Only when it was too late would the bomberos be dispatched to control the damage, asked to put their bodies on the line at no cost to the industry and free of charge to the government.

ACID RAIN

In the summer of 2005, Canizales drove to San Lázaro, a hamlet about 45 kilometers southeast of Nogales. "Hola, señor!" he greeted the first person he met. "Does a train pass through here?" "Yes!" the man answered. "It's there in the back, derailed." Canizales was not thrilled to find what he had been looking for. He climbed on top of the hill and there they were—eight tank containers scattered on the train tracks, three of them punctured. Workers from the Mexican railway company Ferromex were already on scene. He took pictures of black streams running toward the Santa Cruz River. Though sulphuric acid is clear like water, it turns black when contaminated. It was too late to stop the leak. Canizales had to call the gringos; binational agreements mandated that Mexican authorities report releases of hazardous materials likely to affect the United States. But there was no cell phone signal in the area.

Ten years later we were sitting at the wooden table outside a brick shed that housed the fire station in the industrial zone of Nogales, Sonora. A black dog named Negra was resting on the doormat, enjoying the pleasant late November sun, lifting her head expectantly every time someone passed by. She was malnourished and beaten up when she showed up at the firehouse a few months earlier. The guys fed her and she stayed. Two volunteers were working on the trucks—because the troques always needed one fix or another. Some vehicles were donated by US fire departments; others had been bought at reduced prices, usually in Arizona. Engine 26 was from Avra Valley; the brush truck, from Three Points. On its doors, stickers from Idaho, Montana, Utah, New Mexico, California, Louisiana, and South Dakota hinted to the wildland fires it had witnessed north of the border.

When the incident in San Lázaro occurred, Canizales was both an officer at the fire department and the emergency coordinator for protección civil. Better known by his nickname "El Perro" (The Dog), the lieutenant sported slicked-back raven hair and a broad smile, features that cartoonists in the local papers readily exaggerated. He didn't mind: Canizales craved attention and soaked it all up. "Un artista," I heard a fellow firefighter call him. A performer. His flawless English was a testament to the endless hours he spent watching American movies. But the most animated stories were the ones he told in Spanish. After greeting his daughter, who had just clambered onto the roof of the fire engine behind us, he started from the beginning.

On August 11, 2005, he received a call from the Santa Cruz County emergency manager. "Eduardo!" "Hey, Louie, how are you?" "Oye, was there a derailment?" "Ah, no . . . Well, I don't know." "Is there anything in the direction of Mascareñas?" "Let me check on this. 'Bye." The Americans knew that something was going on because the pH in the Santa Cruz River, which, like the Nogales Wash, flows north, had gone down. Rail companies in the US and in Mexico have an agreement with the EPA to notify them of hazmat incidents, but the information goes through the Mexican federal government, and local authorities do not receive the alerts. Ferromex workers were cleaning up the area of the spill without letting anyone know what was happening—secrecy made possible by the overlap of private property and federal jurisdiction.

El Perro only learned about the incident because the Mexican government told the EPA, the EPA told Louie, and Louie dialed his number. Canizales called him back: "Louie, there are no reports." But Louie insisted that there was a derailment and he wanted to know more. Canizales promised to go and find out. He got inside the truck and headed toward Mascareñas. "Louie, do you have more information? There's nothing here," he said, reenacting their conversation. "Nogales, Arizona, was in chaos," he told me. "Nobody knew anything. The state government had no clue what had contaminated the river." By the time Canizales found the site of the incident, he had lost his cell phone signal, so he climbed the highest hill in the area, and then—the way he tells the story—up the cross on top of it, to get a connection. "You should have seen me! Holding onto the cross," he laughs. El Perro called the Americans. "Louie! Yes, there is a derailment. Es un desmadre." Then Canizales picked up his radio and reported what he saw to the Nogales Fire Department. He told them that the containers were already empty. When the teams from Arizona arrived, there was not much left to be done besides neutralizing the water.

The cleanup continued for three days. They were fortunate that it happened during the rainy season. "It rained and rained. Practically, it washed the area."

San Lázaro was not the only incident when the bomberos were not allowed to assist with a toxic spill. The railway is federal property, and the fire department in Nogales, Sonora, is a civil association. Their closest ties to state bureaucracy go through the local offices of protección civil, the agency created in the aftermath of the devastating 1985 earthquake in Mexico City. Though often compared to the emergency management in the United States, protección civil in Mexico "is that and more," explained Vicente, who worked with Canizales when the latter was the director of the office in Nogales. The agency organizes and supports emergency activities on federal, state, and municipal levels. The intention was good: many people who came to help after the earthquake got hurt in the chaos, so the law put protección civil in charge of coordinating response to emergencies. They were also tasked with inspecting industrial sites and manufacturing facilities. But these efforts are thwarted by the agency's dependence on government officials. The director of protección civil in Nogales changes after the election, every three years. The same happens on the state level. "Es una política, pues." It's about politics, the bomberos say: competition between the PRI-istas and the PAN-istas. The fire department doesn't trust politically appointed officials who have no background in handling emergencies. However, when it comes to binational plans, the US authorities continue to insist on including protección civil as the legal representative of the Mexican state, forcing an unstable alliance.

During the time Canizales worked for protección civil—first as emergency coordinator and later as the head of the agency in Nogales, Sonora—the divide between the bomberos and the city government was temporarily closed. Between 2003 and 2006 and then again between 2007 and 2012, personnel easily transitioned between their roles in government and in fire service. Vicente remembers how once, when journalists from the *Arizona Daily Star* came to interview them, they got a call about people trapped inside vehicles being carried away by the arroyo. He and El Perro immediately headed to the scene, taking the journalists along. "They could not believe what they saw. They couldn't grasp how the director of a government office, of protección civil, puts on the gear, grabs a rope and goes to save people in the wash together with his fellow firefighters." For Vicente, as for

Canizales, there was no difference between the two roles. "It's the same. I worked in the office but I continued being a firefighter. So I would hang up my office shirt and put on the bombero uniform and go to the emergency," Vicente said. He and Canizales joined the bomberos together, when they were both sixteen.

It was during Canizales's tenure with civil protection that the fire department accepted the mandate to mitigate emergencies involving hazardous materials. For most of the time since the founding of the institution, bomberos have been there to put out fires. El Perro, remembering those early conversations with the comandante, said, "Our leadership had other priorities. Hazardous materials? What is that? We don't need that. I am concerned about having enough gas to start the trucks." Despite this reluctance to change, over the years Canizales became instrumental in forming the first hazmat team in northern Sonora. In exchange for accepting their role in creating the buffer zone for environmental hazards that threaten their northern neighbor—to stand on the frontlines of chemical, biological, radiological, and other emergencies—they got training, equipment, and a seat at the table during binational meetings. Hazmat earned them recognition from the US government.

As a fluent English speaker, El Perro was one of the first bomberos to be invited to attend hazmat courses north of the border. He began in 1994, with an eight-hour-long First Responder Awareness class. A few years later, Canizales was in Phoenix learning about CAMEO—Computer-Aided Management of Emergency Operations—when somebody pulled him from the room.

It was the first time when they began seeing Mexicans with their nose in these matters. They asked me: "And you? Where are you coming from?" "I'm a firefighter in Nogales." "Do you speak English?" "Yes." They began talking about a chemical contingency on the border. "Let's see, Mexico, do you have a hazmat team?" "What the f— is that?" I said. "No." "Do you have equipment?" "No." "And who responds to chemical emergencies?" "Los bomberos." "But do they have equipment?" "Ehm, no." "Do you have technicians?" "We have what?" They started talking. They said there would be a large-scale hazmat exercise on the border in Nogales, Sonora. I said, "OK. This concerns us." The meeting was over. When I got back here, I told my chief, "Mí comandante, los gringos are saying that we need to create a hazmat team because we will have a hazmat emergency here." "No, no, no, no, no," he said. "We don't know anything about this."

But Canizales didn't give up. In 1999, he went to California to take a course that was part of the "Bombero Program," supported by the Mexican Firefighters Association and run by the San Diego Fire Department. "The term 'hazmat' began to ring a bell." That same year, in preparation for the upcoming large-scale exercise, the EPA organized trainings at the Americana Motel in Nogales, Arizona. That's where El Perro and Louie met. Together they attended the first year-long, regional-level course for hazmat technicians, taught by Phoenix Fire. Several firefighters from Nogales, Arizona, were taking the course; Canizales was one of only two Mexican firefighters who participated. Their graduation as hazmat techs was planned to coincide with the emergency drill in Nogales, Sonora. The exercise, held in 2000, was called "Acid Rain." According to the scenario, a van from a colonia near the Nogales industrial zone had problems with its brakes and crashed into a railway tanker, cracking it open and spilling sulphuric acid, which contaminated the passengers in the van and leaked into the Nogales Wash, heading toward the US. Although Nogales, Arizona, was 7 kilometers away, it was 91 meters below the site where the simulated incident took place, and in the scenario the acid spread downhill and downstream.

With funding from the EPA, Canizales went to Sacramento to attend courses on terrorism and weapons of mass destruction. Another major drill followed: in 2003, Mariposa port of entry was the stage for an exercise that involved a suicide bomber blowing himself up in the US customs inspection area, followed by blasts that would hit a tank carrying chlorine gas. Special effects experts set off pyrotechnic displays that looked and sounded like explosions. A harmless greenish substance stood in for toxic chlorine. It was the first hands-on exercise along the US-Mexico border in which both countries responded to a simulated terrorist attack involving WMDs. About forty different local, state, and federal agencies showed up on the US side, including fire and medical personnel from Tucson, Phoenix, Glendale, and Mesa; twenty Mexican agencies, bomberos and the Cruz Roja among them, came to assist. All in all, about a thousand people participated.[24] Then, in 2009–2010, the first hazmat tech course was held across the line in Nogales, Sonora. "Había lana," says Canizales. There was a lot of money; 9/11 was still on everybody's mind. Resources "for this kind of stuff" were abundant on the US side of the border, and they trickled down south. Even maquiladoras became involved, seeking emergency responder courses for assembly plant personnel who worked with chemicals.

Through a joint initiative, EPA and NORTHCOM have provided emergency response training and equipment to local fire departments in northern Mexico. Echoing trends in the US, where 9/11 prompted the development of a systematic approach to all threats and hazards through the National Incident Management System, they have made efforts to standardize fire service operations south of the border, using IAFF, NFPA, and US fire academy curricula as templates.[25] In a country where many fire departments are run by volunteers, independent of the state, creating a common scheme of emergency response based on a chain of command is a challenging task. Equipment and supplies that American agencies distribute to Mexican firefighters through these initiatives, however, bring more immediate and tangible results. As recently as in December 2014, the program donated one hundred pairs of new boots to Sonoran fire departments, including those in the border towns of Naco, Agua Prieta, and San Luis Río Colorado. Once the Nogales bomberos had completed the coursework and taken the exams to become hazmat technicians, NORTHCOM gave them ten fully encapsulated level A suits. In 2012, in a ceremony in Nogales attended by the city mayor, representatives of the US and Mexican consulates, and federal agencies in charge of environmental protection, the fire department accepted donations of other tools necessary to respond to hazmat spills, including chemical testing kits that can be used for chlorine leaks, gas monitors, an air compressor to refill SCBAs, and confined-space equipment. Thus far the Mexican government has refused to invest in this project.

Canizales is not naive. Bomberos know that they are a human shield that the US federal government won't hesitate to put in harm's way to stop a threat, whatever it may be—a brush fire, an ammonia leak, a bioterrorism attack—from advancing north: downwind, downhill, downstream. Trained by American professionals, they remain volunteers in a country where their government won't take responsibility for their medical care or provide them with compensation. In other words, at no cost to either state, they choose to be on the frontlines, risking their lives. And, if all goes wrong, they can be easily disposed of. Not accountable to any administration, they don't get protection. To repeat what El Perro once told me, they are just "a bunch of cabrones in red trucks" (and now in fully encapsulated hazmat suits) rushing to save lives regardless of the incident.

In the bizarre world of border emergencies, hazardous materials sometimes intersect with the more common US concern in the area—drug trafficking. Canizales showed me photos of a tanker truck carrying sulphuric acid taken in June 2001. "We are at a Mexican army checkpoint near the municipality of Benjamin Hill. They found something suspicious: when the truck was going through the x-ray machine, they noticed that, in addition to the liquid tank, it had another compartment. The military didn't know what it was, so they called Nogales bomberos. 'Hey, we need you to check what it is.' So here we are. This is me." El Perro points to one of the men dressed in white hazmat suits, taking a sample. "The truck had a sulphuric acid placard, and that's what the shipping papers also said." The bomberos took a sample of the milky liquid and did a pH test, which showed that the substance was corrosive. "The pH of 1 meant that it was acid, but we didn't know whether it was sulphuric acid." They recommended that the army transfer the liquid to a different container. It was then that they found a doblefondo, a false bottom: a cylinder within a cylinder, operated by a button. "Ingenious!" El Perro smiled. "Nine tons of drugs hidden inside a truck carrying 7,000 liters of acid."

ROAD TO ROCKY POINT

October 20, 2015. It was almost noon when the bomberos command truck pulled up in front of my home. I threw my leather duffel on top of large bags containing firefighter gear and hopped inside to join Victor, César, Canizales, and a few others. Some of them had not been in this neighborhood since they crossed the border to fight Ellis Fire five years earlier.

We were on our way to binational first responder training in Puerto Peñasco, Sonora, better known as Rocky Point on the US side of the border. Heading north from Nogales we first stopped in Tubac to meet with Louie. Fortunately, Louie was good at waiting: making Mexico and the US work together, at various levels of government, required a lot of patience. In the gravel parking lot, his gray Nissan Sentra, weathered by many years of long rides, was crammed with infant car seats and bags containing reusable hazmat suits. What didn't fit in Louie's car we forced into the back of the command truck, so tightly that there was not a handful of space left. The seven of us squeezed into the vehicles and headed north, then west, and finally south.

As soon as we exited Tubac, we had to pass through the Border Patrol checkpoint on I-19. Though the bomberos could stay within the designated border zone, they did not have the special permit required to take their vehicle further into the interior of the United States. Once issued, it's valid for six months, but it takes too long to get one, which was why, they explained, they were traveling without it. To get to Rocky Point, they usually take the route through Caborca, which does not require them to leave Mexican territory. But the northern route—"por los gabachos"—was faster and safer.[26] The Border Patrol checkpoint in Tubac was the only official roadblock they would have to pass, and Louie was there to make sure they were let through. He got into the inspection lane first. Victor followed closely behind.

"He told me you're heading to Rocky Point and that I should ask you to unload the vehicle," a female officer said to Victor when it was our turn, and pointed at Louie. She was smiling. We laughed, some more comfortably than others, to show that we understood the joke. The agent and the bomberos spoke Spanish, but when she noticed me, she immediately apologized, in English.

"Está bien," I reassured her. "Hablo español."

Language, ethnicity, gender cut us—me and my companions—apart and forced realignments of our positions as we traversed the borderlands. Who they were and who I was—and who we were together—shifted according to the direction we took.

We closed the windows and accelerated onto the highway.

"Puros negritos y una güerita!" Carlos described us. And this time we all laughed sincerely. Chingaderas began. The mood was good.

We made a quick stop in Green Valley, where Louie paid a brief visit to say farewell to his aunt in an assisted living facility, then at the Costco in Tucson, where he bought a large jar of mixed nuts and several cylinders of fuel. "Does he know that it is prohibited to cross it?" El Perro wondered aloud.

We were running late, but nobody liked the thought of hitting the long road on an empty stomach, so we parked at the first fast-food restaurant we found, aptly called "In-N-Out." The bomberos ordered burgers with fries and listened to Louie talk.

"The governor is very supportive of the Border 2020 program," Louie said of Claudia Pavlovich, newly elected leader of Sonora.

The bomberos didn't talk politics. They just listened to what Louie wanted to tell them. That afternoon none of us yet knew how the disagreements between the state government, which was now in the hands of the PRI, and the municipal leadership in border towns, including Nogales and Agua Prieta, which belonged to the PAN, would sour the binational program. At that time, the main concern remained getting equipment and supplies into Mexico. A factory in Douglas, Arizona, donated over a thousand mattresses to the victims of the floods in western Sonora, but,

Louie said, the "red tape" at the Mexican aduana was holding them up on the US side of the border. Louie never hid his criticism of red tape.

By the time we got onto Ajo Way and headed west on Arizona's State Route 86, it was already past two o'clock, but our journey had just begun.

We marveled at the saguaros, decorating the hills past Tucson like candles on a cake. Canizales informed us that it was a crime to steal the giant cacti but that some people were doing it nonetheless.

"No mames güey!" César doubted. "Why would anyone do that?"

"The saguaros are huge!" Carlos chimed in. "And they have spikes!"

"It's like trying to steal chollas!" César found it ridiculous.

I didn't know about jumping chollas yet. It wouldn't be until our return trip to Nogales, driving through northern Sonora via Caborca, that I did not heed to their warnings and, during a short stop somewhere in the Altar Desert, tried to touch one. Pinche cholla!

Time stretched out on the empty highway, and, apart from Victor, who was focused on the road, my companions were dozing off. The desert west of Tucson was expansive and barren for miles on end.

We entered the territory of the Tohono O'odham Nation and passed Sells, distinguishable by humble houses with cement walls and tin roofs clustered closer together.

As we drifted in and out of a conversation about the livelihood of the people inhabiting these lands, the radio chirped.

"Gray truck calling the red truck," we heard Porfirio's voice. He was riding ahead with Louie.

"Go ahead, gray truck," Victor answered.

"Technical stop."

It was a keyword for anything and everything: fuel, food, restroom.

We pulled into a Shell gas station, where Louie was standing in the parking lot with three men I didn't recognize. I approached and he introduced me to the emergency manager for the Tohono O'odham Nation, whom everyone knew by his first name, Larry. Next to him were the public safety director and the fire manager. Larry was new at the reservation. He and Louie knew each other from the days when Larry was the fire chief in South Tucson. Apparently, Louie called Larry to tell him we'd be passing through, and they decided to have an impromptu gathering.

The three officials from the reservation said they were not sure about the meeting in Peñasco. The trinational plan between the Tohono O'odham Nation, the state of Arizona, and Sonoyta, Sonora, Mexico, included in the Border 2020 program, was still pending approval. There was no money, they said. They waited each time before they spoke, their eyes wandering far into the distance. They hesitated. But Louie pressed on until Larry finally agreed.

"I'll try to be there," he said. "We'll take my POV." He turned to the fire manager, expecting his confirmation that it was OK if they went in his personal vehicle.

The men had other things to worry about; things that mattered to them more than the binational—or the trinational, as Louie wanted it to be—plan.

"We need help." The director of public safety finally said what had been weighing on his mind. "Just from the last week, violence is up, homicides are up. There are a lot of migrants coming across."

There was a pause, as if the men were listening to each other's thoughts.

"There's a hazardous materials dump on the tribal lands on the Sonoran side." Louie tried to bring the conversation back to emergency management.

Not invited to this negotiation over politics, the bomberos were inside the gas station, stocking up on M&Ms and sunflower seeds.

The desert landscape was monotonous. To stay awake we shared stories, many of them about the terrain and the blended and blurred space of national jurisdictions—American, Mexican, Tohono O'odham.

"It was initiated by the US Border Patrol," Carlos said about a call for an injured person a few days ago. To get to the scene of the emergency, the bomberos were escorted by officers from both Mexican federal and local police. "It's an area where there is a lot of drugs. It's very dangerous," Carlos explained, turning to me as the only one who might not know.

"We walked about 500 meters off the highway to reach the línea fronteriza. We found the guy there. He had an ankle fracture. He couldn't communicate with us much because he was Hindu."

With the help of a federal police agent who spoke English, they learned that the patient had not fallen off the wall, as it was initially reported. "He said they were coming in a group. He stepped on a stone and twisted his foot and he couldn't continue forward. They [the guides] left him there."

After sunset, he saw the lights of the US Border Patrol and, crawling or limping, reached the border wall. From the other side, the Border Patrol then called C4 to dispatch a rescue team. Inderjeet, twenty-four years old with symptoms of hypothermia and an open right ankle fracture, was immobilized, his leg was splinted, and a federal police truck took him to the Cruz Roja ambulance waiting on the road.

Carlos said that there was another call for an injured border crosser, also South Asian, two days later, but they could not find him and don't know what happened to him. He might have been in US territory.

We reached a crossroads at a place called Why: Ajo was on the right, Lukeville on the left. There was a sheriff's vehicle parked at the intersection facing us. We turned left. The highway continued to be empty, except for Border Patrol trucks parked on almost every road leading off the highway.

"That's because there is a lot of drugs. There's a lot of drug trafficking and indocumentados," Victor commented. Back in the days when he worked for the pharmaceutical company and frequently took this road, he once saw drugs being loaded onto a vehicle in plain daylight.

We were in a landscape extracted from history, made into territory, and divided up into Border Patrol "sections." We had already passed one checkpoint heading west on SR 86; now on SR 85 there was another one. Even though they weren't inspecting vehicles going south toward the border, Victor slowed almost to a halt. The agents standing in the opposite lane didn't greet us. Our companions didn't wake up from their nap.

"Ieva, do you see that mountain range?" Victor interrupted the silence. "That's the línea divisora."

We were back at the border. In Lukeville, a town comprised of a store and a gas station, Louie bought tequila to fill the bulb-shaped bottle everyone knew by the name of "foco." My compañeros got out of the vehicle, stretched, and reached for their cell phones.

"Ya hay señal!" César was excited to hear his phone beep, which meant he had reception. After about six hours of traveling through Arizona and no connection to Mexican networks, the bomberos were thrilled to get back on WhatsApp.

We crossed into Sonoyta in the same order as we passed through the Border Patrol checkpoints: first Louie, then the bomberos. Except here, after Louie went through with a green light, the bomberos got the red signal. All vehicles and pedestrians entering Mexico were subject to this arbitrary selection for secondary inspection at customs. A couple of agents approached the truck. Victor got out and opened the trunk. The rest of us stayed inside.

"They'd better not ask us to unload all that!" Carlos said what we all were thinking.

"Why didn't you check that vehicle?" César pointed to Louie's car. "He's smuggling fuel."

"Pinche pendejo!" El Perro reprimanded César for speaking too loudly.

"Shhhh! Quiet!" Carlos tried to calm them both, lest the agents should hear us.

When Victor returned, he said they asked him why we were crossing the border through Sonoyta. It was far enough from Nogales to warrant suspicion. "Because it's safer, I told them." He also told them that we were on our way to a binational training course and that the aduana mexicana was invited. The agents didn't bother with more questions.

It was dark by the time we reached the fire station in Puerto Peñasco, where preparations for the week's events were under way: hazmat suits were lined up against the wall; a frame for a makeshift decontamination tent was set up in the bay. "Muy suave!" my travel companions said. While they were checking out the equipment, I followed Louie to the chief's office.

Francisco Carrillo greeted us from behind his desk. In Peñasco, he oversaw both protección civil and the fire department. Originally from Guadalajara, Carrillo was a surgeon who began his career in emergency medical services with the Cruz Roja when he was thirteen. He told us that in the last two months they had had six accidents on the railway. "These people come from far away, they have no family members in the area," he said. Carrillo was talking about migrants heading north run over by the train. The tracks that pass through Peñasco lead to Mexicali, just across the border from Calexico, California, about 60 miles west of Yuma.

He told us he recently had to amputate a leg.

In the morning, participants were lining up to register for courses held at the convention center. They wore uniforms with the names of departments and agencies from all over Sonora: bomberos from Puerto Peñasco, Agua Prieta, Cananea, San Luis Río Colorado; state police from Hermosillo; Cruz Roja delegations from Caborca, Santa Ana, and Sonoyta. Two soldiers from the Mexican army. Offices of protección civil in Pitiquito, Benjamin Hill, Ciudad Obregón. Only twenty-two people signed up for the eight-hour awareness-level hazmat course; sixty-eight wanted to take the twenty-four-hour training for operational first responders. Classes for Incident Command System, Traffic Incident Management Systems, and installation of child car safety seats were full.

As the numbers of participants swelled, not everyone was convinced that all of them needed specialized training. While some of those who came worked as emergency responders, others never left their desks to step into the street. But Louie wanted the numbers. He needed the head count to prove to the EPA that the Border 2020 program was working and that there was growing demand for more training. In the after-action report he noted that in 2015 they trained more than 5,500 individuals. And it was only October. He promised the list would be longer before the end of the year.

"This is to avoid being the blue canaries," Louie said.

In hazmat courses, the police are often called "the blue canaries." Like the caged birds that miners used to carry into the shafts and whose death alerted them to the presence of dangerous gases in the tunnels, law enforcement officers are frequently the first on scene at accidents involving vehicles transporting hazardous substances. Without training and without proper personal protective equipment, they risk being unknowingly exposed to lethal doses of chemical, biological, and radiological agents. Firefighters, who arrive later, can read the collapsed body of the police officer as a sign of a toxic emergency. As a former cop, Louie was dedicated to preparing "the blue canaries" to avoid such a fate.

Training continued for three days. Nogales bomberos were not paid for teaching the courses. They did it anyway, saying that it was important to talk the same language with the police and the Cruz Roja, especially further from the border, where first responders received less attention from the US authorities. Bomberos proudly took it upon themselves to create the trickle-down effect, sharing what they had learned with smaller departments in northern Sonora. And they did it earnestly. Although we were staying at Peñasco Del Sol Resort, a popular destination for vacation getaways, the bomberos had no time to enjoy it. As César jokingly said one early morning: "The only pool we will see today is that of decontamination."

The large number of participants overwhelmed the original structure of the courses. The instructors raced against time to get everyone through the practical exercises, dressing them up in level A suits and watching them complete a series of evolutions. There was no shade to hide from the afternoon sun when they climbed ladders, connected hose lines, and struggled to pick up coins with bulky rubber gloves. Canizales wanted everyone to know what it felt like to be in the level A suit. I was scanning the large room for anyone showing signs of heat exhaustion and handed out bottled water.

By the time the emergency drill started, the sun was already going down. It was a full-scale exercise, with an incident command post and tents set up for decontamination. The bomberos from Puerto Peñasco took it seriously and performed well. A few more hours passed. The moon and the stars were competing with light from nearby hotels when we finally left the convention center.

On our fourth day, government representatives, fire chiefs, and other officials gathered for the quarterly Border 2020 meeting. Because of flooding in other parts of Sonora, which became the top priority on her agenda, Governor Pavlovich could not attend. The morning started with representatives of sister cities meeting to discuss how to update binational plans. Several themes dominated: scaling-up from border towns to include the counties and even the state, and developing a database of existing resources in Sonora and Arizona.

"In Nogales, Arizona, and Nogales, Sonora, it has always been firefighters with firefighters," said Bojo, who was in Peñasco on behalf of the Nogales Fire Department. "The plan works because we have known each other for many years. We talk to each other. Comandante has a good relationship with the aduana. In Nogales, Arizona, we know the customs officials very well. Our children go to the same schools. We drink together."

But this bottom-up view, a pragmatic and experience-based knowledge of how things work and don't work on the frontlines, didn't fit with Louie's idea of a universal model. "One plan, all contingencies," he said, determination audible in his words, which ended the meeting.

Although Larry didn't show up, as he had promised, Louie talked about drawing up a mutual aid plan between the Tohono O'odham Nation Reservation, on the US side, and Sonoyta and Puerto Peñasco, on the Mexican side. It didn't matter that Peñasco was outside of the 100-kilometer border zone for emergency cooperation established in the La Paz treaty. It also mattered little that representatives of the Tohono O'odham were not part of the negotiations. Louie hoped that one day they would be sitting at the trinational table.

Those who did the dirty work on the ground also had no say in decisions about the future of the program. As the one who had taught hazmat to the Nogales bomberos, Bojo was disappointed that his former students agreed to playing the numbers game. Concerned for the safety of firefighters, who, unlike other participants in the program, may be called to mitigate an emergency involving hazardous materials, he wanted specialized training to focus on better preparing them. "Firefighters should be teaching firefighters," he said. On paper, the category of emergency responder was getting so broad that it risked becoming meaningless—and, in practice, that was dangerous.

Bojo agreed that police officers, Cruz Roja volunteers, protección civil employees—everyone should learn hazmat awareness so they can recognize potentially dangerous situations and stay away. But it was not their job to risk their lives plugging the leaks. The frontlines belonged to the bomberos.

STAGING

Ray Sayre was on the phone when I stepped inside the emergency manager's office that morning; whenever I came to see him, he was always on the phone with somebody.

The emergency manager's office has no windows. A table of periodic properties of elements hangs above the computer desk. There is a shelf with different pieces of radio equipment, and a red safe box full of black bags. A white uniform shirt hangs over the backrest of a couch that is too small to lie down on. There is another shelf with some books and folders propped up against the opposite wall, where I notice several white binders of "Community Right-to-Know Manual" and "Threat Mitigation Program" and a stack of orange ERGs. That's about all that can fit into this room. The rest of the wall is covered by a full-size nature scene depicting a lake surrounded by a pine forest. Four red fire extinguishers stand by the open door.

Tall and strongly built, with silver-gray hair, Ray spent thirty-five years as a firefighter in Tucson. When he retired, at the rank of captain, and moved to Tumacacori, local fire chiefs "started pulling him hard," he said. Since Louie left the post in 2008, Santa Cruz County had had no emergency manager, and Ray—who had a background in mass casualty incidents and homeland security—was more than well qualified. The chiefs of Rio Rico and Tubac Fire Districts didn't mind that he had no emergency management experience: they kept putting on the pressure until Ray submitted his application and showed up for the interview. He had one condition, he said: "I told them, if you are looking for a paper-pusher, somebody to check off boxes, you've got the wrong guy. If you're looking for the real deal, I'm the boat rocker and I'm gonna get things moving." That's how Ray talked. He's been in charge since April 2013, and not much has changed in the way he handles things. Presiding over the Local Emergency Management Committee meeting in October 2015, he told those assembled why ammonia, which circulates as refrigerating gas in produce warehouses, was a major concern in the county: "Anhydrous ammonia needs no water and it seeks water. And you and I are little water cans. So it will seek you aggressively. In hazmat we call ammonia a TTJD chemical. That means 'Talking to Jesus Direct.'" Local officials listened.

There is a shift of scales and action paradigms as one moves from the perspective of first responders to that of emergency managers.[27] "I come from fire service, which is an operational standpoint. We lay our hands on the situation, we mitigate it. My job as a captain with Tucson was directing my crews to solve the problem. Now I'm more of an orchestra conductor. The concept here is not to get your hands dirty, but to assist everyone else to get their hands dirty in a controlled fashion. It's about building relationships. It's about building capacity. It's about developing trust between many different organizations," Ray explained.

Aid flows across the border asymmetrically: while Mexican responders come to provide manpower to the minimally staffed fire departments in southern Arizona—a situation that seems not unlike the trends in the region's broader political economy, where Mexican migrant workers go north to provide cheap labor in the US agriculture, transportation, or construction industries—the United Sates usually delivers high-tech equipment and shares specialized knowledge. "It's a huge issue," Ray says, that US emergency responders are not able to go into Mexico.

About two years ago, while having dinner at a friend's house, Ray got a call from the bomberos: "Ray, we found this radiation machine. Can you give us some guidance?" he remembered the conversation. With the help of ORTHCOM and EPA, the bomberos had received equipment that could detect radiation, but they couldn't identify the source. "What kind of radiation detection devices do you have?" Ray asked them. "Well, we have a ludlum." "That's it?" "Yeah, that's it." "A ludlum," Ray explained to me, is "a surface contamination detector for decontamination." It was already nighttime, and radiation experts from Mexico would not be able to get to Nogales until the following morning, so Ray directed the bomberos to approach the suspected source with a radiation detector and report whether they noticed any upticks in readings. "At the same time, I'm thinking: I have all the detection technology available. I can meet them at the border and hand them over a hundred thousand dollars of radiation detection gear. But they don't know how to use it, so what's the point? I need to be able to send across somebody who knows how this instrumentation works." Fortunately, the bomberos didn't register any upticks in readings as they approached the radiation source. It turned out it was an x-ray device that a dentist had left behind when he moved out of the house he'd been renting without warning the landlord. "It was ionizing radiation, but it was very low," Canizales told me about the incident.

Radiation may seem like an outdated threat in the United States, where Geiger counters are synonymous with the Cold War era—a period of American history when fear of the nuclear bomb was the organizing matrix of political, social, and cultural life. For the younger generations of emergency managers and first responders, the confrontation between two superpowers is a story they learned from the comic series featuring Doctor Manhattan and the Incredible Hulk. Today, concerns over invisible particles from nuclear explosions have been pushed further down the list of priorities. The mnemonic CBRNE, which is central to hazardous materials training, starts with C (chemical) and B (biological) before it gets to R (radiation) and N (nuclear), as if radioactive isotopes were giving way to anthrax and the Ebola virus.

But the Cold War threat continues to exist in the back of everybody's mind. Textbooks still include the definitions of a "dirty bomb" and warnings about "secondary devices" intent on hurting first responders. As part of the federal government's training programs in the aftermath of 9/11, firefighters from all over the country, including the Nogales Fire Department, have been brought to the Nevada test site. The 3/11 triple disaster in Japan, when an earthquake and a tsunami impacted the Fukushima-Daichi nuclear power plant, causing meltdowns and explosions, renewed concerns about the long-term health effects of radiation exposure. Although there are no nuclear power plants and no large military installations storing nuclear weapons in the vicinity of Ambos Nogales, the risk is always present. As with other threats, the fear of radiation is recast as a matter of border security.

Now and then the news media report that trucks carrying radioactive materials have been stolen in Mexico by thieves who had no clue about the dangerous cargo. Usually, they target the vehicles and don't anticipate the hazards. In 2013, six people with signs of radiation exposure were taken to the hospital when they were arrested for stealing a truck with cobalt-60, a radioactive material used for cancer treatments en route to a waste storage facility in Tijuana.[28] In 2016, Mexican authorities issued an alert for several states when a pickup truck carrying radioactive equipment was stolen in San Juan del Río, in the state of Querétaro. The device, a small yellow container with Iridium-192, was used for industrial x-rays, including testing pipelines for structural problems.[29] The national civil protection agency warned in a public statement that the source "can cause permanent or grave wounds to a person who handles it or is in touch with it during a brief period of time."[30]

It instructed those who might locate the missing device to maintain a security perimeter of at least 30 meters and immediately call federal authorities. Two weeks later the red Chevy Silverado with the radioactive equipment was found untouched. That same year officials issued alerts for the border states from Baja California to Chihuahua when a container holding isotopes of americium, beryllium, and caesium was reported stolen from a government truck in Sonora.[31] It was recovered the following night, left in a black bag on a public bench.

To prevent intentional and unexpected smuggling of radioactive materials into the United States, CBP has deployed radiation monitors at the country's ports of entry to screen trucks and people. Some Border Patrol agents at the checkpoints also wear personal radiation detection devices that track and store dose information for ionizing radiation. Known as PRDs, or dosimeters, these small badges are used by workers in health care facilities and laboratories as well as in nuclear power plants: OSHA mandates that the dose of radiation to an adult body shall under no circumstances exceed 3 rems during a calendar quarter.[32] But the PRDs that CBP agents wear are regularly offset by people undergoing medical procedures, including diagnostic tests that involve ingestion or injection of radioisotopes during heart, thyroid, brain, or other organ scans, which can leave lingering traces of radiation for up to thirty days.[33] When Jim Conklin, the former chief of Arivaca Fire, was driving his wife to a doctor's appointment in Green Valley, they set off the agent's radiation detector at the Border Patrol checkpoint in Amado. The officer ordered a full vehicle inspection. Fortunately, Jim had the doctor's paperwork. A similar thing happened to Billy Bob's mother-in-law, identified as a potential threat when returning from Mexico through the port of entry in Nogales. Firefighters are advised to carry dosimeters because of potential exposure to radiation during the course of performing their duties, but I am yet to meet an emergency responder on either side of the border who wears a PRD.

There was another hazmat incident in northern Mexico that caught Ray's attention. It happened in Nacozari, a small mining town in northern Sonora. "I'd been here for about a month or so and I got a call from Louie," Ray told me. The former emergency manager had anecdotally heard about some very sick people south of the border, some of whom had died. Nobody knew why.

"It got my attention. I invited Public Health. We didn't really know what we were dealing with. Is there some sort of a vector? Is there communicable disease? What was really going on?" They found out it concerned a man who had been illegally mining gold in the wash.

Gold will selectively bind with mercury—it's called an amalgam. If you have a lot of gold particulate, you'll put liquid mercury into it and it will bind. Then you go outside and use butane torches to volatilize the mercury, and you are left with basic gold. This individual had been doing it for a long time. He had a big jar of mercury and he sat it on top of the refrigerator in the house and then forgot about it. The family went to visit somebody in Magdalena and when they came back several days later everybody started feeling bad. They drove to the clinic, where they were told that they all had flu, or something like that, and sent back home. But they all had mercury poisoning.

The man's wife and child died. "The entire house was contaminated with mercury and mercury is very toxic," Ray said. It was another occasion that frustrated him: "I couldn't send technicians over. I couldn't send mercury meters. I couldn't do any of that stuff because we are not covered under workers' compensation." But he helped connect Mexican responders with a toxicologist at the University of Arizona. There were disagreements about the aftermath. "What do you do with this grossly contaminated house in Mexico? You just can't walk away from it because it is an environmental catastrophe, it's toxic. Mercury doesn't go away," Ray told me. The house was boarded and fenced in, and for a while was guarded by the military. There were plans to burn it down, but nobody I asked knew whether that ever happened.

In 2015, when we met, Ray was busy updating the county's multi-jurisdictional hazard mitigation plan, which assesses and ranks vulnerabilities in the area: hazmat spills, wildfires, and flooding were his top three. In 2008, the Army Corp of Engineers inspected the Nogales Wash and concluded, "The walls and roof deck of the covered channel are in good condition, but due to the severe scouring and rebar exposure in the invert, the overall structural stability of the box section has been compromised and its performance under current imposed loads is very unpredictable and a hazardous condition." The International Outfall Interceptor ("a fancy name for a big sewer line," as Ray put it)—the point where all Nogales, Sonora, wastewater concentrates into a 24-inch tube—is a steel pipe that crosses the Nogales Wash at a 90° angle and then runs parallel to or under the wash. When it rains across the line, the water also overflows the sewer system. "Water's got its own knowledge," Ray said, "Water's gonna go, where water's gonna go."

DeConcini port of entry sits on top of the wash and the IOI, above the tunnel that has no concrete floor and no rebar: images show exposed bedrock. Concerns about its structural weakness have reached the offices of political leaders.[34] On June 16, 2016, Arizona senators John McCain and Jeff Flake and state congressional representatives Martha McSally and Raúl M. Grijalva sent a letter to the newly appointed US ambassador to Mexico, Roberta Jacobson, asking her to look into the "critical water infrastructure issue on the US-Mexico border."[35] It notes "increasing stormwater flow from Mexico that is delivered through deteriorating infrastructure" and warns that the Dennis DeConcini port of entry "is in serious jeopardy of collapsing." The letter also points to "longstanding problems with a cross-border wastewater conveyance pipe," which has been "repeatedly threatened by smuggling attempts that can rupture the pipe and contaminate the Santa Cruz River." In the letter, government officials express their awareness of the challenges to coordinate efforts "across overlapping jurisdictions" but "urge the two countries to work together in addressing the problem."

The wash, the tunnel, and the IOI comprise "three layers of nightmare" to the county's emergency and public health officials. But this is not all. "From the hazardous materials standpoint, my biggest concern is the rail yard in Nogales, Sonora, which is upslope from us. As the train goes through Nogales, Arizona, it's pretty slow, 15 to 20 mph, so the speed reduces the risk of derailment. But in Mexico houses are built very close to the rail line. You can't put in another derail because it will flip into the neighborhood. If a train that's not properly blocked, chocked, and constrained gets away, it comes right to the United States and by the time it hits the border, it's doing 50 mph." This is what happened in October 2012. Two cars—a flatbed with a tractor and an "empty" sulphuric acid tank—escaped the rail yard. "Once the two cars got away, the engineers jumped on the locomotive and started chasing it down, trying to hit it hard enough to get the couplings to engage. But that didn't occur." The cars accelerated, gaining speed at a downward slope, and when they reached the border fence, they hit the closed metal gates, forcing them to open.

That night Temo and two other bomberos were on duty at central station in Nogales, Sonora. The runaway train hit the border fence a little after two o'clock in the morning. "C4 told us that there was an explosion en la línea internacional. We were sent to check what was happening," Temo recalls. The three of them headed toward the port of entry. "We stopped at a distance. We didn't know what it was about. We put on bunker gear and SCBAs." Temo walked toward la línea and saw that the metal gates on the train tracks were open. He thought that it was a bomb, that there had been an attack. "The line was empty. There was nobody. The people who inspect vehicles, who do passport control, were frightened and they left." As he got closer, he could see through the open gate into the US where one car had been derailed, tumbled, and was leaking liquid. "We didn't know what it was. Trains carrying sulphuric acid regularly cross la línea. So we thought it was a hazardous materials incident." When the bomberos reached the fence, Nogales Fire Department was already on scene, working on the north side of the border. "We met in the middle. Then we crossed on foot. Together with the firefighters from Nogales, Arizona, we did a 360° survey and we saw that there was no leak, there were no injured people, the crash only caused damage to the infrastructure. There are water pipes supplying sprinklers that are used for emergency decontamination at the port of entry. The gates that the train hit broke the pipes and they began leaking water. It was just water." CBP temporarily shut the border, but it was soon reopened.

Now there is a fork in the railroad before it crosses into the United States: the left branch leads to the border gate, while the right branch ends in a pile of sand. Unless the engineer makes the turn to the left, the train will continue straight and hit the sand barrier. But Ray saw this as a close call. A sulphuric acid container considered "empty" still has many gallons of material residue. Because the railway goes on top of the Nogales Wash, contamination was a serious concern for emergency management. "Acids and water are reactive chemicals," he explains. "There's no warning time. It's not like we can see a fire coming from a distance. You'll have an extensive sulphuric acid mist going all the way down to Nogales. Grand Avenue runs parallel to the rail line, so the hazardous materials plumes will diffuse along the major transportation corridor. That's with sulphuric acid. But it could be chlorine, or it could be nitric acid."

"Let's put this into perspective." He wanted to make sure I understood. "A hazardous materials spill, let's say of chlorine, is considered large when it exceeds 55 gallons. The downwind evacuation distance of a large chlorine spill is 5 miles." A single rail car carries thousands of gallons. "So do the math." When it comes to safety zones, hazmat manuals only distinguish between small and large spills—it doesn't matter that a full rail tank of chlorine carries six hundred times more liquid than what is considered sufficient for declaring a large spill.

To maintain their status as plausible threats, emergencies have to be repeatedly staged. Trainings and drills are spectacles that mobilize fire and police departments, public health authorities, elected officials, and the media to focus on particular dangers to society, at the expense of others. Since the US-Mexico border has never been a site of terrorist attack, to be countered these acts in particular must first be conjured through imaginary scenarios and exercise drills—ritual performance built on anticipation and programmed failure. In Nogales, the biggest to date was the simulated attack involving WMDs in November 2003, which involved state and federal authorities, but border towns regularly stage smaller local exercises. From the perspective of firefighters and paramedics, such performances help keep up their highly specialized skills in working at incidents involving CBRNE, which they rarely, if ever, experience on the job. Emergency exercises also justify continued allocation of resources to mitigating threats that are deemed worthy of being staged. That drills are designed to fail only makes them more effective at what they do; they enact departmental and individual responsibility for providing security against all threats and hazards, and establish guilt for always already failing to live up to these expectations.

In one such binational emergency exercise on July 10, 2015, the tanker trailer involved in a simulated accident at the border crossing between Agua Prieta, Sonora, and Douglas, Arizona, supposedly carried sodium hydrosulfide. A white liquid with an unpleasant odor, it's used in cloth and paper manufacture, the leather industry, and copper mining. When mixed with acids, it releases flammable and toxic hydrogen sulfide gas. The scenario started when a mechanical defect led to a passenger vehicle catching fire in the no-man's-land between Agua Prieta and Douglas. The tanker attempted an abrupt turn to avoid approaching the burning vehicle and hit a flatbed truck carrying barrels of sodium ferrocyanide. All drivers fled the scene. There was a plume of smoke and several bodies lay on the ground. Traffic halted; the port of entry was closed.

The bomberos from Agua Prieta were the first to arrive: three of them approached the scene cautiously, using binoculars to read the placards. On the other side of the border, the Douglas Fire Department was also staging.

They brought their hazmat truck and technicians, who were donning level A suits and preparing to enter the hot zone. Dressed up in full bunker gear, a Douglas firefighter walked up to the white line marking the limit of US territory and stood next to the CBP officers. Chief Luis Rendón of Agua Prieta was the incident commander; he gave orders from under a white canopy tent that served as the emergency operations center. Invited guests and public figures, including several mayors and representatives from McCain's and McSally's offices, observed how firefighters, dressed up in hazmat suits, retrieved the patients; emergency responders from Douglas put one of them on a gurney that they pushed through the gate to the US side of the border; the Mexican bomberos attended to the other victims: dosed them in water from a fire hose to remove potentially hazardous substances on their bodies (it's called "gross decon"), and handed them over to the Cruz Roja. The event would have been confusing had I not had a guidebook to this drill, complete with maps, photos, and information about the chemicals involved. The preparation for the exercise took months even though final details were only agreed upon the previous night, during the asado at Chief Novoa's house in Douglas, where agreements were sealed by tequila shots from Louie's legendary foco.

Knowing what to expect, on the morning of the exercise I crossed the border into Agua Prieta on foot. A group of organizers were already on scene making last-minute adjustments. Two large trailers, supposedly carrying hazardous liquids, rolled into the port of entry on the Mexican side. The Cruz Roja was putting moulage on the volunteers who would play the victims: affixing premade rubber "wounds" and applying makeup. CBP told the US participants to sign their names on a sheet of paper, allowing us to go back and forth across the border without passing through customs inspection and migration control. Invited guests and observers took seats at a designated area behind a chain-link fence on the Mexican side. It all went according to plan except for one detail: during the drill, the Mexican aduana closed the border for eight minutes to evacuate its employees, resulting in a line of vehicles waiting to get into Agua Prieta from Douglas. The plan had been to do the exercise locally. Though the Mexican capital agreed to shut the port of entry, the organizers knew that the US federal government in Washington, DC, would not play along. Louie was worried and rushed to the US side to assure CBP that this would not last long.

Not all drills interfere with everyday life in border communities. Tabletop exercises, or TTX, use technology to simulate emergencies. City managers and other municipal and county administrators often take part in these simulations, as do representatives of federal agencies and fire departments. Unlike full-scale exercises, TTX does not involve rank-and-file personnel. A projector with slides usually suffices to stage the response. Several years ago, Ray wrote a grant to buy a state-of-the-art simulation table for the county. When turned off, it looks like a box filled with sand with a projector hanging above it; when it's on, the device combines real-time GIS data with agent-based modeling for wildfires, floods, evacuations, storms, airborne particulates, and biological and ecological events, all customized for the local community.[36] Ray could point a digital stick to set up a brush fire near Patagonia, a town along SR 82 east of Nogales, enter data for weather conditions (temperature, humidity, wind speed and direction), and watch it spread before beginning to place response units. He let the fire escape the initial perimeter, justifying the need for more resources. Then he projected a map of downtown Nogales on the sand. What would happen if there was a hazardous materials spill at the port of entry? How quickly will the gas clouds travel north? How big will the evacuation area be? What are the escape routes and how soon will they be clogged with traffic? What if the wind changes direction? Ray could change the direction of the wind with one click of the remote control. TTX permits experimentation with a wide range of probable as well as unlikely situations, all tailored to the local topography and climate.

Ray didn't bring his simulation table to Maryland, where he organized an integrated emergency management course for officials from Arizona's border counties and representatives of federal and state governments. Like the first joint US-Mexico emergency management course in 2008, which included several dozen attendees from each side of the border, this event at the National Emergency Training Center was planned on a binational scale. But the Mexican partners didn't show up: there were issues with funding, with the lack of support from the Mexican government, with tepid relationships between firefighters and the political appointees of protección civil; it also took FEMA a long time to process applicants for admissions to the DHS training facility and invitations to foreign nationals were sent out too late for them to get visas and make travel arrangements. Except for Ray and Louie, nobody seemed to notice the uncomfortable absence of the Mexicans. Anticipating this possibility before leaving for Emmitsburg, Ray prepared the bomberos and protección civil to participate in the exercise via WebEOC, a web-based crisis management system. And that's what they did.

The simulated emergency was set a year into the future from the day we were gathered at the NETC: August 19, 2017.[37] It started with tropical depression "Fourteen-E," which gained strength as it moved northwestward and became known as Hurricane Rocco. Rocco produced heavy rainfall in Baja California and Sonora, causing extensive flooding, damaging roads, and knocking out power lines. Flash floods, evacuations, mudslides, first deaths—Ray's scenario for this imaginary contingency was detailed and complex. Following more than 18 inches of rainfall in the past three months, rivers, creeks, and waterways in Santa Cruz County were at elevated levels. Preparations for the storm on this side of the border were under way. Residents went to fire stations to pick up sandbags and rushed to supermarkets for supplies. Rocco entered Arizona as a tropical storm on August 24, overtopping the Nogales Wash and damaging the IOI. The situation was bad—raw sewage was now flowing into the Wash—and the participants broke into groups to discuss existing policies and response structures.

But this was not the end. Ray had prepared "a master disaster." On August 25, another depression strengthened into Tropical Storm Sierra, with wind speeds of over 45 mph. CBP reported that there were 3 to 4 feet of standing water at the DeConcini port of entry, and a couple dozen cars were impaled on border fences. Calls to 911 identified several buildings that collapsed on Morley and Grand Avenues and Arroyo Boulevard. "Extreme overpressurization of the Nogales Wash tunnel has created a collapse of the underground sections along International Avenue, and south into Mexico, along the border street near the border fence." Structural cracks in the foundation raised concerns about a potential breakdown of the port. Rain continued and concrete panels that encase the wash broke free and clogged the bridge at Doe Street. There were reports of bovine carcasses flowing northward. A large cottonwood tree fell into the wash; the bridge collapsed, and a high-pressure natural gas line located on the north side began leaking. Large portions of the city of Nogales and Santa Cruz County were without power. In the meantime, Mexican authorities reported that a bus had tried to pass a flooded road and forty-five persons were carried away by the current; they would soon be launching rescue operations.

Another break-out session for functional groups. Situational assessment: "What changes need to be made within the current infrastructure to better provide decision makers relevant information regarding the nature and extent of the hazard, any cascading effects, and the status of the response?" Infrastructure systems: "Given the weather scenario for this exercise, what else needs to be done to stabilize critical infrastructure functions and minimize health and safety threats in the geographic area?" Long-term vulnerability reduction: "What measures could be taken to reduce the vulnerability from this threat?" The questions were intended to start the discussion—it was not the right place and time to make policy decisions. Ray wanted to show the representatives of city, county, and state governments the dire consequences of not having a strategy. The Nogales Wash Emergency Response Plan, ninety-nine pages long at the time and containing information about everything from primary and secondary incident command post sites to sleeping and food provisions for responders, was Ray's major preoccupation and primary goal during his tenure as the county's emergency manager.

These drills and scenarios don't produce security, which proves to be impossible in a world of multiplying vectors of vulnerability. Rather, exercises create what Joseph Masco calls "a constant state of affective emergency," which drives the potential, the possible, the imaginable into the realm of governance.[38] These drills are sites of convergence between two different approaches to public safety. While the view of those on the frontlines of an emergency—firefighters and paramedics—is pragmatic and detail oriented (they are criticized for having "tunnel vision" and losing situational awareness), the perspective of emergency management is based on a legal and economic matrix, a function of applying resources to mitigate actual and potential vulnerabilities. The tension here is between danger that is experienced here and now and future risk that is calculated and mapped, even if the two have become inseparable.

SECURITY OF THE FUTURE

The built environment of the desert city, with the operational and logistical landscapes of late modernity—roads, pipelines, electrical wires, sewage systems—anchors the discourse of security to the materiality of terrain. An invisible thread connects summer rains, illicit drugs, and radioactive particles with building codes, immigration policies, corruption, addiction, and unemployment. But these pieces of the puzzle are not assembled on an even plane. Some get priority. The government conjures the border as a space of spectacular events, such as drug loads catapulted across the fence or simulations enacting how terrorists would bring WMDs through the ports of entry.[39] The attacks of 9/11 legitimated preemptive politics, in which the threat no longer needs a referent to produce insecurity and justify militarization of public life. Brian Massumi calls this operative logic "autopoietic."[40] Blending crime and disaster, the government approaches the border by anticipating and then combating "nightmarish, if largely speculative, *what ifs.*"[41]

The outsized role the border plays in homeland security should not be surprising. After World War II, American strategists began seeing national territory from the vantage point of an enemy, as a space of potential targets. This spatial logic of domestic security, or what Stephen Collier and Andrew Lakoff call "distributed preparedness," entailed vulnerability mapping—finding and marking nodes in infrastructures that were likely to become targets and assessing potential effects of an enemy attack on specific urban features.[42] With the creation of FEMA in 1979, various emergency management and civil defense functions were consolidated under the rubric of "all-hazards," and the domain of preparedness expanded to include natural disasters. When FEMA was incorporated into the DHS, terrorist attacks were added to the list. Given this broad mandate of emergency management, the border is seen as a source of multiple forms of vulnerability. Some types of response, as we have seen, are at odds. Tactical infrastructure aims to prevent unauthorized migrants, recast as criminals or potential terrorists, from entering the country, but acting on one type of perceived threat it exacerbates others, such as flooding, in ways that endanger local communities. To avoid gridlocks due to incompatible policies, threats have a hierarchy. In the dominant paradigm of national security, focused on enforcing borders against human trespassers, environmental emergencies are of secondary importance.

Moreover, emphasis on emergencies, which creates an appearance that events like toxic spills are nothing more than "accidents," sets them apart from routine exposures to environmental hazards, such as domestic chemicals or air pollution—threats to life that accumulate over time, seeping into bodies unaware of needing protection. Like water and fire, air heeds no jurisdictional boundaries. When in December 2017 smoke from fireplaces and fireworks left a thick haze over downtown Nogales, Sonora, health officials in Arizona issued a high-pollution advisory, warning residents to avoid engaging in any activities that increase dust.[43] It was not the first time they worried about poor air quality in border towns. The toxic mist formed by dust from unpaved roads, smoke from burning trash, and vehicle exhaust enters deep into the lungs of nogalenses on both sides of the border, causing coughing and shortness of breath, worsening asthma as well as heart disease. "Ambient toxicity" is how Gastón Gordillo characterizes the negative tactile pressures the atmosphere exerts on human bodies.[44] Addressing this issue requires binational efforts, and the EPA has listed reducing air pollution as one of the goals for the Border 2020 program, while the government of Arizona has used federal grant money to pay truck owners in Mexico to replace old mufflers with new catalytic converters that reduce harmful diesel emissions.[45] But the matter is more complicated. Not only does the border fail to prevent the circulation of air pollutants, but it can further exacerbate the problem by generating more particulate matter; exhaust fumes from trucks idling while waiting for inspection at the Mariposa port of entry, for example, constitute a major source of toxic emissions.

Although air pollution affects communities on both sides of the border, most of it originates on the Mexican side of Nogales, which has at least tenfold the population of its US neighbor. The Mexican side has also experienced the bulk of emergencies involving hazardous materials. Such uneven distribution of risk is not accidental. Economic rationale and politics have a lot to do with it. Binational trade agreements populated Nogales, Sonora, with maquiladoras, which use large quantities of industrial chemicals to manufacture goods destined for the US market, while leaving safety regulations to the discretion of government officials in Mexico. These industrial chemicals, as well as raw materials, move along the main transportation corridors—the railway and the highway—crossing the border perpendicularly, while numerous warehouses in Nogales and Rio Rico store goods from Mexico before they are distributed around the country. Like air pollution, hazardous materials are therefore a concern shared between the two national jurisdictions. Both parts of Nogales form one binational industrial zone, built on a contiguous terrain at an angle that places the US at a disadvantage: downhill, downwind, and downstream from Mexico.

The border may structure toxic densities, but toxicants erode boundaries.

Emergency responders have long approached Ambos Nogales as a shared space, where water has to be shuttled from one side of the line to fight fires on the other, and where toxic spills have to be contained upstream in order to prevent damage to the entire borderlands ecosystem. Their joint efforts to mitigate structure fires and hazardous materials incidents illustrate a pragmatic approach to the built and natural environment that tries to overcome obstacles imposed by US tactical infrastructure. But this cooperation between the US and Mexico is tilted in favor of the former: hazard control is another layer in the provision of security that has been delegated—and continues to be outsourced—to the US southern neighbor.[46] In an era when there are few social institutions and national infrastructures that are not embedded within the US counterterror apparatus, the task of responding to threats has been passed on to fire departments not only in the United States but also in northern Mexico.[47] The bomberos in Nogales readily put their bodies on the line to do the dangerous work of containment without expecting either government to take responsibility for their treatment should they become injured in the process.

Firefighters in Ambos Nogales tell stories about uncanny coincidences— when events took place following simulations that speculated them as possible scenarios. In October 2011, there was an accident on the federal highway between Magdalena and Imuris: a double tanker rolled over and leaked LPG; a passenger van exploded; and nine people were taken to the hospital. But none of the highway patrol officers were hurt because they had recently taken a hazmat awareness course and knew better than to approach vehicles marked with hazardous materials placards. Another coincidence occurred in Nogales in February 2012, when NORTHCOM gave the bomberos tools for confined space rescue just before they were called to an emergency in the tunnels, where they used the new thermal imaging camera. A year later, the same night they received another donation from NORTHCOM—an air compressor to refill SCBAs—the bomberos needed it at a large fire downtown. Louie likes to invoke these occurrences when he talks at binational meetings, and, as they accumulate, they become urban legends.

One legend in particular stayed with me. A woman came to the fire station in Nogales, Sonora, and asked Canizales to install a secondhand car seat for her daughter. Six months later the bomberos responded to a vehicle accident, when a Ford Explorer blew a tire, skidded, and rolled. The driver and the front-seat passenger were not wearing seatbelts and both women were injured, but a two-year-old girl who was sitting in the back, strapped into a car seat, was not hurt. "You don't remember me, do you?" the injured nineteen-year-old asked Canizales, who was among the first responders helping at the scene. "You installed the safety seat for my daughter." "Somehow, we have karma," Louie says.

An excess in security precipitates its own fulfillment.

PART THREE

Wildland

Wildland, *n.*
Land that is uncultivated or unfit for cultivation: wasteland,
desert.

Webster's Third New International Dictionary, unabridged

A dull, wide waste lies before you, interspersed with low sierras
and mounds, covered with black igneous rocks. The soil is a mix-
ture of sand and gravel; the reflection from its white surface adds
still greater torment to the intense and scorching heat of the sun.
Well do I recollect the ride from Sonoyta to Fort Yuma and back,
in the middle of August, 1855. [. . .] Imagination cannot picture
a more dreary, sterile country, and we named it the "Mal Pais."
The burnt lime-like appearance of the soil is ever before you; the
very stones look like the scoriae of a furnace; there is no grass,
and but a sickly vegetation, more unpleasant to the sight than the
barren earth itself [. . .]; to add to all is the knowledge that there
is not one drop of water to be depended upon from Sonoyta to
the Colorado or Gila. All traces of the road are sometimes erased
by the high winds sweeping the unstable soil before them, but
death has strewn a continuous line of bleached bones and with-
ered carcasses of horses and cattle, as monuments to mark
the way.

LIEUTENANT MICHLER
Report on the United States and Mexican Boundary Survey
Washington, July 29, 1856

LOAD VEHICLES

A "Road Closed" notice warned drivers not to go any further. I stopped, got out of the car, and walked ahead to confirm that a wash had submerged a stretch of the highway. During the rainy season the surface of this twisting road crumbles and pieces float away. "Do Not Enter When Flooded" signs start as soon as you pass the Border Patrol checkpoint in Amado. I'd been taking this route nearly every day and I was aware that arroyos were not the only danger here. When the speed limit goes down from 45 to 20, consider it fair warning. Crosses mark the sites where drivers lost control on sharp curves and sudden slopes. There are cattle too—they freely roam the land and sometimes linger on the road, which snakes deep into the desert. Wildlife abounds: jackrabbits, bobcats, coyotes. But the federal agents scanning the vast landscape through binoculars and night vision goggles are looking for another type of coyote—those that smuggle humans. Migrants and drug traffickers try to cross when the moon is full, the light from the sky guiding them through the treacherous terrain of steep cliffs and snake-harboring ravines.

The road goes to Arivaca, an unincorporated community of several hundred people who made this desert valley 11 miles north of the border their home. Founded in the 1870s, it has long attracted those fleeing mainstream America for a do-it-yourself kind of life: gold and silver prospectors who worked small mines in the surrounding mountains, cattle and horse ranchers, and other frontier entrepreneurs undeterred by the Apache raids.[1] In the twentieth century, they were joined by veterans of foreign wars who came to find peace. The seclusion of the settlement and the proximity to the border drew artists, hippies, and smugglers. Local historian Mary Kasulaitis describes Arivaca as "a remote backwater, retaining the look of a little Mexican village and the flavor of an Old West mining and ranching town with the heart of self-sufficient pioneers."[2] To this day, there is no city government and no police; it takes the sheriff's deputy at least an hour to get here from Tucson. But people own guns and, if need be, can stand up for themselves and their neighbors. There is a rustic cantina, a coffee shop, a small general store, a gas station, an artists' cooperative, and a farmers' market on Saturdays. There's also a school, a post office, a church, a library, a community center, a fire station, a clinic, and a volunteer-staffed humanitarian aid office.

Arivaca has little in common with Nogales. Its rural lifestyle contrasts with the urban assemblage of industry, transportation, and retail that characterizes the binational town straddling the border. This community sits in the middle of "hostile terrain"—the rugged landscape that the Border Patrol operationalized as a key element in the agency's strategic plan to deter unauthorized crossings. Instead of a wall, tactical infrastructure in the area consists of checkpoints and roving patrols that intercept migrants already battered by the desert ecosystem. The mechanism of injury does not produce immediate trauma: wounding here takes time. So does rescue. Once after a failed resuscitation attempt in the middle of Arivaca-Sasabe Road we waited for two hours with a dead body in the back of the ambulance until the sheriff's deputy arrived: vultures were circling above, ants were stirring under our feet; we had no water. Remote places foster an ethos of self-reliance and frontier justice. As legal scholar Lisa R. Pruitt puts it, "Law is less likely to seep deeply into the nooks and crannies of rural space."[3] In the US-Mexico borderlands, material topography and social space inflect legal norms, adjusting them to the pragmatics of survival. The line between immigration enforcement and emergency medical care blurs: the latter often becomes contingent on the former. Alarmed by such ethically and legally suspect alliance, humanitarian volunteers go ever deeper into the desert, to places neither the Border Patrol's all-terrain vehicles nor the fire department's ambulances can reach.

The Border Patrol and the Tucson Samaritans pass each other on Arivaca Road, perpetually competing in their quest to find unauthorized migrants. The former want to detain and deport them; the latter hope to save their lives. Arivacans don't have a consensus about what to do with migrants or with the Border Patrol. Ranchers remember "the good old days," up into the 1990s, when Mexicans would come asking for "work, water, and a sandwich." Heading north to Tucson, they would stop in Arivaca for a few days and resi-

VIEW FROM IRON MONUMENT Nº II NEAR THE EDGE OF THE COLORADO DESERT LOOKING EAST
TOWARDS MONUMENT Nº IV

View from Iron Monument II looking east toward Monument IV (from William H. Emory's report on the United States and Mexican boundary survey, 1987 [1857]).

dents would give them odd jobs. Those Mexicans built their fences and adobes, they told me. But that way of life is over. Arivacans are now concerned about armed traffickers in their backyards and the fences broken down by vehicles that come to pick up the drug loads that ultralight aircraft drop at night. They are no less worried about their community being overrun by federal agents and mass surveillance impinging on their rights to privacy. The trench lines of the US "wars" on drugs and on unauthorized migrants cut through the middle of their homes, without anyone bothering to ask for their approval.

Writer and journalist Charles Bowden, a regular visitor in Arivaca, captured the predicament of this community when he wrote: "You don't get to pick solutions. You simply have choices, and by these choices you will discover who you really are. You can turn your back on poor people, or you can open your arms and welcome them into an increasingly crowded country and exhausted landscape."[4] Some Arivacans are fiercely opposed to the checkpoints and have staged protests that pinned their town onto the news maps of national media. Others say they feel more secure now that they can call the Border Patrol in case of an emergency. "If I found someone breaking into the house, I would call Border Patrol and say that I think they are talking in

Spanish. It doesn't matter if it's true," a rancher once told me, only half-jokingly. The Border Patrol does not engage in domestic law enforcement, but this man knew that the sheriff's office would be reluctant to send a deputy all the way down from Tucson, so he might have no choice but to lie. Like ranchers, emergency responders often call the Border Patrol and not the sheriff's deputy when concerned about their safety.

By the time I got stuck on my way back to Arivaca, I had been living in this desert settlement for about two months. The day I was shown into my rented room at a former assisted living facility, repurposed into a community center, my welcome gifts included a dozen fresh eggs from a local farm and a bag of homemade tortillas. I had a neighbor who hunted with a bow and arrow and sometimes brought me deer meat. He lived in a trailer next door, cut the lawn to keep rattlesnakes away, and stopped by in the evenings to tell me stories about the Mexicans and the Navajos. His father came to the United States as a young boy, he said, "thrown across the Rio Grande." I liked listening to his stories. Once, when pain from a root canal infection made me want to crawl up the wall, I found a white envelope on the kitchen counter: "Lleva" was written on the front, the Spanish way of pronouncing my name; instructions inside directed me to the leftovers of medicinal marijuana he had placed in a coffee can in the laundry room. I felt better just knowing I had a neighbor: he was the only human being within screaming distance, and I missed him when later that summer he returned to his rancho in northern Arizona. The remoteness of the place made me uneasy at times.

Back on the closed road, night was swallowing the remainder of the evening. "Riders on the Storm" was playing on a classic rock radio station out of Tubac, the only one on this side of the border that had a strong enough signal to compete with the accordion-heavy norteño music piercing the airwaves from Mexico. My fuel tank was not more than a quarter full, so I shut off the engine to save what was left for the trip ahead and listened to the loud silence of the desert. I was alone on the road: not even the Border Patrol ventured out when the washes were high.

Cell phone coverage in the area was sketchy too, but I was lucky; the bars on the screen showed a weak signal. I texted Tangye. "Do not cross that wash, Ieva," she texted me back. A paramedic and a firefighter, Tangye was the acting chief of the Arivaca Fire District. She had lived in the area for most of her life and I knew better than to question her advice. I waited inside my car, engine off, the desert heat seeping in, until about an hour later a highway patrol officer startled me by knocking on the driver's side window. "You should probably be able to cross," he said. The wash had receded somewhat, and although I hesitated—my rental Kia Soul was no match for his truck—I tried and made it across. There were a few more arroyos interrupting the road further ahead but I managed to get back to Arivaca before midnight.

The Arivaca Fire Department covers a 612-square-mile area in Pima and Santa Cruz Counties. It was founded in 1986, when money from a federal grant enabled the community to purchase a rescue vehicle, a brush truck, a fire engine, and firefighting and medical equipment. By 1988, there were eleven state-certified EMTs, seven firefighters, and ten volunteers who had completed basic recruit training. For two decades they sold hotdogs, spaghetti, and pies at town fairs in order to buy gear and supplies. Since 2009, when the volunteer department was reorganized into a fire district, they've been getting a share of the taxes and no longer have to depend on fundraising. But, as with any other issue, Arivacans agreed to disagree on the matter. Not everyone liked paying taxes to support local emergency services they might never use.

"When we started the fire department, we didn't know what we were doing," Linda Austin recalled of their early days. Linda, her husband Larry, Roger Beal, and Jim Conklin were sitting in a semicircle formed by two sofas and an armchair in a spacious living room with windows overlooking the desert. It was Linda's idea to invite me to hear the story from the pioneers: at one point or another Roger, Larry, and Jim had all served as chiefs and board members of the local fire department; Linda was one of Arivaca's first EMTs. "We had a lot of fun making something out of nothing. The first year we paid for all the supplies, such as bandages, ourselves," she said. "We took junk from everywhere," added Roger. "It was a very backwoodsy kind of thing," Linda recalled. She explained that Arivaca didn't even have addresses, so they put cones out on the road as markers to guide ambulances coming from Tucson. In the 1990s, when residents were allowed to name the streets, they did not restrain their imagination, and today their houses stand on Broken Dreams Drive, Crooked Sky Way, or Lazy Acres Trail.

About 80 percent of the calls in Arivaca have always been for emergency medical services. The records show that in 1994 the department responded to 109 incidents: 71 for medical emergencies, 25 for fire, 3 listed as "aid and assistance," and 10 false alarms.[5] As first responders in such a remote area, they got to see things their colleagues in urban communities rarely encounter. They also had to take risks that department protocols generally do not permit. For example, when two men visiting Arivaca got into an argument about who would pay for gas and one of them stabbed another with a dagger, they could not wait for the sheriff to secure the scene. The man had a cut in his carotid artery and he was bleeding profusely. As EMTs tried to maintain pressure on the neck, blood spurted through the patient's mouth. The helicopter broke the time record, arriving in twenty-three minutes.

In the late 1990s, these emergency responders began seeing big groups of border crossers involved in rollovers near Arivaca. In one incident at the bottom of Milepost 3, nineteen people were packed into a suburban "like sardines," one of them recalled. Another time they responded to an accident involving a small car that carried eight adults, including a pregnant woman and a child. When R.D., who worked as an engineer in San Diego, California, moved to Arivaca and became a volunteer with the fire department as an EMT, this is what he saw:

> You wouldn't believe how many people! Fifteen, sixteen people on the pickup—that's a pretty good load of people. When the average person weighs 150 pounds and this truck is doing 65, 70, 80, 90 miles an hour trying to run away from the Border Patrol and they blow a tire and the next thing you know we have a rollover and people scattered for fifty yards—bodies, some of them running . . . some of them were still ambulatory . . . they were taking off and I couldn't handle them because it wasn't my job to chase them. Border Patrol was right on scene. There's been people apneic and pulseless and I was assessing the patients though I knew there was no helping them. There were some people that had broken bones, but it wasn't life threatening, so I would go on to the next patient and help them as much as I could. People had problems with breathing or were bleeding really bad, and I would attempt to stop the bleeding and make sure they have a clear airway and make sure they were comfortable, that somebody was holding C-spine. I was nothing but an EMT Basic but the amount of experience that we got out here . . . I've splinted broken femurs, I've splinted arms using a stick. We used what we had—duct tape, cardboard.

During the "car wreck phase," as emergency responders call this period, Border Patrol agents "were observers and pursuers": unlike today, they did not have EMTs and were not helping with the patients.

As a teenager Tangye used to babysit the kids of Arivaca's fire chief while he and his wife ran calls. Although she had family in the police—her grandfather and her brother were cops—she was never interested in law enforcement. Tangye wanted to join the military, but they wouldn't take her because of asthma. For a while, she lived in Tucson and considered becoming a nurse. It was not until 2004, when she returned to Arivaca, that she got into the fire service. She completed her EMT training and, three years later, finished paramedic school and graduated from the fire academy. She is proud that she is not the only firefighter in her family; her great grandfather and cousin were firefighters in Colorado, and her husband's uncles in Indiana are all firemen. But she never emphasizes the fact that she is the only firewoman among them—and one of only a handful of females in the fire service across southern Arizona.

Tangye is blond, wears dark sunglasses, and drives a giant red Toyota truck with IAFF and Rio Rico Fire Department decals on the back window, an anti-Obama sticker on the bumper, and her name on the license plate. When I met her for the first time, we sat outdoors at Sweet Peas Cafe during the Friday Night Fish Fry, watching her five-year-old son Colin play in the backyard. She has three other boys: fourteen, sixteen, and seventeen. Several years ago, a severe allergic reaction to an antibiotic caused seizures that broke her spine and she spent a couple of weeks in a coma, but when she recovered, Tangye returned to emergency services. She spoke to me on the second day of her triple 24-hour shift. From the roster of about thirty active personnel, at least two emergency responders are on duty at all times. "They call me the black cloud because all the bad calls happen when I am on," she said

"People in the East have a lot of misconceptions about it," Tangye said. She pointed south to the mountains and the border hidden behind. She gets many calls to help unauthorized migrants, or "UDAs," as first responders more commonly refer to them in Arivaca. "The majority are Mexican or from Central America, but not all. I've had some Chinese. I've had someone from Czechoslovakia—blond-haired, blue-eyed. I've had someone who walked from Ecuador—that was a long, long walk." "OTMs" is the term that the Border Patrol uses to talk about migrants who are "other than Mexicans." Tangye was comfortable with "UDAs" and "OTMs," but speaking with me she called them "border crossers." "Not to offend you," she explained when I asked why.

"The terrain is very rough," she said. "If you don't know the terrain, I wouldn't walk out here at night. But they do. They fall off cliffs or they trip over rocks." She has seen many patients with dehydration and heatstroke, as well as hypothermia. "I even got rhabdo. Three of those in the past year." Patients with suspected rhabdomyolysis need aggressive fluid replacement to

Sign announcing Border Patrol checkpoint on Arivaca Road.

reduce kidney damage from toxins that dying muscle fibers release into the bloodstream. Before Arivaca began providing advanced life support (ALS) services, patients who were severely dehydrated or who were involved in serious motor vehicle accidents had to be flown to the hospital by helicopter. "Now with ALS I'm able to stabilize them and then transport to Tucson." Until the opening of the hospital in Green Valley in 2015, the closest facility to Arivaca was St. Mary's, about 60 miles away. Banner South, which has a lockdown unit for patients in Border Patrol custody, is about the same distance. It took over an hour to reach either of them. But it can be another hour to get to the location of the patient, often "out in the sticks." Approximately 12 percent of an average of 210 calls that Arivaca Fire responds to each year entail flying the patient to Tucson by helicopter.

Tangye was the first person to tell me about the positive side of Border Patrol checkpoints, which many in her community detest. "I want to live in the United States. It's as if you had a checkpoint at the end of your driveway," one of Arivaca's former fire chiefs complained. But Tangye noticed that with the checkpoints, tragic vehicle accidents with multiple casualties—the kind that R.D. talked about—have stopped. "Now they are running through the desert but they are not running that amount of people. It's one truckload at a time instead of six or seven." The routes are still active, but since the checkpoints came in, Tangye hasn't seen a border crosser killed in a motor vehicle accident. Hints to what it was like earlier can be found in the papers:

February 24, 1998. A pickup truck overturned on a sharp S-curve on SR 286 near Arivaca Junction, between Sasabe and Three Points.[6] Eleven unauthorized migrants were taken to hospitals in Tucson, and two more later showed up at a ranch 10 miles north of the accident site to ask for help. Border Patrol spokesmen said that the truck rolled over about a mile and a half from where agents watching the highway had seen it pass by but before they could give pursuit. Mexican consul Carlos Torres Garcia said interviews with nine deported accident victims indicated they were hiding in the bed of the pickup and could not see what lay ahead.

June 18, 2000. Eleven Mexicans were injured in a single-vehicle rollover near Milepost 24 on SR 286 north of Sasabe.[7] "Patients were strewn about the scene," said Captain Louis of the Rural Metro Fire Department. Arivaca Volunteer Fire Department, the Border Patrol, and the Arizona Department of Public Safety were also on scene. Four ground ambulances and four helicopters were dispatched to transport the injured to Tucson-area hospitals.

August 8, 2002. "A truck carrying at least 14 illegal aliens, 10 of whom were riding in the truck bed, crashed on Arivaca Road."[8] Border Patrol spokesmen said that the woman driver was a US citizen, while the passengers were all Mexican nationals.[9] Some of them fled into the desert. In another accident on the same day, a 1987 Pontiac was speeding northbound on SR 286 when a rear tire lost its tread, the driver couldn't control the vehicle, and it rolled several times about five and a half miles south of Three Points.[10] Four people who were ejected died in the crash, and two others were taken to UMC by helicopter.

February 21, 2003. Fifteen men suspected of being illegal immigrants were in a Ford F-250 when the pickup truck rolled over on Arivaca Road near the Pima–Santa Cruz county line.[11] Pima County sheriff's spokesman said the driver was traveling "at an excessive rate of speed" when he entered a dip in the road that was followed by a curve to the left and lost control of the truck. The truck rolled, throwing passengers onto the road, while the driver fled into the desert. Thirteen injured, two or three of them critically, were taken to the hospitals in Tucson and Nogales. They were all from various towns "deep in Mexico," the deputy told the press.

January 10, 2005. A Chevrolet Suburban carrying fourteen people rolled over after rounding a tight curve on Arivaca Road, leaving seven critically injured and one dead.[12] Border Patrol agents found the Suburban upside-down in the middle of the road shortly after the crash. "There were just bodies all over the place," according to Arivaca fire chief Tilda Martinez, the first paramedic to arrive on scene. Seven southern Arizona rescue agencies responded. "Some of the rescuers' pants had bloodstains up to the knees from kneeling on the bloody pavement to help victims," the newspaper reported. Helicopters came from as far away as Willcox and Casa Grande to carry the most critically injured to Tucson-area hospitals.

In their collision reports, the Arizona Highway Patrol doesn't use identifiers that would help distinguish whether an individual involved in a motor vehicle accident "is or is suspected to be an undocumented alien."[13] With no official statistics to draw from, all that is available are the estimates provided by the press: the *Arizona Daily Star* reported that thirty-two border crossers died in car crashes in 2004 alone.[14]

Dispatched to calls that didn't look like anything they were taught in basic training, emergency responders in rural communities had to improvise. Tangye told me about a rollover accident in 2006; the Arivaca Fire Department was dispatched for an MVA on SR 286 near the main entrance to the Buenos Aires Wildlife Refuge. The Border Patrol had been following a white pickup truck loaded with drugs, and, when they attempted to pull them over, the driver tried to flee, but lost control of the vehicle. It rolled several times. Tangye was one of three volunteers on site:

> I remember the first thing I saw as I was walking toward the scene were pot bales strewn about the landscape. They were everywhere. USBP was armed and needed everyone's names for documentation. My job was to attend to the trapped occupant. My partner and I used our extrication tools to remove the driver side door and the roof of the vehicle. The driver's seat was broken and, because we had to stabilize the patient, we used what we had near us. That "something" happened to be a bale of marijuana as it was the right size and weight. I've learned in this business to use what you have available.

The driver had a severe head injury and was unconscious; a helicopter transported him to UMC. The second patient was taken there by an ambulance. As far as Tangye knows, both of them survived.

Tragic vehicle crashes have also occurred on roads east of I-19. A particularly bad incident happened in June 2009, when a Ford Excursion carrying twenty-four people rolled over on SR 82 near Sonoita. Carmen, who at that time was an EMT with the Tubac Fire District, was one of the first people on scene. "I was brand new. I remember getting off the ambulance and it was like a war zone. Bodies everywhere." The first patient she saw was a fourteen-year-old. "Her face was just . . . like if somebody got a knife and just sliced her up." Then, as she started walking, Carmen found people with head injuries: "There was brain matter on the ground," she remembers. She was there with her captain, and, until other emergency responders arrived, they counted on the Border Patrol agents for help. When Sonoita Fire arrived on scene, they took over incident command, while Carmen and her captain continued doing triage and providing medical aid. Eleven unauthorized migrants were killed in that accident. In their reports to the media, officials from the Arizona Department of Public Safety denied that the truck was being pursued, but one of the survivors, a Mexican national, said a Border Patrol vehicle had been following the SUV, which accelerated and, due to the oversize load, blew a rear tire and rolled multiple times, ejecting most of the passengers.[15]

The field of causality in rollover accidents includes the type of terrain and the kinetic energy produced by the speed of the vehicle and the weight of the cargo. It entails the shared responsibility of human smugglers, who load too many migrants in one truck (mass), and the Border Patrol, who chase the van (velocity). The weather, too, plays a role in acceleration because it changes the surface of the road. As an emergency responder, I understood these dynamics. The same highway, SR 82, runs in front of the Nogales Suburban fire station. Chief Parra told me about numerous vehicle rollovers in our jurisdiction. During the rainy season about twenty years ago, he said, a DPS officer was chasing a car on the highway when he lost control, flipped over, and died on scene. The road has stretches so winding and narrow that, for their own safety, the police don't pull over speeding drivers because there's nowhere to stop.

Accidents also happened on South River Road, which until a decade ago was unpaved. "Now people fly through there, but back then, when it was just dirt road, oh God, it was really bad: a lot of dust, and when it rained it got all muddy and you could slip and slide," Chief Parra told me. Some of those accidents involved vehicles with drugs or migrants pursued by the Border Patrol. Erected at a place they call Dead Man's curve, a white cross with a flower wreath commemorates one such incident. It was a

Sunday afternoon about a decade ago. "He was carrying a load and he had some illegals in a camper in the back," Chief Parra recalled. He was being chased by the Border Patrol and he lost control on that curve. The truck flipped over a couple of times and landed on its roof. The guys that were in the back all jumped out and they were kind of OK, but the driver got pinned under the truck. He died." Emergency responders could not move the truck until law enforcement had taken pictures and finished their report. "I don't know if that also went to court, if the Border Patrol got too close or was going too fast," Chief Parra said. Since the checkpoints were established, rollovers have become less frequent because unauthorized migrants keep off the roads. Our chief nevertheless made us practice extrication. CBP readily supplied confiscated vehicles for firefighters to train on.

THE MAN IN BLACK DRESS PANTS

June 12, 2015. My phone rang at 4:57 P.M. Tangye was in a rush, but her voice was calm and clear: "We have a call, probably a UDA. Meet me at the station." I ran to the car. Since I lived just down the road from the firehouse, I beat her there. Trevor had started the ambulance, and, as soon as Tangye's red truck rolled into the parking lot, we were set to go. The call for heat exposure at Milepost 3 on the Arivaca-Sasabe Road came from the Border Patrol. We were told that their EMTs were already taking care of the patient. The road is usually empty in that direction, so Tangye didn't turn the lights and siren on.

It took us about half an hour from the time Tangye got notified until we reached the scene. Trevor knew where to stop: two Border Patrol vehicles were parked side by side south of the road that cuts two otherwise indistinguishable chunks of the desert. The agents had brought the patient to this spot, which Tangye appreciated. Some years ago, when she was dispatched for "rescue nature unknown" and reached the location on Arivaca Road, she was informed that the patient was near a cattle tank behind a hill, about a mile away from where she stood. There were only three of them in the ambulance that time, so they decided to go off road and get as close as possible to shorten the distance they would have to carry the injured. Unfortunately, the department's new four-wheel-drive ambulance hit a rock, which pierced the radiator and put the vehicle out of service. They had to continue on foot. Once they found the patient, he was severely dehydrated, with an obvious ankle fracture. After splinting his leg and administering fluids, they packaged him and carried him to the road, a mile away. Tangye wanted to avoid getting into such situations if at all possible.

The agent who met us explained that the man they found had been walking for five or six days, that the group leader had abandoned him, that he was trying to call 911 but he did not have a cell phone signal. When the Border Patrol got to him, he was in a bad shape: limping, dizzy, nauseous. He ran out of water four days ago and had been drinking what he could find left in the desert. The agent informed us that the last time the patient urinated was in the morning, and that his urine was dark yellow. He knew that asking questions about the color of the urine helped diagnose the severity of dehydration. Prior to our arrival, Border Patrol EMTs inserted an IV needle into his right arm and administered two bags of normal saline. He looked much better now, they said.

The patient was strong enough to walk over to the ambulance and lie down on the gurney.

"Tell him to scooch up a little bit so he is more comfortable," Trevor said. He didn't speak Spanish. I translated and the patient moved as instructed.

He was wearing black laced leather shoes with thick gray socks and black dress pants with a black leather belt. But he had no shirt on. A plastic light blue rosary hung on his naked chest.

"Which way is Arivaca?" he asked me. I was sitting next to the gurney facing him, while Trevor was setting up the cardiac monitor, wrapping the blood pressure cuff around his left arm ("Tell him to keep his arm straight," he directed me) and placing the pulse oximeter on the index finger of his right hand.

"That way," I said, pointing east, in the direction from which we had come. "Where you trying to get there? To the camp?" I asked.

Located off the road south of Arivaca, the "camp" is a collection of tents where volunteers with the humanitarian organization No More Deaths provide migrants with food, water, and medical care. My neighbor called this aid center the "muertos camp"—the camp of the dead. Often migrants are in grave condition when they reach it; they vomit blood, they are dehydrated; their feet are so blistered that they resemble raw meat. And, as soon as they recover, they are on their own: the volunteers aren't allowed to help them in their journey north. But while inside the camp they are temporarily safe. Based on the same principles that protect the Red Cross in war zones, No More Deaths has an informal agreement with the Border

Patrol that the latter will not interfere.[16] The man in black dress pants said he was trying to find it.

"They told me to follow the Baboquivari," he said.

As the most recognizable shape in the desert landscape west of Arivaca and north of Sasabe, the 7,730-foot-tall granite monolith known as Baboquivari Peak is a reference point to those who cannot carry a compass in their pocket. The Tohono O'odham consider this mountain sacred—the home of their deities and the place where people may have once emerged from the insides of the earth. I remembered how the Samaritans taught their volunteers to give directions by referencing landmarks such as this.

While Trevor and I were preparing the patient for the long ambulance ride, Tangye was talking to the Border Patrol agents outside. "Which of you is escorting me to the hospital?" I overheard her ask them before she shut the back door.

The patient was slightly tachycardic (heart rate of 115), but had normal blood pressure (136/92). Tangye hooked him to a bag of lactated ringer's (LR) solution.

"When was the last time you had anything to eat?" she asked.

"This morning. I found an energy bar."

He understood English, so Tangye asked him to speak to her in English. She needed to gather his medical history.

"My Spanish is muy poquito," she said.

"How come you don't speak Spanish?" he wanted to know.

"Do I look like I speak Spanish?" she asked.

"No, but you could," he said.

Tangye didn't argue. She turned to Trevor: "Get my book." He passed her the pocket-size handbook entitled *Spanish for EMS Providers.*

"Tiene dolor de estómago?" Tangye knew where to find the questions she had to ask.

He nodded. Tangye flipped to another page:

"Tiene hypertensión? Diabetes?"

"No, no hypertension, no diabetes. No HIV."

"Oh, you know that?"

"Yes, I got tested." Then, after a brief pause, he said: "We can also speak Italian."

"So you speak Italian too?"

The patient was coughing heavily and Tangye asked him how long ago his cough started.

"Long time ago," he said. He complained of sore throat and said he had green sputum.

"Do you have night sweats?" Tangye was now following the protocol for soliciting the history of present illness for a person suspected of having tuberculosis.

He nodded, though it wasn't clear to me whether he understood what she was referring to.

"Have you lost weight recently?" Tangye asked, and then turned to me.

"Ha perdido peso últimamente?" I translated.

He nodded again.

"Have you been tested for TB?"

"TB?"

"Tuberculosis."

"No."

"Trevor, check his temperature," she told the EMT.

"99.8."

"OK, I'm putting a mask on him." Tangye placed a green HEPA mask to cover the patient's mouth and nose. He continued coughing—in deep, tearing bursts—all the time we were with him. We didn't wear masks.

Trevor got into the driver's seat while I stayed with Tangye and the patient in the back of the ambulance. We were ready to head north to Tucson.

"I am a smart Mexican. But not smart enough to cross the border," the man said once we started moving.

"Not at this time of the year," Tangye replied. "Respire profundo," she said, instructing him to take deep breaths while she listened to his lungs. Then she lifted his mask and placed a nasal cannula set to deliver supplemental oxygen at 2L/min.

Tangye filled out the patient care report, which included his signs and symptoms, medical history, and the treatment he received. There were still blanks left on the form.

"Fecha de nacimiento?" She asked for his date of birth.

"August." He showed her three fingers: "Tres. Three. 1976."

"Thank you."

Tangye asked for his first and last name and our patient introduced himself. I will call him Manuel. Manuel said he was from Puebla. "Near Mexico City," he specified, uncertain about how well we knew his country's geography.

"Medications? Allergies?" Tangye continued with the questionnaire.

"No medications, no allergies." Manuel said he took a pill for sore throat and something else for his legs, but he could not remember the names.

"Ha tenido vómitos?" Tangye asked whether he had been throwing up.

"Sí."

Manuel turned to me and said that he had a daughter who was born in the US. She was now living in Puebla and she had just had her quinceañera. "The sweet sixteen," he explained, comparing the Mexican tradition to celebrate the girl's fifteenth birthday to a similar practice popular in the United States. He wanted to bring his daughter with him to the Estados Unidos. We talked in Spanish.

"Anything pertinent?" Tangye asked me, looking up from the computer screen. She was filling out paperwork.

"No," I said. "Just talking about his daughter."

Tangye evaluated the neurovascular status of his hands ("squeeze my fingers") and legs ("push up, push down"). Manuel said that both of his feet hurt. He had changed socks four days ago. Though he likely had blisters, the soles of his shoes were intact, and Tangye decided against removing them now that he was en route to the hospital.

Manuel had told the Border Patrol that he had abdominal pain, so Tangye examined it by applying gentle pressure. It didn't hurt now. Manuel pointed to the lower left side and told us that he had pain there yesterday. His last bowel movement was three days ago.

"Dolor de cabeza?" Tangye asked about headache.

"No."

"Dolor de garganta?" Sore throat?

"Sí."

After a brief pause, Manuel asked:

"Why 'tierra salvaje?'"

We didn't immediately understand what he was referring to.

"What wild land?"

He tilted his head toward Tangye's uniform, which had the logo of the Arivaca Fire District: the Maltese Cross–shaped symbol consisted of a stylized desert image surrounded by four words: Arivaca, Fire, EMS, Wildland. "Wildland means *incendios forestales*," I explained. Forest or brush fires. Even though in this situation *salvaje*—"wild," or "savage"— more accurately described the treacherous desert landscape that nearly killed him.

As we headed north on SR 286 toward Tucson, Manuel faced the back window and could see the Border Patrol vehicle following the ambulance for the entire length of the trip. The highway is less curvy here, but it is hilly and patched up; stripes and blotches of the darker cement plugging old holes continue from the Sasabe port of entry to Three Points. All of us in the back jumped when Trevor didn't slow down for a dip once or twice. But Manuel did not complain. Motioning toward the Border Patrol escort behind us, he said his head was banging on the roof when the agents were transporting him to Milepost 3 on the Arivaca-Sasabe Road.

We passed a checkpoint, no different from the one in Amado, without coming to a halt, but I saw the Border Patrol escort stop and the agents talk to their colleagues guarding the roadblock.

"Tiene frío?" I asked Manuel. The AC inside the ambulance was on and he was shirtless. But he shook his head.

"Where's your shirt?" asked Tangye.

Manuel again thrust his head toward the Border Patrol escort: "They have it."

"So you have been coughing for a long time? Have you been to the doctor?" I was worried about his cough.

"What doctor in Mexico?" Manuel replied rhetorically.

The journey took us over an hour, and, to fill in the silence, Manuel shared some pieces of his life story.

"There are eleven of us," he told us. Eight brothers and three sisters. "But I have the prettiest wife," he said. "She is white, also from Puebla. She looks like a model. You'd see if I could show you a picture on my cell phone."

As he was talking, Manuel's mask began slipping off and Tangye readjusted it.

"I have a big nose," he joked, blaming it on his facial features. "My wife calls me 'mi negro narizón.'"

Manuel was living and working as a cab driver in New York City when 9/11 happened. "It was very sad," he remembers. "I cried." The daughter who had just celebrated her quinceañera was born in New York, but a few years after 2001 they moved back to Puebla. There, he worked as a taxi driver and practiced his English talking to tourists.

Manuel spoke eagerly, so we continued asking him questions.

"How did you get here?" I inquired.

"How much did it cost?" Tangye wanted to know.

Manuel said he had agreed to pay $7,000 for the trip from Puebla to New York. He traveled by plane from Mexico City to Hermosillo. In Altar, he got into a van with thirty other people and headed to El Sásabe.

"The mafia and the police are the same in Sonora," he said. He told us how during the ride from Altar to El Sásabe they passed a police checkpoint and the mafiosos in charge of the smuggling operation paid a bribe to the agents. Using his cell phone, he took a picture of the group's leader. Manuel said that as soon as he got to a detention center he would turn him in. "I have his name and his photo on my cell phone," he told me.

"Isn't it dangerous for your family in Puebla?" I asked.

"I don't know," he answered quietly. It seemed he hadn't considered that. But now he was getting worried. Manuel said he wanted to call his wife and warn her not to pay the smugglers. He was afraid that they would get in touch with her and tell her that he'd successfully crossed the border into the United States. Unfortunately, his cell phone battery had died in the desert, so even if he had found a signal he could not have called 911.

He continued his story: they got to El Sásabe Monday night and crossed the border early Tuesday morning.

When Tangye asked Manuel about the plastic rosary that he had on his neck, he said he found it in the desert.

"I have also found those," Tangye noted.

"When I found it, I knew that it would change my luck," Manuel told us. "I was trying to find them," he motioned with his head to the Border Patrol escort. After discovering the rosary, he climbed up the hill and saw the patrulla. He said he waved and the agents came to him.

"It's most important to be alive," I said. I didn't think it was appropriate to ask about the other members of his group; we were emergency responders, not law enforcement, but the boundaries are thin sometimes. Tangye didn't ask about them either.

By the time she'd hung the fourth bag of IV fluids, we were entering Tucson.

"You still don't want to pee?" she asked in amazement. "That's been 3 liters!"

Then she picked up her cell phone and dialed the hospital's number to give her medical report:

This is Arivaca Fire Rescue 502. I have a twenty-minute ETA to your facility with a thirty-nine-year-old male, heat exposure. Patient is in Border Patrol custody. He's been walking five days, ran out of water on Tuesday, has been drinking water he found along the way. He last peed this morning and his urine is dark yellow. He is a TB suspect: positive for cough since December, positive for fever (99.7). He has no other history. Patient takes no medications, has no allergies. Vital signs: blood pressure 119/73, heart rate 109, respiration 14, and he is currently sat 98 on 2 liters per minute; finger stick is 85. He has an 18 gauge in the right AC. He received 2 liters of normal saline prior to arrival and I've given him 1 liter LR; he has the second liter TKO.

It was past 7:00 P.M. when we reached the ambulance intake at the south campus of the University Medical Center, better known as Banner South. Tangye and Trevor lowered the gurney and we headed for the main entrance to the emergency room. A Border Patrol agent caught up with

Tangye to ask her whether she needed a copy of the TAR, the transport authorization request. She said she did and expressed her surprise that they had it ready so quickly. "Usually I have to wait," she told me. Without this piece of paper the fire department could not bill the government for providing care to an unauthorized migrant.

Once inside, we continued down the hallway and through a set of gray metal doors with "Restricted Access" written in red, until we entered the security unit for patients in law enforcement custody. An intoxicated woman lying on a bed in the hallway was shouting at the staff.

Each room had gray metal doors and large glass windows, and Manuel was sent to the one on the far-right end of the hallway. Except for a bed, the room was empty. It had bare beige walls and it was cold. While the nurse left to find an IV stand for hanging the drip set, a young woman who spoke fluent Spanish brought a computer station to register Manuel in the hospital's system. A female Border Patrol agent stood watching us from behind the tinted glass window on the right side of the room.

"It's safer to keep them there than let them sit in the room with the patient," I overheard one nurse tell her colleague when the latter expressed concern about the agent not having a badge to open the door. Ordinarily, agents sit in the same room as the patients, but the nurses wanted to protect her from possible TB exposure.

Tangye and the nurse both received copies of the TAR, and the nurse told another staff member to double-check the patient's data to make sure everything matched.

Meanwhile, Trevor went back to the ambulance. He had to clean and disinfect the patient's compartment, discard used medications, put all equipment back in place—standard practice after every call. But because of possible TB contamination, Trevor was particularly scrupulous.

After leaving the hospital we stopped at a gas station to buy some water and snacks for the road. It was a long trip back to Arivaca: we didn't return until after dark, around 9:00 P.M. Fortunately, nobody else got sick or injured during the four hours the community was left without its only paramedic, and backup more than half an hour away.

BOUND BY LAW

I had been gone for a week and Tangye told me that I had missed several more runs for injured migrants. We sat talking outside of Arivaca's only coffee shop, shielded from the sun by Aleppo pines that grow tall in the desert, where few other trees dare. "Border Patrol found him walking on Arivaca-Sasabe Road," Tangye said about her last call. "His sneakers had no sole. That's how far he walked." She recounted the rest:

"Fifty-three-year-old male, possible dehydration." That's what came by dispatch. Possible? There's no possible! I got out there and he was bad off. He had been walking for a week, separated from his group three days prior. He had no food for three days and he was drinking cattle tank water, which is always a mistake. He was complaining of generalized body aches and abdominal pain. He got 3 liters of fluid: a liter of lactated ringer's and 2 liters of normal saline. His veins were still flat, I couldn't . . . Border Patrol EMT was on scene first and he started an IV, but the gauge was too small for dehydration because you need to run fluids. I couldn't get another line. He had amber-colored urine, he told us. That's indicative of renal failure. He was in rhabdo. I took him to Banner South. He was lethargic. If I asked him a question in my broken Spanish, he would answer, but he didn't have his eyes open the whole time. He was just sort of sleepy. His ECG was showing peaked T waves; that's dehydration there! His blood pressure was low for his age, 104/70, and I couldn't get him up above that. He deteriorated once we got to the hospital. They moved him to ICU. That's the difficult thing; there's nothing more that I can do for that but give fluids.

Tangye continued:

The next day, Saturday, we got called out again for another UDA, a twenty-four-year-old male. Another rhabdo. That's what kills them ultimately out here in the desert—severe dehydration. They [the Border Patrol] were at the very edge of my response area: Highway 286 Milepost 23. I only go to Milepost 24. So that's almost 12 miles from the junction of Arivaca-Sasabe Road and SR 286. It's a 30–35 minute response from here to there. They kept calling: "You have ALS today?" "Yes." "What's your ETA?" And then I knew he was bad off. But again there is nothing I can do when they are severely dehydrated but give them fluids.

Tangye has many stories like this. "The hottest I've ever seen anybody out here was 106°F. I didn't even think that was viable with life. It's hyperthermia for sure." When their core temperature is this high, people don't sweat anymore. They are usually tachycardic and confused, and may have seizures; 104°F is the cutoff for making a formal diagnosis of a heatstroke in a human being. If sustained, it leads to organ failure and brain damage. It's death by slow roasting. Luis Alberto Urrea described the process in his account of Mexican migrants who were abandoned by their coyote and spent more than four days in temperatures reaching 115°F, lost and wandering in the desert southeast of Yuma in 2001: "Proteins are peeling off your dying muscles. Chunks of cooked meat are falling out of your organs, to clog your other organs. The system closes down in a series. Your kidneys, your bladder, your heart. They jam shut. Stop. Your brain sparks. Out. You're gone." In that incident, fourteen died. Eleven were treated for severe dehydration and kidney damage.

Chances of survival in the desert are measured in degrees Fahrenheit. In mid-June 2015, the thermometer inside a vehicle in Green Valley showed 124°F. Once, on a hot day like that, an Arivaca resident saw three migrants being loaded into a truck in the parking lot next to the library: two squeezed in the front seat with the driver—"the lucky ones," she told me—and one climbed into a large toolbox in the bed of the truck. "A hot day! I don't know how far they were going or if they made it."

Years ago, when Nogales firefighters pointed an infrared heat sensor toward the front passenger seat of a Ford Mustang, it read 156°F; the temperature inside the trailer of a commercial truck—similar to the one the Border Patrol stopped on SR 82 to find ninety-one undocumented migrants only days earlier—was 140°F degrees.[17] High temperatures strand LifeLine and LifeNet helicopters on the ground. It's thermodynamics: intense heat decreases air density, which reduces thrust and lift required for helicopters to take off. With flying out of the question, on the hottest days rescues from the canyons proceed on foot and may take hours.

It is 102°F in Arivaca when I pull into the gravel parking lot by the station. The lot is full—training day: firefighters connect the brush truck to the tender, put a smooth-bore nozzle on an inch-and-three-quarters hose line, briefly turn on the engine pump, and then disassemble everything. Water is scarce here, so they use as little as possible. Next they clean the station and the rigs. Arivaca Fire has fourteen vehicles, but in mid-2015 about half of them are out of service: some for small issues, like tires or a broken light, others for more serious problems with the transmission or engine.

Since the former fire chief handed in his resignation over a month ago and Tangye won't step in to fill the position until late June, there is nobody in charge of the daily operations. SCBAs are nearing their expiration date and have to be replaced—the same with turnout gear, which was purchased ten years ago. The agenda of the Arivaca Fire Board meetings also includes discussions about attracting more EMTs to work in the community, increasing taxes for the residents, offering subscriptions to those who live outside of their immediate coverage area, and writing new grant proposals. There are even suggestions to request funding for buying night vision goggles. "Bioterrorism is not going to come through the port of entry. It's going to come through the rural area, like Arivaca or Sonoita," one of the board members reasons. If used right, the discourse of counterterrorism and the vulnerability of the border can be productive in getting departments resources they want. It may be more difficult to prove the need for specialized devices in a small rural community than in a busy urban corridor such as Nogales, yet it was an appealing strategy.

"Bound by the law," Tangye says without hesitation, when I ask her why she calls the Border Patrol when she suspects the patient may be an undocumented migrant. According to their records, in 2012, Arivaca Fire responded to 39 calls involving patients in Border Patrol custody; in 2013, there were 11; in 2014, 15; by the end of 2015, 24 out of 192 runs made would be for patients in Border Patrol custody.[18] The records don't say whether it was emergency responders who contacted the Border Patrol or whether the Border Patrol asked for an ambulance. The latter scenario is much more common: in calls involving unauthorized migrants, federal agents are often already on scene. The former situation raises questions about the ethics and legality of making medical care contingent on the patient's arrest.

Tangye could not point to a particular legal document that spells it out. Rather, it was the unlawfulness of their action—allegedly entering the country without legal authorization—that made her reporting them to immigration enforcement the right thing to do. "I can't discriminate and I wouldn't discriminate against anybody. If you need help, I'm gonna help you. I don't care if you are from another country. It doesn't matter," she tells me. She didn't think of it as profiling: she felt confident she could recognize a UDA. It comes down to the location: if she was dispatched to a gas station for "a Hispanic person who speaks English," she wouldn't question the person, she says. But it would be different if she was sent to the middle of the Arivaca-Sasabe Road and there was no vehicle nearby. "If I find somebody out there walking in the desert, in tattered clothes and shoes, you know, they have that look about them, then I'm gonna wonder why are you out here."

We are talking in the day room, which in this firehouse also serves as the kitchen. The US and Arizona flags frame a large flat screen TV that hangs on the wall above two white folding tables. The rest of the furniture includes three recliners and a desk with a printer. The walls are decorated with a couple of district maps and a bulletin board that contains announcements and posters. The one from the US Department of Justice, Civil Rights Division says: "If you have the right to work, don't let anyone take it away." Below it, another poster alerts: "This Organization Participates in E-Verify." Identical posters in Spanish hang next to the English ones. EMTs are stepping inside to grab a cold drink from the fridge or use a restroom before they go out into the bay again to work on the trucks.

"It's more for safety," says a young, white, male EMT who joins our conversation.

Most EMTs come to Arivaca straight from school and use it as a stepping stone to gain experience before they can find a full-time job elsewhere. Often from Tucson, they don't know the service area well and don't stay long enough to learn about the local topography or the local people. In 2015, EMTs were paid $8.06 per hour for sixteen-hour shifts and were only required to work two or three shifts per month.

"The illegals started Jalisco Fire. We had to stay there working all night and we found two AK-47s," another young EMT says.

Tangye didn't disagree with the first EMT; she often called Border Patrol because otherwise she would have to wait an hour for a deputy from the Pima County Sheriff's Office. But she corrected the second: "Those were smugglers, not UDAs. These are two different things."

There were times when unauthorized border crossers did start fires. Once, when a crew from Arivaca was on their way to a fire in the Papalote Wash area, they came across a migrant who was throwing up along the side of the road. They stopped to help him and he admitted that he had started the fire to get attention. Back at the station, while they waited for the ambulance to arrive, the patient took off without notice. Another time they were dispatched to a fire out near the dam on Arivaca Lake. En route, they came across a sick border crosser. Once again they stopped to render aid to the patient and he said he had started several spot fires to call for help.

Emergency responders in Arivaca disagreed over whether they had to report their patients to federal authorities. One of the department's EMTs was volunteering with an organization that provided help to unauthorized migrants; at least one more supported them. Run by No More Deaths and People Helping People, the humanitarian aid office in downtown Arivaca occupied a one-story building with signs warning the Border Patrol not to enter "without a lawful search warrant" and a colorful mural depicting animals in a landscape no longer regulated by "Stop" signs and orange traffic drums. "Imagine peace and justice in the borderlands," a banner announced, both in English and in Spanish. When they found a migrant in need of medical attention, some Arivacans did not call 911, but dialed the local number of the humanitarian aid office instead. They suspected that volunteers took the injured to the "camp." Since transporting undocumented aliens "in furtherance of their illegal presence" is a crime, they preferred not to know the details.

Arivaca ambulances used to regularly come to the No More Deaths camp to pick up critical patients and take them to the hospital. But this has changed. The volunteers have become more reluctant to call 911 because the arrival of the fire department would likely entail the involvement of the Border Patrol. They blame local emergency responders for colluding with law enforcement and taking on the role of immigration police. Emergency responders, in their turn, criticize the humanitarian aid groups for ignoring the well-being of the people who need critical care at the hospital. "I don't want somebody to die because they won't make a phone call because they didn't want Border Patrol involved," Tangye said. Injured migrants know the cost of going to the hospital: the only way out leads through a detention center. Sometimes, humanitarian volunteers are convinced that a migrant needs advanced care for a serious injury or illness, but they would never call 911 without the patient's consent. One of them once told me she spent thirty minutes arguing with a woman who had a collapsed lung. She eventually agreed to go to the hospital and was later issued a U visa, reserved for victims of physical and mental abuse who agree to assist law enforcement.

"They have their beliefs and I am bound by law for mine," Tangye rephrased what she said before. "The law" here does not refer to a concrete piece of legislation, but rather to the idea that border crossers did something illegal. Following the law is only part of the story, however. On those rare occasions when the Border Patrol is not on scene when emergency responders arrive— for example, when the humanitarian volunteers call 911 upon encountering a critically ill or injured migrant in the desert—firefighters and EMTs contact the federal agency not because they are "bound by law" but for reasons that are more pragmatic than they initially admit: money and safety.

In order to bill the federal government for medical services provided to border crossers, emergency responders must have the transport authorization request, or TAR. Departments handle this differently. Some have strict policies. "The first thing I ask them [border crossers] is whether they are under arrest. If they are not, I call Border Patrol," said Joseph DeWolf, the chief of Sonoita-Elgin Fire District. Before assuming this position, DeWolf was part of what he called "corporate America" and had a reputation of being an efficient manager. The fire district covers 350 square miles, but the department provides ambulance services to an area twice as large. Here, rocky desert terrain with ocotillos and mesquites—the familiar landscape around Arivaca—gives way to flat grasslands. These days there aren't as many calls to help "international hikers," as DeWolf calls border crossers, in part because the Border Patrol has their own EMTs, he suspects. There is a Border Patrol facility with four hundred agents right across the street from the fire station in Sonoita, at the intersection of SR 82 and SR 83. "Those guys are awesome," DeWolf said about the federal agents. "They give us aid on a daily basis. They help us with traffic control on car wrecks." Since the sheriff is located in Nogales, which is forty-five minutes away, the fire department also relies on the Border Patrol for safety when responding to domestic violence situations, a practice that was familiar to emergency responders in rural areas. "We use Border Patrol," De Wolf said. "They have night vision goggles and all the fun toys that we can't afford." In turn, the Border Patrol calls the department when they find people who must be transported to the hospital—"the serious cases," DeWolf said.

There used to be an alternative. A program known as Section 1011, "Emergency Health Services Furnished to Undocumented Aliens," reimbursed ambulance services, hospitals, and physicians that treated unauthorized migrants.[19] Doug Diezman, a paramedic in charge of coordinating EMS at the Three Points Fire District, said that if the patient acknowledged that he or she was in the country illegally, all the paramedic had to do was check off a box on a special form and the government later reimbursed the department at Medicare rates. Even then it was less than 50 percent, he estimated. But Arizona exhausted its Section 1011 funds in November 2014, and health care providers were instructed not to submit any new requests. The Border Patrol has become their only recourse for getting reimbursement for patient care. Unless the department has a TAR number, the cost for the call—including fuel, medications, and time—is on them. But small communities, like Arivaca, Sonoita, and Three Points, have few taxpayers and can't afford to have their fire departments make numerous uncompensated calls. It's a thorny issue to all concerned.

Three Points has a second name: Robles Junction, in honor of Bernabe Robles, whose Sonoran family is said to have crossed the border on donkeys in 1864, and, as the American success story goes, acquired land, built a ranch, and lived prosperously.[20] More than a century later, "prosperous" would not be an accurate way to describe the settlement bearing his name. Blocks of modest single-story dwellings and mobile homes, pickup trucks parked in front. Simple roadside ads along the dusty highway that leads to Ajo: Haircut, Propane Gas, Family Dollar, Dollar General, Serenity Baptist Church, VFW post, childcare center, and a couple of gas stations. Some homes are used as drop-off spots for drugs—others, for unauthorized migrants. Some for both. There are meth labs. Nearly everybody has guns. "Tucson thinks of us as drugs and crime and bodies in the desert or stuffed into the trunks of cars," a local activist told the *Tucson Weekly*.[21] In sum, Three Points is an odd place with a sketchy reputation.

The Three Points Fire District covers 207 square miles and serves a population of about twelve thousand people. "Most of them are working class. Economically depressed," was how Doug put it. A Vietnam vet, in the 1980s he became a volunteer firefighter and EMT, then completed the paramedic course at St. Mary's Hospital. Before coming to Three Points he worked in the ER and was a flight medic.

"The number of incidents involving unauthorized border crossers 'eased' about eight or ten years ago," he told me. There are now fewer accidents with injuries than there used to be. It happened when the Border Patrol changed its policy on chasing and the checkpoint on Sasabe Highway went up. The Border Patrol boosted manpower in the area. "Big kudos to BORSTAR. I know they saved lives," Doug said, referring to the Border Patrol's Search, Trauma, and Rescue team.[22] These changes significantly cut down the amount of trauma calls the fire department responds to. Vehicle accidents now more often involve drug runners. But they still see people in the desert who need medical attention for injuries from exposure to heat or cold.

In order for the Border Patrol to pay for transport and care provided to the patient, they had to establish that the individual was here illegally and take them into custody. But the Border Patrol was incurring huge costs, so, Doug said, they "used to play this game": when the ambulance arrived on scene and emergency responders asked whether this was a UDA call, the Border Patrol would say that they had to investigate. Even when the fire department asked where the patients were from and the latter answered that they were from Guatemala and that they had no documents, this information was not sufficient for the Border Patrol to take them into custody.

Until the mid-2000s, the agency took a hands-off approach to migrant care. The sick and injured were an inconvenience to the Border Patrol, which justified "informal humanitarian exceptionalism": officers in the field were instructed to avoid establishing alienage, thereby refusing to take responsibility for migrants that were in need of medical care.[23] They would call 911, allowing local fire departments, ambulance companies, and hospitals to take over. But these policies changed when the Border Patrol reoriented its mission toward terrorism prevention. Beginning in 2005, agents were asked to establish the alienage of all migrants, even those who needed emergency medical care. Advanced treatment became contingent on arrest.

But not all fire departments followed the same path. Rio Rico did not have a rule mandating emergency responders to call the Border Patrol when they provided care to unauthorized migrants. "Within the fire service we don't hold any law enforcement title," an official with Rio Rico Fire told me. "If the patient needs assistance, their nationality has no bearing on us." Emergency responders did not know whether their patient was a legal resident until they reached the hospital. "If they are not, we gather as much information as we can and then our billing department contacts the federal government. I guess the shortcut would be calling the Border Patrol. But that would be beyond what we would do," this veteran of the fire department said.

"With that issue [referring the patient to the Border Patrol], you are making the EMS people become involved with immigration enforcement," a fire captain in Nogales told me. "The only reason we do it is so that we can get paid." However, the imperative to provide care allows emergency responders to sidestep any financial or other considerations. "We've gone out to places where people were in extremely bad shape and taken medical custody of them, knowing that we should have called the Border Patrol," Billy Bob said, then added: "If I'm gonna mess up, I'm gonna mess up to the good side.'"

The first commandment of emergency services is "scene safety." Whether it is a fire or a medical injury or illness, if the scene isn't safe, you don't go in. By definition, no emergency scene is entirely safe. The rule is there simply to remind firefighters, EMTs, and paramedics that they should try to minimize dangers—make sure they know the escape routes, don the proper PPE, and maintain situational awareness. This rule can also be used against them if something goes wrong: a legal tool for government entities and private companies that puts the blame for work accidents or line-of-duty deaths on emergency responders, who, they may allege, failed to make sure the scene was safe, for example, didn't wait for law enforcement to arrive before they intervened to stop arterial bleeding from a stab wound.

Most firefighters and paramedics in the border zone don't consider their work any more dangerous than the profession of an emergency responder already entails. "I have lived my whole life in this area and I've never had an issue with border security," a Rio Rico firefighter once told me. "You see certain programs that are offered on cable, like *Border Wars,* and you are sitting there and thinking, 'How long did it take to get a half-hour segment?' Because, honestly, that is not what we see here." Chief DeWolf of Sonoita had a similar take: "We are in a dangerous field," he said. "Anything we do is dangerous. So is there more danger [on the border]? From what? No. It's just like domestic violence. Is that a dangerous thing? Yes. Is an immigrant walking across the border dangerous? Not necessarily. Some of them are coming for work; some of them are visiting family—whatever they are doing. Are there dangerous ones carrying weapons out there? Yes. But again we are not supposed to put ourselves in that position. That's what Border Patrol is for. Let them secure it. Let them make sure there is no weapons. And then what's the danger?"

It was usually from female firefighters—and not all of them—that I heard about concerns for their safety when they respond to calls in remote border areas. The day after newspapers reported that two Mexican nationals were convicted of murdering Border Patrol agent Brian Terry near Rio Rico in 2010, I talked about it with Carmen, a paramedic at the Tubac Fire District. The men who were sentenced, Ivan Soto-Barraza and Jesús Lionel Sánchez-Meza, were part of a "rip crew" that crossed illegally into the United States seeking to steal drugs from smugglers in a known target area close to Peck Canyon.

"Is it dangerous?" I asked Carmen about her work. She had already told me how she fought her way into the boys' club, proving to male firefighters that she had the same skills, and how difficult it was to be a Hispanic female paramedic serving a predominantly white retiree and snowbird community, where a patient once refused to let her treat him because she was "a girl." Carmen toughed it out. She was not the kind of person who was easily deterred—or alarmed. She was used to going out to the mountains to help border crossers wounded by the rugged terrain. But there are some areas in the district where she was more cautious, she told me. Peck Canyon is one of them. "You never know what they are carrying. A lot of those people carry guns. We don't carry vests. We don't carry guns, of course," Carmen said. "It's not required for us to call Border Patrol—that's not my job. But when you see them there and you don't know what they really want, you get that gut feeling, from some of them, that you don't trust them. Unfortunately, you don't. Especially when you know that they are already doing something wrong, and at night, in the middle of nowhere. We don't have radio service there, we didn't have cell phone service. It's just my partner and I. Good thing I trust my partners," she laughed.

"We've been around for so long that we know when they are drug dealers, drug runners, or when they are just coming to find a job," she said. "How do you know?" I asked. "The way they are dressed. It's kind of funny, but . . . the smell: they've been out there for days and days . . . How they look: if they're very dehydrated, if they're sick. Most of the drug runners, they are still kind of clean, they don't stink as bad, and they are hydrated. They carry cell phones and they call 911 so we can go pick them up. And, of course, they have the red lines here, where they carry the packs," Carmen pointed to the area where the shoulder straps leave marks on the bodies of drug mules. "So they'll complain about their shoulders."

"I've never had a UDA be aggressive," Tangye told me. "Typically, when I arrive on scene, they are grateful that someone is there to help them and they are very tired. The ones that I don't like—that make me nervous—are the smugglers." Though she can usually tell them apart, sometimes she fails:

Throughout the years I can tell the difference between the two, but sometimes you can't. I have a long transport time, so I'm in the back of the ambulance with somebody who is potentially a violent criminal. Sometimes Border Patrol will tell me. And sometimes they won't. The last time, when I took the patient with the Clorox overdose, they escorted me up [to Tucson]. I had an hour and a half transport because I was coming out from SR 286. When I got to the hospital and took the patient out, the Border Patrol agent who had escorted me met another agent and they were talking about the patient. I asked them about it, and they said, "Oh it's not a major issue: he's just got several drug possession charges and a rape conviction." And I said: "What?

An ambulance and a rescue helicopter during an incident on the Arivaca–Sasabe Road.

You guys didn't tell me that? You didn't think that was relevant information? I was at the back of an ambulance with this patient for an hour and a half. You should have been in the back with me." I didn't have a problem, but potentially I could have.

The lines between the traffickers and the migrants, the "deserving patients" and the "dangerous criminals," have never been definitive, but they are getting blurred even further, putting rescuers in a position where they are torn between their mandate to help anybody and everybody and the number one rule of responding to an emergency—scene safety. Firefighters, EMTs, and paramedics have seen what people are capable of. There's the bad: more migrants are now forced to carry drug loads as a form of payment for the crossing, and those who refused have been tied up to the border fence. "Like piñatas," Sheriff Estrada said. He reported two such incidents west of Nogales in the past year. But there's also the good. A paramedic in Rio Rico recalled how a woman traveling with her son got into a rollover accident on Ruby Road. She died in the crash, but the boy, seven or eight years old, survived. An unauthorized migrant happened to come through. He couldn't talk to the child—the border crosser spoke Spanish, the kid knew only English—but he decided to help. He built a fire, covered up the mother's body, and in the morning went out onto the road and sat there waiting for the Border Patrol. "They would have never found them," she said. "The car had rolled so far off of the area that no one would have ever seen it there. But this guy turned himself in to save another. So there's good. There's a lot of good out there, too."

WATCHOUTS

"I've been on wildland fires when we came across bundles of drugs," Oscar said. "You find that and you think: Son of a gun! We just found 500 pounds of marijuana, and there's nobody around us, and radio communication is almost nonexistent. You really can't touch it. You just try to mark where it is and tell law enforcement. At the same time you are hoping that whoever dropped it off is not around the corner."

Oscar is stocky, clean-shaven, and, had we not met at a fire station, I might have mistaken him for a law enforcement agent. Instead, he is a firefighter and a paramedic at the Rio Rico Fire District, where he's quickly climbed through the ranks to become an officer. RRFD is an all-hazards department with three stations, forty members, and a 36-square-mile response area. As in other nearby communities, about 80 percent of their calls are for medical emergencies. In 2014, the district launched Arizona's first Community-Integrated Paramedicine program, which involves first responders making non-emergency home visits to help patients manage their disease or chronic health issues so that they don't have to call 911 and return to the hospital as frequently.[24] The department provides technical rescue and does vehicle extrication: the I-19 corridor that cleaves the district is notorious for deadly crashes—during his first five years as the district's chief, Les Caid saw more rollovers and auto accidents on the freeway than during a quarter of a century he worked in Tucson. Like other departments in southern Arizona, Rio Rico also assists the US Forest Service with wildland fires.

Every wildland firefighter in the country knows the 10 Standard Firefighting Orders and the 18 Watchout Situations: base all actions on current and expected behavior of the fire; identify escape routes and safety zones; post lookouts when there is possible danger; fight fire aggressively, having provided for safety first; and so on. The Forest Service developed these guidelines to reduce firefighter injuries and fatalities, even though it is nearly impossible to fight a wildfire without violating at least one or more of the commandments.[25] In addition to the "Ten" and the "Eighteen," firefighters who are sent on assignments near the US-Mexico border receive cards listing the 19 International Border Watchouts:

1. Expect high-speed driving and law enforcement pursuits
2. Expect drivers to be distracted
3. All aircraft operations have increased collision risk
4. Radio frequency interference from Mexico likely
5. Radio/cell phone dead spots increase employee risks
6. Cell phone connections to Mexico likely
7. Language barriers increase risk
8. Threats to employees are present 24/7/365
9. You are not clearly identified as forest service employee
10. Every visitor contact has potential risk
11. Higher occurrence of unexpected visitor encounters
12. Traditional responses may not be appropriate; check your gut
13. Responding to situations inconsistent with assigned authority and training
14. Night operations require special considerations
15. Unattended vehicles will be damaged or stolen
16. Illegal uses in remote areas likely
17. Heightened risk of biological contamination
18. Always know your location and be able to describe it
19. Let others know your expected route and destination (check-in/check-out)

The US Forest Service created this list following the publication of a report about dangers to firefighters in the Arizona border region.[26] While there were no incidents in which firefighters had been assaulted or threatened, fire response and law enforcement officials identified several aspects of cross-border activity that firefighters must account for: they may encounter armed smugglers; unauthorized border crossers who avoid contact with firefighters may be killed by fire suppression activities, such as setting backfires; and there may be interference with radio communications when smugglers use the same frequencies. Representatives from several land management agencies worried that firefighters could be distracted by the presence of illegal border crossers. Their morale slumped when firefighters discovered bodies of unauthorized migrants, the report notes; moreover, it suggested, focused on their own safety, they may be less invested in fire suppression.

Suspicions that unauthorized border crossers started wildland fires prompted the Government Accountability Office to examine data on incidents that occurred in the Arizona border region between 2006 and 2010.[27] It counted 422 human-caused wildland fires that burned one or more acres on federal or tribal lands; of the seventy-seven fires that were investigated, illegal border crossers were suspected of causing thirty, all of them located within 40 miles of the border in the Coronado National Forest, Buenos Aires National Wildlife Refuge, and Organ Pipe Cactus National Monument. Half of these fires resulted from efforts to signal for help, provide warmth, or cook food. The 2006 Black Mesa Fire, which burned about 170 acres, started when one person traveling with a group of about twenty individuals got injured and could not walk further; before they continued their journey, his companions started a fire to keep animals away and to attract attention in the hopes that someone would rescue the migrant. The 2009 Bear Fire, which burned 15 acres, was likely caused by a campfire: investigators found discarded bottles and food wrappers with Spanish-language labels at the site where it started, in an area adjacent to a known trail. To deal with improperly extinguished campfires, the Cleveland National Forest in California created a border fire prevention crew that hikes daily on known migrant trails and takes care of abandoned campfires. But there is no such crew in southern Arizona. Instead, seasonal firefighters who come to the area to work for the Forest Service get a card with the 19 International Border Watchouts and a small map printed on a sheet of paper that indicates "Elevated Risk Area" south of I-10 and I-8. A message in capital letters warns: "SMUGGLING AND ILLEGAL IMMIGRATION MAY BE ENCOUNTERED IN THIS AREA." Firefighters are advised to seek guidance from local dispatchers.

Most of the fires in this area are of "human cause," Martin told me in May 2015. Some of those are "people in distress or lost." Martin, who looks more like a cowboy than a wildland firefighter, has worked at the Buenos Aires National Wildlife Refuge for over a decade. He told me about the time when, in order to be rescued, border crossers set an old empty building on fire. He also recalled how a person who was shot set fire to signal for help; they named it "Six Shot Fire." Martin said, "People we find, who don't run away, need help." Unlike their urban counterparts, wildland firefighters are not trained as EMTs and do not provide medical care. When they come across somebody who is injured, they call an ambulance from Arivaca. But other "human cause" fires are set up to deflect attention. Martin referred to them as "diversionary fires." Oscar called them "distraction fires." Drug smugglers use this tactic to draw as many resources as possible to one area, while they take the load across through a different, unmonitored, route. "If it's out in the west county, then they are probably trying to divert through the east county," he explained. These are only suspicions, though, since most fires are never investigated.

"Most of the winds here come from the southwest. Fire can start in Mexico and we can't do anything about it. We wait for it to cross into the US," Oscar said. But in the borderlands it can be hard to tell where one country ends and another begins. Once you get further into the mountains, the boundary is no longer obvious. "We had a fire crew on the west side of I-19, in the Potrero Canyon, that was detained by Mexican soldiers. They were in fire gear—green pants, yellow shirt, helmet—working the fire, and the Mexican government detained them for about five or six hours," Oscar recalled. It has happened the other way around, too, according to Vicente. He said that Mexican bomberos were fighting a brush fire when the US Border Patrol approached them. "What are you doing?" the federal agents asked them. "We are working on the fire," the Mexicans replied. "You are in the territory of the United States," the agents told them. "We are sorry, we didn't know." Canizales said they were digging a fireline and did not realize they were about 2 kilometers inside lado gabacho. When the US Forest Service arrived, they informed the Border Patrol about the binational agreement. "OK, carry on," the agents told them.

The agreement between the US Forest Service and the National Forestry Commission (CONAFOR) in Mexico stipulates that the agencies can combine resources to fight wildland fires within 10 miles of the border. In April 2011, the Bull Fire, which started in Mexico southwest of Nogales, crossed the border into the Coronado National Forest lands on the US side. Two hundred and fifty people, backed by three helicopters and two airplanes, fought to contain the fire, which charred 24,000 acres in Sonora and Arizona.[28] Out of the base camp at Calabasas Park in Rio Rico, forty Forest Service firefighters were sent to join the crews of Mexican bomberos fighting the fire south of the border.[29] During such cross-border operations, CBP follows the Forest Service protocols and sends personnel to set up a temporary port of entry at Peña Blanca Lake, a convenient place to clear helicopters flying firefighters and equipment back and forth between the US and Mexico.[30]

A month later, in May 2011, a fire that started in the Tumacacori Mountains merged with another fire in the Atascosa Mountains, forming what became known as the Murphy Complex Fire. It burned over 68,000 acres in Arizona and, when a segment of the fire jumped the border into Mexico, consumed approximately 2,750 acres in Sonora. US authorities were worried that the fire could swing around to the west and burn back into Arizona at Sycamore Canyon. Louie, who at the time worked for the Tubac Fire District and served as a liaison between the incident management team in Arizona and their counterparts in Sonora, contacted Comandante Hernández and Lieutenant Canizales to ask for help. There were no available CONAFOR brigades in northern Mexico, so volunteer firefighters stepped in. While US helicopters flew loads of water across the border and dropped them onto the fire, fifteen bomberos from Nogales, Sonora, provided manpower on the ground.

Louie fondly remembers this fire as another example that underscores the significance of binational cooperation. As he spoke, he showed me maps and pictures of the incident on his laptop computer:

> There is a fire that is in Arizona and Sonora, and in Sonora it's heading to the west. If it gets to a certain area, it's going to explode. We need to get it taken care of, so I call Eduardo. "Eduardo, we need some help over here." "OK, Louie." "Now, Eduardo, call me when you get home at night." "OK, Louie." They went out. Ten o'clock that night: "OK, Louie. We are OK, we are safe." Second day: "OK, Louie. Yeah, we are done for the day." Third day: "OK, Louie. Yeah ... We are on our way home." Fourth day, around five o'clock in the afternoon: "Louie! Louie!" "Que pasó, Eduardo?" "Louie! Louie!!!" I think, "Oh, shit!" "Eduardo, que pasó? What's happening?" "Louie! Mission accomplished!" I could have killed him. He was just so excited, but I could have killed him! The US says: "How did they do that?" I mean, they went out there, worked their butts off, took care of the situation.

"All of this burned for the gringos. And this is what burned for us." Canizales showed me the same pictures, months later and on the other side of the border. "Just a small piece." The incident commander told them to dig a line and they did, supported by US helicopters flying about 2 kilometers into Mexico to deliver water drops. Every day Canizales crossed the border to meet with the authorities at the incident command post located in Arizona. He got the instructions, the plan for the day, and returned to Sonora. "I grabbed the raza de aquí y vámonos!"

Even before the Murphy Complex Fire jumped across the border into Mexico, the bomberos offered to assist American crews battling it in Arizona, but they were not allowed. In the US, wildland firefighters must complete a training course that certifies their basic knowledge about forest fires and their physical preparation for the job. The bomberos had crossed before to help the Nogales Fire Department on Ellis Street, but that was possible because of the agreements at the municipal level. The Forest Service is a federal agency; the bomberos could be a legal liability for them. This issue made officials realize that they needed to train together so that they could join forces on more types of emergencies. The following year twenty-two bomberos from around Sonora—most were nogalenses, but a few came from Agua Prieta, Imuris, and Cananea—gathered in Rio Rico for a four-day wildland firefighting course taught in Spanish.[31] Now they have training equal to that of wildland firefighters across the US.

"Fire was not even on my radar," Oscar told me. He was determined to go into law enforcement, a career he began at the age of eighteen as a dispatcher for the Santa Cruz County Sheriff's Office. Two and a half years later he moved to Phoenix, where he worked at a hospital as a Spanish translator and later in security. As EMTs and paramedics were coming in and out of the ER, he could not understand what they were talking about—"To me it was gibberish," he said—but he noticed that people greeted law enforcement and firefighters differently: "It was night and day." When he returned to Santa Cruz County, Oscar took a job at his parents' company and started volunteering for the local fire department. He finished fire school, completed an EMT course, and was offered a permanent position at RRFD.

Though he loved working for the fire service, Oscar felt something was missing. "That desire to be in law enforcement was in the back of my mind. It wouldn't let me go." Several years later he tested for the Border Patrol and got in. "I thought that was what I wanted to do," he said. The Border Patrol academy in Georgia lasted five months. Since they weren't sworn officers, recruits would be sent out of the academy wearing a uniform and carrying a fake gun. One time during basic training Oscar had to go to an off-site hospital for a checkup. "When I was sitting there, people would move away from me. I greeted them, but they would not sit close to me. I was alienated," he recalls. Oscar said he didn't understand what he was doing wrong. "It wasn't until some firefighters came in, and there was a mother and her little boy sitting there, and she goes like, 'Look, son, look at the firefighters!'" Oscar realized he was wearing the wrong uniform. "That night I called my chief and said I think it's time for me to come back." He quit the Border Patrol academy and returned to Rio Rico, where he's stayed ever since. He doesn't regret his time in the academy: "It's an honorable job. We need law enforcement. We need individuals to do it. But it's just not what I thought I was supposed to be."

As a firefighter, Oscar regularly works with the Border Patrol and the sheriff's office: they help with traffic control during motor vehicle accidents on the highway, provide security in potentially violent situations, and add to manpower in rescue operations. But he's seen how their presence can make patient care more difficult. Once Oscar was dispatched to an area about an hour away from his station, at the very end of the paved road:

> Sheriff's office called us out for an individual who was not feeling well. When we got there with the fire truck and the ambulance, we saw the sheriff's deputy standing by his vehicle, a good 25–30 yards from the patient, which I thought was interesting. Being a paramedic you learn about scene safety. I am thinking, law enforcement is there, so the scene should be safe, but in my opinion, he was a little further than where he should be. As we approached the individual, we saw he had multiple black ink tattoos that looked home-made: from his neck all the way down to his torso (he didn't have a shirt on), his arms, his back, I mean, even his face was all tattooed.

Oscar got closer and introduced himself. He said he was from Rio Rico Fire. "Are you OK?" he asked. "No! My legs hurt, my back hurts, I haven't eaten for a couple of days, and I haven't been drinking any water," the man replied. The deputy, who remained behind the door of his patrol car, shouted to Oscar: "Are you OK?" "Yeah, code 4, we are OK," Oscar responded, then turned to the patient:

> I said: "Can I ask you a question? Is there a reason why you think the deputy is staying away from you?" He said: "Yeah. Because that bleep-bleep-bleep is too afraid of me." And I go: "Why would he be afraid of you?" And he throws up some kind of gang sign and says "I am MS-13."

MS-13, also known as Mara Salvatrucha, is the name of one of two notorious gangs—*maras*—that originated in the United States and in recent years unleashed violence in El Salvador and neighboring countries in Central America, forcing youths who don't want to join or pay extortion to flee north.

The firefighter knew that the gangs were dangerous, but he didn't step back from the patient:

> One thing that I appreciated learning in Border Patrol and the sheriff's office was seeing how certain individuals treat people in custody in a really negative way. And I thought: you know what, there are some of them that are messed up, but I am not a judge, I am not the jury. I tell my crew: treat the individual, not the situation because you don't know the situation. Our job is not to place judgment. Our job is to treat the person.

Per protocol, when patients are combative, Border Patrol agents or sheriff's deputies ride in the ambulance with emergency responders. But, as Oscar noted, this can make it more challenging to provide treatment. "The minute you pull out law enforcement from the back of the ambulance, the person calms down and realizes, 'Oh, these individuals are here to help me.'" Oscar said he told the marero: "Listen. I am not here to judge you. I am here to treat you. You let me know what you need, I'll take care of you. But the code goes the same way: you disrespect me, we'll have an issue." He remembers the marero replying: "That's why I appreciate you: because fire doesn't judge who I am. That guy over there, staying behind his car, judges away."

AID IS NOT A CRIME

The meeting at the church in South Tucson began with a moment of silence: for those who were in the desert and those in detention. Twenty-six Samaritans sat on rows of benches forming a semicircle. They talked about their trips, nine over the past week. A woman said she saw "recent activity" about a mile east of Sasabe. Some others reported that they found backpacks bought in Altar at the site they visited: the bottles were empty, they said, and the tarp and the blankets underneath it were gone. The bottles near Milepost 7 on Arivaca Road were also empty. Right at the border they found a couple of backpacks with their shoulder straps cut. Another group did an exploratory trip on the east side of the Arivaca Road, looking for the missing links on their map, which shows the trails connecting black dots, each assigned a number: these are the drop spots—the GPS-coded locations where they leave water and food for the border crossers. "There was plenty of debris all along the trail," they said. "It is clearly being walked." They reported that sausages, fruit cups, and energy bars had been consumed. Five people who had gone out earlier that day found eight water bottles empty, with their caps on, lined up. "A lot of fresh debris," one of them said, "including a black jug."[32]

Frustrated with hardline government policies that let human beings perish in the deserts, mountains, ranches, canals, and rivers of the southern United States, civil society has stepped up to defend migrants' rights. Since the 1990s, when "prevention through deterrence" became the cornerstone of Border Patrol strategy, humanitarian aid organizations have been working to prevent unauthorized border crossers from dying.[33] They search for lost migrants, set up water stations, provide first aid, leave food on the trails, and recover the remains of those who lost their hope—and their life—along the way. The Tucson Samaritans, founded in 2002 and first known as the Samaritan Patrol, is one of these humanitarian groups. When they started, they didn't think that there would still be a need for them in 2015, but they were wrong. Today, they scour rough dirt roads in two donated four-wheel-drive vehicles and walk the trails of the inhospitable terrain, carrying first-aid kits, communication equipment, maps, and water. In the large stretches of the desert between Tucson and Sells, Sasabe and Three Points, Nogales and Green Valley, and Amado and Arivaca, as well as in the Buenos Aires National Wildlife Refuge, they are the "healing presence along the border."[34] They also visit the Kino Border Initiative's migrant aid center—el comedor—in Nogales, Sonora, and bear witness at the Operation Streamline court in Tucson.[35]

At the meeting, the Samaritans also discussed their latest run-in with the Border Patrol. A camera caught three volunteers close to the border and eight individuals on the other side of the line, and the Border Patrol thought that the volunteers were the guides. When they learned that they were Samaritans, one of the agents allegedly said that "the Good Samaritans weren't that good" because they were supplying drug smugglers. The encounter did not escalate. The Border Patrol seemed to be content with their joke and let the volunteers go. But that hasn't always been the case. In 2005, when two Samaritans were driving three very sick migrants to Tucson—one of them vomiting, another with bloody diarrhea—the Border Patrol arrested them and charged them with one count each of "transportation in furtherance of an illegal presence in the United States" and "conspiracy to transport in furtherance of an illegal presence in the United States"—felony charges that could lead to fifteen years in prison.[36] These charges were dropped, but federal agencies, including the US Fish and Wildlife Service, have cited other humanitarian volunteers in

Arizona for "littering." Two were convicted for placing water jugs in the Buenos Aires National Wildlife Refuge. The case went to the Ninth Circuit Court of Appeals before it was overturned in a 2-to-1 vote.[37]

Borderlands fall into the gray area of the law—a territory where humanitarian activists and Border Patrol agents compete in defining practices in ways that fit their respective interpretation of right and wrong. While the Samaritans and other advocacy groups defend their actions of helping injured migrants and providing them with water by claiming that humanitarian aid can never be a crime, federal government agencies—the Border Patrol, the Bureau of Land Management (BLM), the Fish and Wildlife Service (FWS), Buenos Aires National Wildlife Refuge (BANWR)—frame them as discrete illegal acts subject to prosecution: "transporting aliens" and "littering."[38] Volunteers are blamed for assisting the cartels by providing them with resources. They routinely find water jugs they leave in the desert to save dehydrated border crossers slashed or their contents poured away. In 2012, to learn who was destroying the bottles, No More Deaths set up a hidden camera in one of the locations along a migrant trail. The footage showed three Border Patrol agents, two men and a woman, coming across a dozen one-gallon jugs, then kicking them down a ravine, bursting them open.[39] In 2016, one of the water stations maintained by Humane Borders in an area near Arivaca was found pierced by bullets, and a dead coyote was placed near the water tank.[40]

I was sitting in the third row next to Bob, a soft-spoken and resilient Samaritan, who, in his mid-sixties, spent most of the days hiking the desert trails carrying water and collecting trash, visiting the detainees at Eloy, and helping out at el comedor in Nogales, Sonora. Bob told me he's given water to the Border Patrol—twice in the last several months. "We help everyone," he said, and smiled.

When I returned to the Southside Presbyterian Church on a Sunday in June, I brought a gallon of water. Because many Samaritans are retirees and some leave Arizona to spend summers up North, during the hottest, deadliest, months of the year the group needs help. I came for the volunteer orientation. We placed the water jugs we were asked to bring next to other supplies in the shed behind the church, where the Samaritans also kept food, socks, and blankets that they took on their trips to the desert and to the shelters south of the border.

There were ten of us: two college students from a public university, one of whom was an EMT; an older gentleman and his grandson; one recent law school graduate from Michigan and two of his friends who were working for a nonprofit providing free legal services to detained immigrants in Arizona; and a couple of young women who arrived late and missed the introductions. We were handed yellow slips of paper to provide information about ourselves: What activities were we interested in? What medical training did we have? There were options for MD, NP, RN, EMT, and wilderness first responder. Could we speak Spanish? We filled out and returned these slips.

Over the next several hours the new volunteers completed a crash course in borderlands history, immigration law, and medical aid. John Fife spoke first. A retired Presbyterian minister, he was one of the founders of the 1980s sanctuary movement that helped undocumented Central Americans seeking refugee status in Tucson. In the early 2000s, he participated in forming the advocacy group No More Deaths and to this day he continues working with different humanitarian organizations in the border zone. He told us about the Treaty of Guadalupe Hidalgo, about the origins of the Border Patrol, about the Bracero Program, and about Operation Wetback—the story about "the hypocrisy of immigration policies" that he had rehearsed many times before.[41] We gathered around the maps he had laid out on the table and listened to him explain how the "prevention through deterrence" strategy worked: when the fence was built in Nogales, migrants moved to Douglas–Agua Prieta area; when the fence was built there, they went through Naco; once that corridor was closed, they moved to Sasabe. Now their only route was through the mountains. Border crossers have been "funneled" to the most dangerous terrain. The Border Patrol underestimated the pressure of poverty, Fife said. They didn't understand that parents would do anything to feed their children.

No More Deaths and the Samaritans are organized as "civil initiatives," exercising "the legal right of civil society to directly protect the victims of human rights violations." The former reverend explained this by reference to the Nuremberg Tribunal, which prosecuted Nazi officers who said they obeyed orders and the laws of the state. Human rights law triumphs nation-state law, and perpetrators of violence can be convicted. He told us that civil initiative was not the same as civil disobedience; it did not involve breaking the law to achieve justice. Rather, it was the same claim to legality used by the sanctuary movements in the 1980s: resisting in ways that pushed the government to fulfill its legal obligations to protect human rights.[42] Although by June 2015 the two organizations had been issued thirty-seven citations for littering in the public land controlled by BLM, FWS, and other federal agencies, the courts have upheld their right to help victims of human rights violations. "Water saves lives," Fife said, closing his remarks.

Bill Walker, an attorney who represented humanitarian volunteers in several dozen misdemeanor cases they faced over more than a decade, spoke next. "What is not a crime?" he asked. After gathering some answers—providing aid, giving water—he said: "Humanitarian aid is not a crime. Humanitarian aid is never a crime. You can give water, food, medical care—treat blisters, take blood pressure, hydrate them." But there were things we could not do. Harboring or hiding migrants from the Border Patrol is a crime, he explained. Transporting is a crime when it is "in furtherance of illegal presence." If an undocumented migrant is being taken to the hospital, that's not "in furtherance of illegal presence," so it's not a crime. But the Samaritan protocol instructed that if we came across an injured person, we should call the medical team; the medical team will either give permission to treat the person there or transport to the hospital, to the camp, or to the clinic. "Our protocol keeps you safe," he told us. Going through the checkpoint, volunteers should be transparent and tell the Border Patrol that they are transporting a sick person. "Don't let them hide," Bill said. "When we act responsibly and honestly in the desert, the Samaritans are gaining allies among the Border Patrol."

Norma Price, who had spent twenty-five years as a physician in Atlanta, Georgia, before she retired and moved to Arizona, was in charge of medical training. The purpose of the Samaritans, she said, was to "prevent deaths and be a witness in the desert." This mission statement appeared on a slide that was projected on the back wall of the church. The group has one doctor and five nurses; most other volunteers are wilderness first responders and only treat migrants who have minor problems. She presented a list of the most common medical issues. Everybody out there is dehydrated, she said. It is impossible to carry enough water to last several days. Dehydration puts people at risk of heatstroke in summer and hypothermia in winter. "If they are semiconscious or confused, you have to call 911. They need to go to the hospital." The same goes if they have muscle cramps and can't urinate—call 911. "Kidney failure is the major cause of death later for people who have crossed the desert."

She clicked the next slide: an image of a rattle snake. "What do you do?" she asked. After a few seconds of silence, nobody responded, so I said: "Call 911." "There is absolutely nothing you can do in the field," Norma agreed. Those patients must go to the ER. During her thirteen years with the

Samaritans, she has only seen three snakebites. "Any injury to the lower extremity puts the person in danger of death because they would slow down." The Samaritan protocol lists nine situations that warrant calling 911: in addition to snakebites, these include chest pain or any severe pain as well as if the person cannot breathe, cannot talk, cannot walk, cannot eat or drink, cannot urinate, is "unstable" (for example, has dropping blood pressure), or when the migrant asks to call 911.

"Ask about their age," Norma instructed us. The Samaritans used to see mostly younger and more fit crossers, but there are more elderly now, people who have been deported from the United States and who are trying to go back home. The elderly, she said, are at greater risk for illness. "Ask how many days they have been in the desert. Ask how much water they carried. When was the last time they urinated? What color was their urine? If it is brown, they need to go to the ER immediately." Norma projected the medical procedure flowchart on the screen.

"If you can't treat in the field, call 911, with the patient's consent, unless they are unconscious." When she called 911, she gave the dispatcher her full name and her location: either the GPS coordinates or the milepost on the road. "If the dispatcher asks, 'Is this one of those illegal aliens?' you can say: 'I don't know. There is a sick person here who needs to go to the hospital.'" She continued: "Wait with the patient until the ambulance arrives. If the ambulance doesn't arrive (for example, they are delayed because of an MCI on I-19) or if there is no cell phone coverage in the area to call 911, then you can put the patient in the car and drive to where you can get a cell phone signal. As soon as you reach an area with cell phone coverage, call the dispatcher, tell them that you are driving a red Samaritans vehicle, plate number so and so, and that you are transporting a patient to St. Mary's Hospital. Ask the dispatcher to send you an escort." The Border Patrol can stop Samaritans on their way to the hospital or to the camp, and there is nothing the volunteers can do if the agents decide to take the patient over from them.

Although all volunteers agree to follow the medical procedures outlined in the protocols, patient assessment always involves discretion. Some conditions, such as minor foot injuries, may not yet be severe enough to warrant transportation to the hospital, which in practice almost always means that the Border Patrol will have an opportunity to detain them. However, if untreated, even mild conditions can lead to critical, life-threatening situations. Anything that impairs mobility, including sprains and blisters, presents a risk for those crossing the desert through remote areas, where they may not be able to call emergency services when they need help. Under these circumstances, the by-the-books definition of a medical emergency is impractical. But how does this ambiguity fit with the law? When is the act of transporting an injured border crosser to the hospital a crime as defined by Title 8, U.S.C. §1324(a), because it is "in furtherance of" their "unlawful presence in the United States," and when is it a life-saving humanitarian intervention?[43] The answer depends on legal minutiae.

In contrast, the answer to another question was unequivocal. When the training was over, we followed Bob outside, back to the shed where we had left the water jugs, and, before we dispersed, he told us one last thing: "When people hear about us going out there in the desert, they ask, 'Do you carry guns?'" He reassured us: "There is really no need for that."

LAND OF MANY USES

September 6, 2015. Having finished her shift, Tangye was waiting for me at the Arivaca fire station. It was her day off, and we decided to go on a road trip. Her son Colin, now six, would be going with us, she said, as would her husband, Dave, who didn't like the idea of her driving there by herself. "There" was the border, about 11 miles south of Arivaca. Dave was wearing a gray T-shirt with logos from a real estate conference, black pants, and a camo baseball hat. At first I didn't notice that he had a 9mm handgun strapped to his right thigh. Two AR-15s on the backseat were harder to miss.

Colin climbed inside Tangye's truck and sat next to his father. The boy thought we were going hunting and sounded disappointed when Dave explained that we were not.

"I haven't renewed my hunting license this year," he said.

"Why do we carry the guns then?" asked Colin.

"Because we are going to a dangerous area," his father replied.

The boy was not content with the answer. He said there was no reason to take the guns if we were not going hunting.

"Remember well what I am going to tell you," said Dave. "It's better to have the guns and not need to use them than not have the guns when you need them."

We drove out of town and turned left toward Arivaca Lake. The first stretch of Ruby Road is paved, but the ride was already bumpy because of large cracks and holes in the asphalt. Unlike Arivaca Road, the lifeline that connects the community to the rest of the country, Ruby does not get patched up after the arroyos carry away pieces of the pavement during the monsoon rains. The road is named after a mining town long since deserted. We passed several abandoned silver and gold mines along the way. Today, the road is primarily used by the Forest Service, the Border Patrol, and the traffickers they are after.

"I would not go here at night," Tangye repeatedly told me.

As soon as we passed a Border Patrol surveillance tower, the asphalt abruptly ended and we continued on dirt. We left Pima County and entered Santa Cruz. "Tubac covers this area, but they never come this far," Tangye said. It is the Arivaca Fire Department that ends up responding. There are no mile markers, so when she gets a call, usually from the Border Patrol, they use landmarks to determine the location of the patient. The most prominent of those is the mesa known as Montana Peak. I heard that you could see the Sea of Cortez from up there. Tangye heard that the hippies climb it to mourn the dead.

"Land of Many Uses," a sign announced as we entered the Coronado National Forest.

It was only my second time out in the desert south of Arivaca. A few months earlier Mary and her husband Rob took me to the ruins in the San Luis Mountains. That time we had two vehicles, both four-wheel drive, in case one of them broke down: sharp stones on dirt roads we followed to the outlying ranches could easily pierce a tire. We carried safety flares to call for help in case of an emergency. Rob also had a handgun strapped to his belt. Walking in the ruins along what looked like an active migrant trail, we found empty cans of pinto beans as well as water jugs. We also passed open mine shafts with warning signs: "Danger! Peligro! Abandoned and inactive mines are death traps! Don't get trapped! Stay out! Stay alive!" They had an image of a skull to communicate the idea to those who may not know English or those who don't know how to read. But covered by tall grass and shrubs, these shafts must be invisible at night. "They are laying their lives on the line," Rob said about the migrants who cross these inhospitable lands, "just to get a job." Although we didn't see any Border Patrol once we got off the Arivaca-Sasabe Road, three large tires with hooks indicated their concealed presence; agents tie these to their trucks and pull them to smoothen the surface of the dirt road. It's called "a drag." The following morning, they check the land for footprints.

Tracking our route was difficult without a cell phone signal. Tangye drove us past the ruins of houses miners had built, past an old orchard with two pear trees and a large blackberry bush, past old cars, sometimes just their rusted carcasses. Fugitives from the law can hide here for years without being discovered. Arivacans talk about them, but they are not the kind of people who would turn anybody in.

When we made a right turn toward Warsaw Canyon, the road became worse and we were bouncing in our seats, trying to avoid getting our eyes poked by the branches of mesquites that reached inside through open windows.

The first side road that we took led nowhere—it kept winding up a hill, too difficult even for Tangye's 4x4 truck. We returned to the place where it forked and tried the other route. When the truck couldn't advance any further because the terrain was too steep, we got out and walked, up a hill and then down. Cattle grazing in the valley lifted their heads and regarded us before resuming their business.

It took us a while to see the border fence running across the green shrubbery: the crisscrossed posts of Normandy barrier and four-strand barbed wire behind it.

"It's Mexico there," I said to Colin, pointing to the shrubs behind the fence.

"Where?" the boy was incredulous.

He also sounded disappointed. It was hard to tell the two countries apart. Mexico looked just like Arizona, nothing special. And the fence? Even he could easily pass through. And he was only six.

Dave didn't come with us to the line. He waited on the top of the hill, watching over the area. When we got back, he told us he saw a vehicle stop on the Mexican side of the border while we were down by the fence. "There are scouts everywhere," he said, and Tangye agreed. When we were ready to leave, we noticed rocks spray painted with green dollar signs next to where we had parked the truck. Somehow we had missed them when we arrived. Dave guessed that they told people coming across that they were now in the US.

We didn't encounter anybody until we were back on Ruby Road. We didn't even pass a single Border Patrol vehicle. "The Border Patrol are hit and miss," Dave said. "Sometimes they are there; sometimes they aren't." We finally saw one once we reached the paved road closer to Arivaca.

The rocks with dollar signs that we found at the border were about equal distance to Nogales in the east and Sasabe in the west. Not more than 15 miles, as the crow flies—or the drone. But much longer if you walk or drive. These are the depths of the Sonoran Desert, where the four-strand barbed wire fence, in some areas reinforced with vehicle barriers, remains the only marker of the international boundary. This is where, as Bowden wrote, "new

Americans are being forged in a burning desert."[44] Policed by *bajadores* (rip-off crews) who rob and assault migrants deterred by the tactical deployment of the steel wall in nearby towns, this place is too dangerous, too rugged, and too remote even for the Border Patrol, who comfortably sit and wait at the checkpoints, in the shade, for those that make it through here alive.

But it would be impossible to follow the border to reach Sasabe. There are areas where trespassing is not allowed. In 2006, CBP restricted public access to the stretch of the Buenos Aires National Wildlife Refuge—about 3,500 acres of land—near the border. I have only been there once. In a white truck with Arizona Fire District logos, Martin drove south on SR 286, turned left at Sasabe, passed a Border Patrol vehicle guarding the road, greeted the agent, and turned right. We found ourselves on a dirt road that follows along the 12-foot-tall pedestrian fence running through the desert landscape. That day Martin told me that the border fence and the dirt road make a good fireline. Through agreements between the US and Mexican authorities, firefighters from the Coronado National Forest can suppress fires across the border. His crew at BANWR, however, is not allowed to go into Sonora.

Martin lives a few miles north from the main entrance to the refuge. Visible from the highway, his house is surrounded by a barbed wire fence— the first time I passed it, I thought it was a jail or a detention facility. He owns horses, but that's not why the property is fenced in. "The house has been broken into," Martin explained. One day a few years ago he came home from work and found flat tires on his car. Inside, his computer was smashed and his shotgun was missing, as were his knives, a new bow, and money. He called the Border Patrol and, with some insistence on Martin's part, they soon found a guy wearing his clothes and carrying his shotgun. They tracked him from Martin's home to the place where he was apprehended with Martin's possessions. But no charges were pressed. Since the man was not a US citizen, the Border Patrol released him to ICE. Martin is still upset about that. He says he smelled burned tortillas and found cut onions in his kitchen. "People who had broken into my home spent the day there." He suspects there were more of them than the one who got caught.

Sasabe is the last outpost, where Arizona butts against Mexico and the lands of the Tohono O'odham Nation. It is the outer limit of Arivaca Fire Department's territory. When I drove there on Memorial Day, the roads were deserted. The only vehicle I passed shortly after leaving Arivaca was an SUV marked by a bright red sticker with a cross on the door—the logo of the Tucson Samaritans. I didn't meet any Border Patrol until I reached Sasabe, almost an hour later, and even then their vehicle was parked behind the gate at the station, no agent in sight. Last time I had taken this route, about two weeks earlier, heading north on Sasabe Highway toward Three Points, I passed three or four civilian vehicles, including a lorry hauling bricks, and close to two dozen Border Patrol trucks. The activity was unusual, likely related to the federal operation near Arivaca: a bust of a house holding both migrants and drugs that my neighbor later told me about.

A post office, a gas station, a general store, and a schoolhouse are not sufficient to merit Sasabe the title of a town. Debbie, a blond, light-skinned fourth-generation Mexican American, is one of eleven people who officially live here. She owns the store, a family business since 1932, selling soda, canned food, propane tanks, firewood, and cowboy hats. In late fall and winter, hunters come down to shoot deer and javelina and stop by for beer and snacks. The rest of the year, her customers are the neighbors she knows by name, from both sides of the border. It was her grandfather and great aunt, both from Mexico, who founded Sasabe a century ago.[45] Working at the store alone since her mother died, Debbie has witnessed Mexican families drop off the sick at the port of entry and US fire departments send ambulances to pick them up. The only doctor in this area lives across the line in El Sásabe, Sonora. But the clinic provides very limited care and the doctor is not always there, so patients who need emergency or specialist care must go to Caborca or Hermosillo, or to Tucson.

I drove slowly south toward the border, and stopped when I saw signs welcoming me to Mexico. At this small port of entry it was not clear where the US ended and Mexico began. Noticing my hesitation, two CBP officers came out of the building and approached the vehicle. I explained that I wanted to go across to El Sásabe, where I knew Grupo Beta had an office, and they were kind enough to let me park my car in one of the rows for secondary inspection, under the roof, where a few other vehicles stood shielded from the sun. There were no people around in this quiet, lonely outpost. In 2015, on average fifty-five cars and two pedestrians passed through this port of entry daily.[46] In comparison, each day that year Nogales registered approximately 9,500 passenger vehicles and 8,580 pedestrian border crossers, in addition to 876 trucks, two or three trains carrying over two hundred containers, and nearly thirty passenger buses.[47]

Opened in 1916 and for decades used for transporting cattle across the line, today the Sasabe port of entry leads nowhere: the Mexican government had planned to pave the highway to El Sásabe, which was supposed to bring more Sonoran commerce through the port. With these expectations, the US invested several million dollars to upgrade the facility in the early 1990s.[48] But Mexico didn't keep the promise. Having nothing else to do, agents meticulously inspect every vehicle, which their colleagues in busier ports, such as Nogales, could never aim for. They stop trucks hauling mesquite firewood or adobe bricks from the factory in El Sásabe north to Tucson, and sometimes find bales of marijuana hidden with the legal cargo. They also stop southbound traffic, looking for weapons and cash. But, aware of how easily they would be caught crossing through Sasabe, smugglers generally choose other, busier, ports to transport contraband.

The CBP officer pointed to a white house a stone's throw away on the other side of the border. "The Grupo Beta office," he said. He advised me to stay on the sidewalk, even though there were no moving vehicles in sight. I walked into Mexico through a metal gate that I unhooked and then closed behind me.

"Grupo Beta?" I asked a lone customs agent at the Mexican aduana, and he signaled that I should keep going; it was the next building on the right, a white one-story structure surrounded by orange vehicles with Grupo Beta signs. I chatted with two young men standing in front of the building until Hector Salazar, the encargado, came outside and told me to follow him to the office in the back.

Only three men work at the outpost in El Sásabe. The US does not deport people to this border town, so the primary task of the Betas is to rescue migrants who are injured in the desert. Most of them come here from Altar. Every Tuesday, volunteers from Humane Borders drive down from Tucson with almost 300 gallons of water to refill the holding tanks in the yard— water that the Betas provide to migrants. There is no shelter where migrants can stay overnight. All the agents can do is give them water, beans, and snacks. "Only for those who need it," Hector clarified. They also give out blankets; I noticed a stack of them in his office. The Betas don't detain border crossers. It's about "trust with the migrants," Hector explained.

The cell phone reception is very sketchy in this area. If they have a signal, migrants who need help call the centralized emergency line in Nogales, which then dispatches Grupo Beta to do search and rescue. The Betas are part of the Instituto Nacional de Migración (INM) and work under the Secretariat of the Interior. While some see them as helping migrants, others blame them for being the Mexican equivalent of the Border Patrol. In El

Behind Grupo Beta office in El Sásabe, Sonora, with US-Mexico border fence and the Baboquivari Peak in the background.

Sásabe, they have nine vehicles, one motorcycle, and one all-terrain quadrocycle. Usually they are called for people hurt on terrain that is difficult to access. If migrants need medical care, the Betas load them onto their pickup trucks and take them to the hospital in Altar or Caborca. Once they had an individual with a pelvic fracture that they could not move to their vehicle, so they called the federal police helicopter from Caborca. El Sásabe has municipal and state police as well as a military base, but they do not have any equipment to aid the Betas in rescue operations.

Hector gave me two brochures. The larger one describes the activities of Grupos Beta and migrants' legal rights in Mexico. It has a directory with phone numbers of consulates and other institutions that provide help. The smaller one, which easily fits into a pocket, is a brief survival manual. "Amigo migrante, nuestros consejos pueden salvar tu vida y la de tu familia." Advice that can save your life and the life of your family. The dangers migrants encounter are divided into five categories: "transport" entails falling off the train or suffocating in poorly ventilated vehicles; "animals" has a photo of a snake; "rivers" includes a warning that the water level in the arroyos can rise in just a few minutes; "desert by day" and "desert at night"—temperatures reach up to 122°F and fall down to 14°F. Migrants are advised to bring warm clothes, long pants, comfortable closed-toe shoes with thick socks, gloves, hand lamps and matches, 4 liters of water, *suero* (an electrolyte solution), and canned or prepackaged meals. Sweets and high-calorie foods "will help maintain normal body temperature," the brochure says. Even if they could afford to buy these supplies, sold at inflated prices in Altar or elsewhere along the border, migrants could not carry that much. The brochure does not mention the human factors: polleros that rape women and abandon groups, narcos that make migrants carry drugs, bajadores who wait to assault them, the Border Patrol who have discretion to use force—the ecosystem of violence that thrives on despair. There is a short telephone directory in the back—for those lucky enough to have battery power and cell phone signal when they most need.

Several bomberos I met in Nogales worked for the Betas before they joined the fire department. When I spoke to him in 2016, Armando told me what he remembered about his posting in El Sásabe, more than a decade earlier. The Betas could make arrests if there was a crime, he said—for example, a sexual assault or violent robbery. They had the authority to detain polleros and charge them with human trafficking. But it was "a double-edged sword": "You couldn't detain a migrant. But if you detain a pollero, who assaulted the migrant, you had to convince the migrant not to go, to wait a few days, to file a complaint." In cases where migrants didn't want to delay their trip across the border while the case was being processed, their assailants were released. "It was very difficult," Armando said. But there were some success stories; the few polleros that were prosecuted are probably still serving their prison sentences. Armando left the Betas because of what he referred to as "malas prácticas." "We were there to help people," he said. But several years after he joined he started seeing how agents were looking for personal gain. "I never liked to be involved in situations that may cause legal problems," he told me, without going into detail.

Armando came to the Betas from the Cruz Roja in the early 2000s, at the time when the organization was undergoing changes on the national level, rebranding itself from a police force to a rescue group. They threw away law enforcement–style uniforms—black pants and khaki shirt—and stopped carrying handguns. More paramedics, legal experts, and psychologists joined the ranks of what until then had been a police-dominated institution. The office in Nogales was tasked with overseeing the stretch of about a hundred kilometers from the Santa Cruz River in the east to the San Miguel gate in the Tohono O'odham Nation Reservation in the west. When they decided to open a provisional post in El Sásabe, federal and municipal agents from Nogales, Agua Prieta, Sonoyta, and other areas were rotated to staff it.

Armando and other agents lived together in a rented house. "Four walls and a roof and the most basic stuff," is how he described it. The first thing they did when they got home in the evening was to check underneath their beds for snakes. Prices in the only store in town were too steep, so they took turns driving to Caborca or Tucson for groceries and cooked their own meals. "We compared it to being in a war zone in Afghanistan. There was nothing there. You were alone." The Betas converted an open canopy into a makeshift hospital, with mats placed on cement floors. Sometimes they had fifty or more people under the tarp. It could take them up to two hours to transport the critically injured to the hospital in Caborca, about 100 kilometers away. The Betas did not have an ambulance, only four-wheel-drive jeeps and pickup trucks that they use to this day, so the patients who had an IV drip set for fluids were helped to the backseat, while those with fractures were strapped onto a backboard and secured to the bed of the truck. Once, when they found a severely dehydrated pregnant woman in the vicinity of the San Miguel gate, far away from the roads and right on the international border, Armando asked a US Border Patrol agent to call BORSTAR and fly her out to the hospital in Tucson. But that was unusual. Arrangements for transferring patients over to the US did not exist in El Sásabe.

Nobody wanted to stay in this outpost for more than a month, a few at the most. Armando was sent out there twice. "It's a drug corridor," he said. Drugs come by sea to Puerto Libertad and El Desemboque, and then are transported by land to Caborca and through Pitiquito to Altar, from where they are taken up north; or they are sent through Magdalena to Tubutama and then to the border. When Armando was in El Sásabe, it wasn't that ugly, he told me. "We knew that there were pollero groups, but we had a deal: you do your job, but don't mess with mine." At the checkpoint, the Betas counted the men, women, and children, and told them what to do if they got lost or found themselves in "other types of situations." "And off they go. We didn't confront them. That wasn't our assignment." Matters had gotten worse since then. In 2009, when the Sinaloa Cartel still held a strong grip on the crossing points in northern Sonora, but the fighting with Beltrán-Leyva Cartel had begun, the group in El Sásabe maintained a low profile. Either, as the agents then said, because it was too dangerous to mess with the narcos, or, as others have suggested, because there was a tacit agreement between them.[49] While on shift, the Betas no longer ventured outside of town, where, they knew, the paths of migrants and drug smugglers intertwined.

Even though the power dynamics between the narcos have since shifted again, the situation in El Sásabe didn't seem to be much different. In 2015, it made the news when seven bodies with signs of torture, including one that was decapitated, were found west of town, in Rancho La Sierrita. It wasn't the first time law enforcement had been to this staging ground for drug and human smuggling. Even the price migrants paid to cross here was well known: $7,000—the same as Manuel told us his trip from Puebla via Altar and El Sásabe had cost. In 2011, the authorities rescued 132 people from Mexico and Central America held in La Sierrita. They were back in 2014 to recover thirty-nine more. During this raid, a Mexican helicopter accidentally crossed into the US; the ranch is only 500 feet from the international boundary.[50]

For emergency services, El Sásabe is a no-man's-land. The Cruz Roja used to have a mobile clinic there, but it has since been moved to Altar. The closest fire department is in Pitiquito, a 138 kilometers away; Caborca is another 10 kilometers farther. Both Pitiquito and Caborca, like many other towns in northern Sonora, are the legacy of Father Kino's missionary work in the late seventeenth century. Caborca is larger and more prosperous than Pitiquito. It was made famous by Rafael Caro Quintero, a powerful narcotraficante who controlled large swaths of Mexico in the days before the cartels splintered and started fighting. It's the seat of landowners who grow cattle and produce in the fields that extend into the desert—green stripes on a beige canvas. The town has a well-equipped fire department: several newer fire engines, a water tender, an American-style ambulance. Bomberos from Nogales came to give classes in Caborca, a practice that was part of their mission to create what they saw as "a domino effect": teach what they learned from the gringos and share donated equipment with the neediest departments. Pitiquito, by contrast, is tiny—a few thousand people clustered into single-story adobe and cement houses, arranged in rectangular blocks and surrounded by the desert, as if the town had been accidentally dropped by the side of the Carretera Federal 2, just a few miles short of reaching Caborca. A year ago, through the state firefighters' association, Nogales bomberos helped Pitiquito acquire a new fire engine.

"We have been to El Sásabe," the comandante told us when Bojo, Captain Lopez, and I stopped by the fire station in Pitiquito in 2017. We saw the new fire engine, with a single inch-and-a-half attack hose thrown on top, parked in the yard. There were nine volunteers on the books, who shared four air-packs, and they were proud to have the "jaws of life"; the bomberos respond to over half a dozen vehicle accidents a month. The times they went to El Sásabe were for rollovers. Because of bad roads, it takes them nearly two hours to get there. But the distance is not the only obstacle. It has been too dangerous for a while. "We couldn't go because if you go, you wouldn't be able to come back," the comandante told us. He even stopped visiting his family in Sáric, the last town on Route 42 before the turn-off to El Sásabe. In 2010, a shootout between members of the Sinaloa Cartel and the Beltrán-Leyva Cartel, with their allies from the Zetas, left over twenty people dead near the village of Tubutama, on the way from Pitiquito to Sáric. "Punto tan caliente," is how Armando described Tubutama when he told me about the times he drove past it to reach El Sásabe for his assignment with the Betas. By 2017, things had improved slightly, but the bomberos from Pitiquito would not make it to El Sásabe in time for a structure fire or to save a life in a vehicle rollover.

For border crossers, El Sásabe, Sonora, to Sasabe, Arizona, is a one-way corridor. It only leads north. Either you make it to your destination—Phoenix or New York, or wherever else work or family awaits—or you spend months or more in detention and are then dropped at the port of entry in Nogales. They quickly learn where to go first.

SOME PILL TO HELP US WALK

June 18, 2015. Not a single seat is left in the humble dining hall decorated with murals of campesinos harvesting corn in the fields. Above rows of wooden tables, ceiling fans spin frantically, failing to disperse the hot summer air. Except for when they raise their hands to ask for another serving of "agua"—a muddy brownish drink made from mixing water with oatmeal—the men eat their breakfast quietly. There are women too, but they sit at a separate table in the back, where the image on the wall portrays Jesus and the Apostles at the Last Supper. Some of them are here with children. At least one is pregnant. Today's meal consists of eggs with spinach, rice, and beans. Visible through the gap under the tin roof covering this soup kitchen, a green sign with an arrow announces "Frontera USA."

El comedor was started by the Missionary Sisters of the Eucharist before it became part of the Kino Border Initiative, a binational humanitarian effort named after a Jesuit who spent his life in the Sonoran Desert before the nation-states that divided this land to assert their sovereignty even existed. Twice a day, with the help of volunteers, the nuns prepare hot meals to "migrantes deportados y en transito"—migrants who have been deported and separated from their families as well as those who are en route to el norte, fleeing violence, economic turmoil, natural disasters. El comedor is where the displaced meet. In 2015, the sisters served over forty-two thousand meals.

Some of those inside have spent weeks or even months traveling on foot, by bus, and on top of notorious freight trains. There are good reasons why they call these trains "*la Bestia*" (the Beast)—a steel monster that ferociously takes the limbs of those who try to ride it toward a better life. They come from central and southern Mexico, El Salvador, Honduras, and other parts of Latin America, and this is their last rest stop before they try to cross. Though they carry backpacks, their jeans and tennis shoes are better suited for a walk in a city park than a strenuous hike across the hostile terrain of the US-Mexico borderlands, where everyone and everything conspires to kill trespassers: a blister or a sprained ankle can be a death sentence if the injured can't walk fast to keep up with the group or if the guide decides to abandon them. According to the Pima County Medical Examiner's Office, the remains of 135 migrants were found in the Tucson Sector in fiscal year 2015.[51] Dehydration and heatstroke are common culprits.

Others already know about the mortal dangers awaiting migrants in the desert. Women swallow birth control pills, aware of the fact that many will be raped before the end of their journey. It's probable that some already have been: most cases are never reported, but by rough estimates, between 60 and 80 percent of migrant women and girls are sexually assaulted in Mexico.[52] They also know about the cages mounted on the beds of the Border Patrol trucks, custom-made to be uncomfortable, so that during rough rides on unpaved roads the captives bang their heads on the roof. Transparent bags with their names and their meager belongings that some deportees have brought to el comedor are tokens of their encounter with la migra, a reminder of their time in detention. Between July 2014 and March 2015 more than one-third of 7,500 migrants who participated in the survey at el comedor reported abuse or mistreatment by US authorities: inhumane detention conditions, verbal abuse, racial slurs, physical assaults. When they are apprehended, migrants are frequently separated from immediate family members and travel companions, and they are deported to a different geographical area from where they were caught. The Border Patrol has a name for this practice: the Alien Transfer Exit Program (ATEP). ATEP aims to "break the smuggling cycle by physically separating aliens from the smuggling organizations."[53] Left without anyone they can trust, deportees are more susceptible to attacks and robbery in Mexico.

I first came to this aid center for migrants in June 2015, as a volunteer with the Tucson Samaritans. El comedor is more than a soup kitchen. Taking turns with No More Deaths, the Samaritans bring cell phones so that migrants and deportees can call family members in the US or in Latin America, free of charge; some ask them to transfer money to buy food and clothes or pay the coyote; others are desperate to inform their loved ones of their whereabouts, or simply want to hear their children's voices. Volunteer nurses and doctors also provide medical aid to the sick and injured. That's how I got involved; they didn't mind having a Spanish-speaking paramedic. This was my first day.

At nine o'clock in the morning the heat is already suffocating. Sarah and I sit by the shelf with medical supplies. Tags on transparent plastic boxes hint as to the contents inside: "feet," "wounds," "pain," "skin," "allergies," "blood pressure," "diabetes," "stomach," "eyes," "gauze," "ointments." Sarah is training to be a nurse. She does not speak Spanish. Some deportees talk to us in English. With others, I conduct patient interviews in Spanish and translate for Sarah. We clean infected wounds and advise how to treat blisters. We send most people away with a few doses of ibuprofen and over-the-counter cold remedies. It's as much as we can do, even though we know that pills, cough drops, ointments, and gauze only deal with signs and symptoms, one body at a time. They have no effect on the political and economic conditions that have forced people to leave their homes and put them in harm's way. It's a temporary medical solution to cover up injuries of violent displacements.

A young man leans toward me and talks in a hushed voice. He shows me a bottle with prescription medications. "I have HIV," he says. The pills are antiretrovirals. Since he does not have a local address in Nogales, the doctors at the hospital could only give him one month's supply. In Acapulco, Guerrero, where he is from, four encapuchados forced his father into a car and decapitated him; he is not going back, he said. One of the volunteers is going to help him file for asylum.

A former militar from Central America complains of lingering pain in his feet. He jumped off the train when the pandilleros tried to rob him, and injured both legs. He never saw a doctor. He says he can manage the pain with pills, and he is not giving up on his plan to cross the border. In the military, he tells us, he learned how to navigate the desert, how to use a compass. He is sure he can make it. We give him ibuprofen.

A young woman is two months pregnant. Three days ago she tried to climb the border fence in Nogales, when she fell down. "It was just a meter and a half," she says, explaining why she did not go to the hospital. But yesterday she started having pain in her lower back. We encourage her to see a doctor. She asks for medication. We double-check the instructions: ibuprofen, which is all we have, is not recommended during the last trimester of pregnancy; consultation with a health professional is advised for use earlier during pregnancy. But she doesn't want to hear about going to the hospital or seeing a doctor. "Take one or two every six hours. Don't take more than six in twenty-four hours," I explain, as Sarah pours a handful of red tablets into a small plastic box. I read and translate the warnings on the label, and she nods that she understands.

A young man just deported from the US has sore throat. But we are distracted by the bones in his forearm, dislocated and sticking out at the wrist. He tells us he broke his arm when he fell off the fence. He is from Monterrey but he chose to cross in Arizona and not in Texas, because of the cartels that operate in Nuevo Laredo and Reynosa. The Border Patrol found him and he was flown by helicopter to Tucson, he says. He shows us a piece of paper with a prescription for ibuprofen from one of the hospitals up there. His family lives in Washington, DC, he says.

Another man complains of toothache. He lived in Phoenix for nearly thirty years until one day he was caught driving without a license, spent three months in detention, and was deported. "I have nothing in this country," he says about Mexico. His wife and children live in Arizona. He is waiting for a friend who expects to be deported to Nogales in the next few days. They will cross back together. He can't go through the desert, he explains, because he has hypertension. But his buddy knows the way through Ciudad Juárez. I give him ibuprofen. "This will numb your teeth," Sarah says as she hands him a tube of Orajel.

Then there is a young Salvadoran who is feeling dizzy. I invite him to sit down, wrap the cuff around his left arm, and measure his blood pressure. He was in a hospital twenty days ago, where he received IV fluids. He shows us a prescription with the Cruz Roja logo, which contains a list of medications for an intestinal infection. He says he had been traveling for weeks— on foot, by bus, and on top of La Bestia. He had nothing to eat for at least two days. We have no glucometer to check for hypoglycemia. We worry about electrolyte imbalances and anemia. One of the volunteers agrees to take him to the hospital. While he waits for the ride, he sips water mixed with suero.

Many more migrants traveling through Mexico on their way to the US today are women and children compared to decades past. Some of them are off to El Norte to join their husbands and fathers, who have already found a niche in the undocumented workforce. They may have been preparing for months or years. But not everyone has time to plan for the perilous journey. Those in a hurry, most of them young, are fleeing gangs that have instilled fear and unleashed violence, destroying their communities. The hondureños, their urban styles setting them apart from the rural folks in el comedor, are on the run for their lives. A small group of them is getting ready to cross later today.

Two men approach Sarah and me as we are sorting the medical supplies: "Can you give us some pill to help us walk?" one asks.

"There is no magic pill," I tell them.

I explain that they have to drink water, that the headache is caused by dehydration and that drinking enough water will prevent it. I also instruct the men that they must drink clean water because the water from the cattle tanks will make them sick. They listen, even though we all know that it is impossible to carry out my advice. To survive in the Sonoran Desert an average person needs to drink over a gallon of water a day—that's more than migrants can carry for a trip that usually takes at least three times longer. Some coyotes give their pollos Sedalmerck, a pill also known as "triple stackers," which combines acetaminophen, caffeine, and phenylephrine. Discovered in Mexico in 1932 and marketed as an energy-boosting analgesic, it gives them energy, but it also dehydrates them faster. All I can give them are several tablets of ibuprofen, for minor aches and pains. As I glance at the nearly empty bottle in my hand, I am relieved that there is nobody else waiting to see us today.

By now most of the migrants have left. Many are on their way to the Grupo Beta office, where they can take a shower and get help finding shelter. We will probably not see them again when we return to el comedor next week. Others will take their seats at the long tables, eat a warm meal, call their relatives, swallow some pills to cope with pain, and be on their way out. Recycling of displaced lives.

June 25, 2015. Motors of tractor-trailers hauling freight toward the Mariposa port of entry drown Sister María Engracia's voice as she leads the prayer before breakfast. Meals in plastic plates flow down the rows of tables. Men and women raise their empty glasses asking for more "agua." It looks like wastewater from dirty laundry or from a puddle on an unpaved road, and one of the guests politely asks for "regular" water. When they finish eating, the migrants walk outside to the street and tell the man who stands guard at the entrance to put their names on various lists: one list for making a phone call, a different one for medical aid. There may be other lists—for filing a complaint of abuse, for help with cashing checks. Several volunteer to wash dishes.

At the first-aid station, Sarah and I talk to a young guy who says he has a stomachache. He has not been eating. "Does anything make it better or worse?" I feel stupid asking the standard questions for patient assessment. It got better yesterday, after he had a meal, he says. But it is still bothering him. "You should eat, and drink a lot of water," we say. "If it doesn't get better in a few days, then you should see a doctor."

We don't know what treatment migrants can get at the hospital in Nogales. The Salvadoran from last week, the one who was dizzy and had blurry vision, looks somewhat better. The hospital gave him fluids, he says, as he extends his right arm and points to where he had the IV. But they didn't know what was wrong with him. He has an appointment later today to get the results of his blood test. He still feels weak, as if his neck is not strong enough to hold his head, he says.

The man who approaches us next stands apart from the others. José Cortez Gutiérrez is not one of the migrants. He wears a white shirt and a straw hat, and on his chest carries a laminated photo with a plea: "Ayúdame a encontrarlo!" Underneath appear telephone numbers of the agency for disappeared persons in Culiacán, Sinaloa, and the state investigative police in Villa Pesqueira, Sonora, among other places where he has already filed denuncias. Don José's twenty-one-year-old son, Juan Carlos Cortez Franco, disappeared on May 2, when he and a group of jornaleros boarded a pickup truck bound for Hermosillo.[54] All of the workers—there were about a dozen of them—went missing. Don José, who lived in Oaxaca with his wife and two daughters, has come to look for his son. He walked across Sonora, visiting truck stops and police stations, handing out flyers in public buses. Tired and broke, he slept in public plazas, ate at shelters. He asks us for some medications to help with the pain that he has all over his body: his legs, his back, his shoulders all hurt "from walking," he says. His head hurts, too. He shows us an old scar. "I was in a coma for two months," he tells us, without elaborating. I pour a handful of ibuprofen pills into a plastic box and give him the instructions on how to use it.

There are more people that ask for help: a young woman with dust allergies complains of sore throat; a very quiet young man has a stomachache; another young woman shows large blisters on both of her feet. One of the migrants who has been slicing the peppers for the afternoon meal cut his finger, which bleeds profusely. Sarah cleans the wound and applies three

Band-Aids to stop the bleeding. "Put pressure on it." "Lift your hand up." She shows. I translate.

The ex-military man who had jumped from the train when he was attacked by gangsters is still here. He is waiting for the heat to subside before he leaves for the desert. I don't ask him whether he has the compass he said would help him find the way.

July 2, 2015. Bob picks me up at the Pilot stop off I-19 and Ruby Road, and we are at el comedor at our regular time. Six tables are almost full, only several seats in the back and at the women's table remaining. It doesn't matter how many people come to el comedor each day: the sisters always make room for everybody.

The morning address to the migrants starts with a role-play. The padre and one foreign volunteer are federal police; one of the women who works at el comedor and several migrants are passengers in a taxi. The federales stop the taxi at the roadblock and ask for their identification. The passengers argue that they are inside Mexico and don't need to show their documents. They say they are going to Agua Prieta to work in the maquiladoras. The young men are all family members of the older señora. She is the one arguing with the federales; they don't intervene.

"Cómo vés?" asks the padre playing the male agent, as he turns to the gringa, his junior partner.

"Me parece muy sospechoso." She says it looks suspicious.

The federales accuse the woman in the taxi of being a pollera. They ask her to step out of the vehicle and take her in for further questioning. Other men in the taxi are let go.

The play goes on with new twists in the story: the policía are asking for a bribe (they call it a "fee") from the woman in exchange for releasing her; she says she has no money, so they tell her they will keep her locked up until her family members agree to pay. The altercation continues. Next we see the woman trying to file a complaint of abuse. The person taking down her information asks what police she is referring to. "It was the federales," she says with confidence. He then asks her to provide the names of the officers and the vehicle's plate number, but she doesn't have that information.

The performance ends and the nun talks about the lesson: migrants should know their rights and record the details when they see them being violated.

Breakfast is served. Then we repeat our routine. Bob, who is providing phone service, is also giving out "harm reduction kits"—plastic ziplock bags containing a few packets of petroleum jelly, cloth to filter water, two vials of Clorox (each enough to disinfect 1 gallon of water), several Band-Aids, instructions in Spanish, and a whistle, to call for help. Sometimes there is a fresh pair of socks. Students at the University of Arizona began making these kits in 2013.[55] No More Deaths continues their initiative. Sarah and I check what we have in the plastic boxes at the aid station. We came prepared: she opens her backpack and pulls out supplies donated by her classmates in nursing school: gloves, IV sets, even a tracheostomy cleaning kit; I place a large bottle of ibuprofen in the "pain" box. I bought it at the pharmacy before crossing this morning, aware that we may be running out of pills. We both have our stethoscopes.

We give ibuprofen to a man with a toothache and to Don José, who complains of headaches. The woman we saw last week says she still has a sore throat; the lymph nodes on her neck are swollen and painful, but Sarah does not see the white patches in her throat that could indicate strep. We give her some cough drops and a few doses of DayQuil, not enough to last two days. One man's legs are all bitten by spiders, swollen; we ask him to wait, as we are with another patient, but he leaves before we can examine him and doesn't come back. There is a man who traveled by train when a metal object fell on his left foot, severing half of the nail on his big toe. Sarah cleans the injury and instructs him to do exercises. Another man says he showered at the shelter and heard rumors about fungus; he is concerned he got it on one of his feet. "You probably wouldn't have it on one foot only," Sarah explains, but gives him a tube of cream and powder to absorb moisture and instructs him to dry his feet well after he washes them. He is wearing three layers of socks because his shoes are too big for him.

Shoes.

I remember Araceli's sneakers, black with red stripes, stained with blood.

Epilogue

THE GREAT NEW WALL

We descended down the escalator in silence, aware that we were entering a tomb. Over three hundred emergency responders lost their lives here on a September morning, nearly seventeen years ago. We read some of their names inscribed in the dark granite panels surrounding two reflecting pools that fill the void left by the collapsed towers. The events of 9/11 put firefighters on the frontlines of the US War on Terror, which changed the meaning of emergency. Captain Lopez, Alex, Bojo, and Angel witnessed how they transformed the border in Nogales, but until this cold and windy day in the spring of 2017 they had not set foot on "ground zero." Wrapped in scarfs they rarely needed in the desert, the four came to pay respect to the brothers who never returned from that tragic call.

At an exhibit deep inside the 9/11 memorial museum, a recording of the dispatcher's voice directing a long list of ladder and engine companies to the World Trade Center plays over and over again. In the same room, the chirping PASS device sends chills to those who know that this alarm means the firefighter has not moved for thirty seconds. Many of those who died were crushed by the falling towers, several of their dusty helmets displayed in the cases behind glass. My companions paused to examine the twisted steel columns that held the two skyscrapers and the mangled body of Ladder Co. 3, one of several fire trucks that bear the marks of destruction. But they did not even stop at the part of the exhibit that presents the political narrative, from the development of al-Qaeda to the US government's response after the attacks. As those who do the manual labor of rescue, they were attracted to the material texture of violence, not its discursive renderings in the national story of terror and counterterror.

Even if that story can bury them alive.

Pensive and somber, we stood inside America's gaping wound less than a week after the CBP solicited proposals to design President Trump's signature campaign promise: "the big, beautiful wall."[1] Folded into the narrative of homeland security, the bid also emphasized its tactile qualities and aesthetics. Half of the eight wall prototypes unveiled in the San Diego border area later that year were made of reinforced concrete, and the other four were built using mixed materials, including steel. They all met the principal requirements the government had outlined for the new barrier along the southern border: 30 feet tall, they were "physically imposing in height" and made it difficult, if not impossible, "for human to climb to the top of the wall [. . .] unassisted"; they prevented "digging or tunneling below it for a minimum of 6 feet" and deterred "for a minimum of 1 hour the creation a [of] physical breach of the wall (e.g., punching through the wall) larger than 12-inches in diameter or square using sledgehammer, car jack, pick axe, chisel, battery operated impact tools, [. . .] or other similar hand-held tools." The bid called for designs that could be constructed on 45-degree slopes. And, last but not least, "the north side of wall (i.e., US facing side) shall be aesthetically pleasing in color, anti-climb texture, etc., to be consistent with general surrounding environment." Since the nearly 2,000-mile-long border crosses varied terrain, the color and texture of the barrier would change accordingly.

During the first few months after the announcement the media was awash with commentary from politicians, human rights activists, lawyers, environmental advocates, and community leaders, most of them opposing, but some supporting, the building of the barrier. As he was handing over the office to the incoming administration, CBP commissioner Gil Kerlikowske said that anyone familiar with the terrain along the US-Mexico boundary recognized that erecting a wall there would not be feasible. Judging by the numbers the government used to measure it, security on the border has increased, he noted, but what is a secure border remains unclear: "Definition is in the eye of beholder," the official told the press.[2] Meanwhile, wildlife conservationists filed a federal lawsuit to halt any work on the wall until "the government agrees to analyze the impact of construction, noise, light and other changes to the landscape on rivers, plants and endangered species—including jaguars, Sonoran pronghorns and ocelots—and also on border residents."[3] Artists and architects offered their imaginative takes on what the border wall could look like—from a binational city and a "regenerative co-nation" shared by citizens of both Mexico and the United States to a line built from millions of pipe organs.[4] Such experimental designs were not a new phenomenon: *Borderwall as Architecture* includes proposals for a "xylophone wall," a "burrito wall," and a "greenhouse wall."[5] The most recent push to build a wall and the hardening of the government's anti-immigrant policies merely proliferated such subversive responses. French artist JR, reacting to the Trump administration's decision to rescind the DACA program, installed a monumental photograph of a smiling baby peering over the border fence and held a binational picnic on a large tarp depicting the eyes of a "Dreamer," one in Mexico and one in the United States.[6]

The proponents of the wall sought a structure that would not rely on razor wire or electric shocks to deter people from crossing: it would be too embarrassing to see wounded bodies on the evening news—or on social media. It had to be a "humane obstruction," as the owner of one construction company explained: "I just didn't want to wake up on a Sunday morning and read about, you know, a dozen Guatemalan kids that were electrocuted or seriously injured. That would not have been something that my conscience would [. . .] allow."[7] This double imperative of the wall—it must be effective at stopping unauthorized entry but also elegant—calls for a particular security aesthetic: a barrier that appears innocuous even though it is intended to harm.

Since the government has recently hinted that a physical wall will not stretch along the entire border, the prototypes merely remain contestants in a surreal national pageant. But this bizarre spectacle hints to the weaponization of terrain well under way in the region, where both the built environment and natural topography are already being used to enable and facilitate violence. The present fence separating Ambos Nogales, comprised of concrete-and-rebar-filled steel tubes, meets most of the desired specifications for the new barrier. It may not be "aesthetically pleasing" for those who live on the north side, but at least they rarely see the wounded. Mutilated bodies are made invisible: some vanish in the desert and turn up years later as bone fragments reassembled in forensic labs; others are picked up by ambulances and rushed to hospitals, where doctors attend to their fractures and replenish their dehydrated bodies with fluids before ICE locks them up in detention centers. People who have been hurt by the wall live in the shadows of public spaces, with renal failure or a permanent limp, bound to a wheelchair or missing a finger. Some are afraid to seek treatment because they still don't have documents to live legally in the US; others are unable to find or afford long-term care once deported to their country of origin. The numbers of those injured by the wall don't exist; no agency would be proud to make such figures known.

Rescue obscures the politics of wounding. For emergency responders, trauma is routine, a result of energy transfer when a body collides with a surface. Accidents are programmed into the built and natural environment. The mechanism of injury establishes causation between the types of forces involved and specific ways they damage the body. Ordinarily, it matters little who unleashes those forces. Presence or absence of intentionality has no effect on treatment. Emergency responders follow the law, not question it; they avoid politics, even though their refusal to take sides is inevitably political. But they are not blind. They see the rocks sticking out of cement along the border wall. Whether they blame the immigration policy or the people who disobey it, they know a human being won't survive without water in three-digit temperatures for long. They work at the threshold of the state, where it both wounds and cares. Legal exceptions allow the government to operate on what may seem like contradictory principles—extralegal punishment for trespass followed by legally mandated provision of aid—but in fact sovereign power relies on the complementarity of these impulses.[8] Tactical infrastructure simultaneously produces victims and marks them as criminals, erasing the Border Patrol's responsibility for wounding. It allows disguising state violence in the form of accidents.

The idea of building a wall on the US southwest border taps a potent symbol to assuage people's deep social and economic anxieties by displacing those fears onto a remote frontier that allows drugs, alleged gang members, and simulated terrorists to seep through. It is a metaphor that conjures up threats and calls for protection, a distraction—or diversion—from the state's failure to ensure the well-being of its citizens. Supporters see the wall as a defensive structure necessary to safeguard their jobs and their values—a means to rescue what's left of the "American dream" through enclosure. Listening to Attorney General Jeff Sessions at a press conference in Nogales call the border "ground zero" in the fight against criminal gangs and cartels that "rape and kill innocent citizens" and "profit by smuggling poison and other human beings," they may be angry rather than afraid.[9] But many Americans would agree with him that this "lawlessness" has to end and that the border wall could help. More than a decade has passed since Janet Napolitano, then Arizona governor who later became secretary of homeland security, said,

"You show me a 50-foot wall and I'll show you a 51-foot ladder," but fortification remains the centerpiece of Washington's border policy. It stays because it is popular: the "big, beautiful" wall is the white picket fence of an American middle-class suburb refitted to the scale of the nation-state—a pleasant-looking symbol of property and prosperity. It should keep others from taking away what's ours. This logic of defense hinges on hope and persists in false promises that are hard to recognize and harder to abandon. The offensive character of the wall—its capacity to wound and kill—is obscured by its symbolic, ideological, and aesthetic qualities.

Trump's "big, beautiful" wall is sometimes compared to the Berlin Wall, the monstrous emblem of the Cold War and a powerful reminder of divisions in the not-so-distant past. But any wall is more than a trope. The material barrier has tangible presence in the communities it separates. "In Berlin, there was a wall between citizens of the same community, that split families, like it's happening to us here," Comandante Hernández said about Nogales. The fence of steel and cement bisects the social fabric of the border town the same way the East was once severed from the West. What history books forget to mention is that firefighters played a direct role in saving people who suddenly found themselves on opposite sides of the Iron Curtain. In 1961, when the "Wall of Shame" sealed off one half of the city from another, fire brigades in West Berlin used rescue nets to catch people who tried to escape East Berlin by jumping out of buildings on Bernauer Strasse, one of the streets that marked the fault line. Political circumstances are different now: while the communist government of East Germany built the wall to keep people from fleeing to the West, which welcomed the few that broke free as survivors, the United States uses the barrier to stop those trying to outrun violence and criminalizes many who manage to succeed. Still, the scenario on the ground is eerily familiar. Half a century later, firefighters are still rushing to the borderline to rescue people who are wounded by weaponized terrain.

A placard at the entrance to the central fire station in Nogales, Sonora, announces their mission: "to save lives, protect the environment, and preserve property in situations that threaten [. . .] our community." It says that the service firefighters provide—rapid, professional, and humanitarian—"does not distinguish on the basis of race, religion nor social class." The roots of public service, which for the longest time depended exclusively on volunteer labor, run deep in the history of Ambos Nogales and extend across the line. Both in Mexico and in the United States, albeit to different degrees, municipal fire departments have ties to the state and work in concert with government institutions, such as protección civil and emergency management. But firefighters are first and foremost members of the local community. Emergency responders take the side of the people—residents and migrants, Mexicans and Americans, those with and those sin papeles. Everyone has the same red blood and a heart that is a muscle the size of a fist. Their ethical mandate to save lives has as its referent humanity at large, superseding national governmental agendas. And yet politics and rescue are inevitably intertwined: the state *makes* emergencies—it produces injuries and disasters, defines what counts as exceptional, and decides on the priorities of caregiving.

Since September 11, 2001, security measures along the US-Mexico border have swelled faster than in any other period in history. The Real ID Act of 2005 indefinitely waived close to forty laws, including those protecting public drinking water supplies, endangered species, and Native American graves, to allow the federal government speed up the construction of fortifications that currently extend to about 700 miles of fence.[10] Following 9/11, emergency responders watched the fence in Nogales get higher, longer, and deeper, and federal agents in their local communities multiply. Firefighters, EMTs, and paramedics lived through the immediate impact of these security upgrades: the spread of fear, the new types of trauma, but also the temporary increase in training opportunities and available resources. The border became a vulnerability—a porous perimeter that could conceivably let terrorists wielding biological, chemical, or nuclear weapons slip through—and was swiftly turned into a stage for demonstrating national preparedness. Emergency responders assumed the role of frontline subjects of the security state: they began participating in large-scale theatrical performances simulating future threats, and in their daily routine gradually started accepting the distortions to their professional ethics. In the border zone, policies designed to fight terrorism supplanted all other concerns over public safety and the enforcement of other laws.[11]

Despite the uncertainty about US-Mexico relations and the escalating anti-immigrant rhetoric, emergency responders from both sides of the line continue to work together. Camaraderie is as strong as ever, and professional ties help them overcome obstacles posed by the security apparatus. This is a case in point: in April 2017, when five Mexican firefighters from Cananea and Hermosillo wanted to attend a CPR course held in Sierra Vista, Arizona, but did not have visas, CBP in Nogales issued them humanitarian parole. Such arrangements are possible because of personal relationships and mutual trust developed over the years between local emergency responders and federal officials who live in the community. The same logic does not apply to decisions made outside the realm of the local: one of the Mexican bomberos who came over to fight the historic structure fire that burned several houses in Nogales, Arizona, and helped with other binational incidents was denied a new Border Crossing Card when the one he had held for ten years expired. He is no longer allowed to enter the US.

At stake here is the definition of security. In the border zone, protection from manmade or natural disasters, which falls under the purview of public safety, cannot be confined within the contours of the state. Borders, by their mere existence, create incentives for transnational crime; and they don't stop hazards from crossing over and impacting the people and environment on the other side. Residents of the borderlands are safer when local emergency responders operate on a binational scale. Even though this scheme partially outsources the function of threat containment to the neighboring country, where the government can avoid responsibility if something happens to those placed on the frontlines, the underlying notion—that hazards are not confined within the perimeter of the nation-state—is a step forward.

However, security is more than public safety. It also includes social and ecological well-being. For the state, the concept of security serves as the cornerstone of its policies directed at hardening the border (threshold as a stumbling block) and the central notion justifying the production of "accidental" human casualties (threshing as trampling and beating). But for the residents of binational communities as well as for those who are passing through, this rhetoric—and the apparatus that it has given rise to—is an equally powerful source of the opposite: uncertainty, vulnerability, danger. Living in Nogales, I learned that people on both sides are better off when the line that separates the US and Mexico is more and not less permeable to emergency responders. Porous borders leak aid, reviving an older meaning of threshold in Spanish— *umbral,* as entrance through which light passes.

Franz Kafka described the task of building the Great Wall of China as being so hopeless that it had to be done piece by piece. Jubilant celebrations were held to mark the completion of each new section, and then the workers were shipped off far away to start over. "On their journey they saw here and there finished sections of the wall rising up; they passed through the quarters of the higher administrators, who gave them gifts as badges of honour, and they heard the rejoicing of new armies of workers streaming past them out of the depths of the land, saw forests being laid low, wood designated as scaffolding for the wall, witnessed mountains being broken up into rocks for the wall, and heard in the holy places the hymns of the pious praying for the construction to be finished," he wrote. "All this calmed their impatience."[12]

The US-Mexico border wall will never be finished: topography makes it impossible and unnecessary. Like the Great Wall of China, it is constructed piecemeal, and to boost the faith of those who participate in this Sisyphean effort, as well as to assuage the impatience of those who strongly support the project without having ever seen the border, politicians make speeches against the background of the ever taller and more technologically sophisticated fence. To the public, the material form of the border wall is less important than the metaphor. The metaphor unites the nation; it provides historical continuity and marks the territorial boundary of state sovereignty, offering imaginary protection against the people from the south that many only know through their negative representation. But the steel barrier cleaves communities and mutilates bodies. And further from the towns, its lone sections stand awkward, abandoned, and slowly falling apart in the middle of the desert, too remote to reach and maintain; a testament to the absurdity of the project and a memorial to broken dreams.

ABOUT THIS PROJECT

There were two things I was afraid of when growing up: fire and needles. I used to keep a plastic bag ready to stuff my favorite toys in case there was a fire and we had to make a quick escape in the middle of the night. At least once I ran away from school to avoid going to the nurse's station for a required immunization. My parents were called in. There was a drama. Much later, once I moved to the United States and to a second-floor apartment, I kept a linen rope under my bed to repel down the window, if need be: it wasn't ideal, but I thought it was better than not being prepared. Back then I could not have fathomed that some day I would become a firefighter and an EMT/paramedic; that I would stand in a burning building watching the flames ripple across the ceiling, sparkles falling on my face shield, mesmerized; that on the ambulance and in the emergency room, needles would become routine, and that my classmates and I would practice inserting IVs into each others' arms—many misses, many bruises.

I first became interested in firefighting while doing dissertation research with local media in Puerto Iguazú, Argentina. On their daily beat, news reporters I followed in this border town often stopped at the fire station to interview the chief about the latest emergency. Together with one of the journalists we once spent the night shift with firefighters for a story about their routine. Months later there was a powerful storm, with strong winds that picked up rocks and tore off roofs. The building where I lived swayed, windows shaking, and my linen rope (yes, I had one there too) could no longer provide the illusion of protection, so I decided to go to the only place I deemed safe: the firehouse. Instead of letting me shelter inside the station, the chief told me to get on the fire engine and accompany firefighters who were sent to patrol the flooded neighborhoods. Somewhere at night in that heavy rain I lost fear and found fellowship. I was training to become an anthropologist, but I wanted to be a firefighter.

As I kept returning to the firehouse, I decided to do something that would benefit the volunteer department, and they liked the idea of a documentary. While working on the film *Bomberos* I spent weeks in the midst of a sweltering subtropical summer interviewing firefighters, recording how they responded to emergencies—flood evacuations, motorcycle crashes, occasional fires—and shared the daily chores at the station. We soaked cervical collars in soapy water to scrape off dried blood and use them on new patients; we ran to answer the phone to hear false alarms; we watched a lot of TV. In a town with frequent blackouts, at the station with no air-conditioning, we drank ice-cold tereré to cool off on days when the forecast warned about temperatures exceeding 100°F and near 100 percent relative humidity. When due to a power outage the town's water supply was cut off, we hung a fire hose through the bathroom window and used water reserves in the tanker to take quick showers. We trained, too. On the weekends, we attended courses taught by ER doctors at the local hospital. Other days, wearing donated and badly fitted turnout gear we ran in circles, walked on logs, and crawled through tunnels. For the men and women in the Puerto Iguazú Fire Department, their service was a vocation. When I finished my dissertation fieldwork and returned to the United States, I could no longer imagine my life without this camaraderie.

And so, back in Massachusetts for the last year of graduate school, I took an EMT class, where our instructor taught us to do chest compressions following the tempo of the Bee Gees' "Stayin' Alive," and joined the Cambridge Auxiliary Fire Department. We trained in forcible entry techniques and participated in wilderness search and rescue drills; we were dispatched to structure fires to do overhaul and roll a lot of hose; we were sent to crime scenes to run the lights while police detectives collected evidence. There was my first fire: I remember engines, ladders, ambulances clogging the narrow streets of Cambridge and commotion as firefighters carried out their tasks. When we went inside the house to help clear the debris, I recall standing in the kitchen on the second floor, surrounded by charred chunks of wood and puddles of water. Several photographs were pegged by magnets on the door of the fridge—portraits of a family that had just lost their home. I grabbed the shovel and began throwing burned pieces of furniture and heaps of ash out through the window. The following morning I taught my first class at Brandeis University, a course on the anthropology of violence and the media. But my body was still overwhelmed by the sensory experiences of the fire's aftermath and my mind still lingered in that burned building. I could not see the connection between what I had experienced and what I had to talk about in the classroom.

I lived a "double life"; my family and friends, some fascinated, others perplexed or even concerned by my new vocation, joked that it reminded them of Dr. Jekyll and Mr. Hyde. During the day I continued writing my dissertation and teaching classes, but in the evenings I spent long hours with auxiliary firefighters walking up and down the streets of Cambridge discussing how to break in or break down different types of doors. We drove to Home Depot to get tools that we would then fine-tune in the firehouse basement, while showing off new flashlights, high-voltage detectors, and other gadgets. We learned tying knots: bowline, clove hitch, figure 8 follow through, and "handcuff knot," which made the young volunteers giggle. Those days I carried a portable radio, hoping I would never miss a call requesting the auxiliary. Sometimes those calls came in on Friday evenings, while I was having dinner with friends; other times it was weekend mornings before dawn. I had a bag with my uniform ready to go and rushed to the fire station in East Cambridge, where we picked up our rig. LP2 was an ambulance repurposed into a "lighting plant," and for the most part that was what we did: light the scene, provide rehab, do overhaul—we got the leftovers of fighting fires. But we were wannabes and we did it all with pride.

One weekend I was invited to participate in rapid intervention team (RIT) training at the Massachusetts Firefighting Academy in Stow. Dressed in full bunker gear, on air, we each took a tool, and, in teams of four, entered a four-story building filled with smoke, with a mission to find and rescue a "fallen firefighter"—fortunately, our victim was just a human-size sandbag dummy; unfortunately, it weighed over 60 pounds more than I did. We repeated the drill for four hours, changing scenarios and team roles. "Cambridge!" the instructors shouted, and I knew they were addressing me, for I was the only one from the city. They ordered me to hurry up, to catch up—I was new, not part of the graduating class, and this drill remains one of the most difficult things I've ever done. The axe felt heavy. My knees ached from repeatedly banging them onto cement floor as we went up and down the flights of stairs on all fours, never letting go of the wall and of the rope connecting us one to another. I could not see anything and I could hear very little. It was hot. It was awkward to breathe through the SCBA. There were moments when I thought I could not move an inch further and contemplated ripping off the mask to inhale fresh air. But between public shame and possible heat exhaustion I chose the latter. When we were done, some of the recruits were throwing up. Firefighters have died during intense training exercises like this. Between 2001 and 2010, the US National Fire Protection Association (NFPA) registered 108 firefighter deaths related to training, most from cardiac arrest, some from heat stroke.[1]

Pulled ever deeper into this new fascinating world, I completed a couple of operations-level hazmat courses. Even the dry incident management curricula did not deter me. I spent one or two shifts a week with the crews of Ladder 2 and Engine 3 in East Cambridge. The city became more tangible to me as I learned how to anticipate the next emergency. When it started to rain, firefighters expected the dispatch to announce a car accident; on cold windy days they fidgeted with the settings on their radios to make sure they were listening to the right channel—they wouldn't want to miss a structure fire. Their bodies and their tools were fine-tuned with the urban environment, synced and tied to it.

In 2012, when I began teaching at the University of Florida, I became a volunteer at the fire department in Micanopy, an old Florida town located between the Paynes Prairie and I-75 about fifteen minutes south of Gainesville, with an old cemetery sheltered by Spanish moss-covered oaks, a gas station serving juicy brisket and ribs, and a strip club my peers would visit for "safety inspections" when I was not around. I would come down once or twice a week for a daylong shift. On Wednesdays, which were our "truck days," we spent several hours cleaning Engine 26 and testing equipment: PASS alarms on SCBAs, rescue saws, air bags. Although some days were like pages torn out from a book of hell—call after call—it was more usual for us not to get a single call and have to occupy ourselves with runs to get coffee and ice cream, working out in the gym, or dozing off in the recliners in front of the TV. It was a great place to study, which was important to me since I had just enrolled in paramedic school.

The paramedic school was in Orange Park and I did my field internship with the Jacksonville Fire Rescue Department, followed by a series of clinical rotations in the area's hospitals. Rescue 4, the ambulance unit that I committed to, was stationed in a poor neighborhood with a bad reputation, and we ran calls nonstop, day and night. During those months I learned technical skills: how to listen to lung sounds with the stethoscope and how not to miss a vein sticking the patient's arm with a needle in a moving ambulance. But there was nothing that challenged my book-based knowledge more than conversations with Jesse Modican—firefighter, paramedic, hazmat technician, and a member of the regional urban search and rescue team. He was our chief in Micanopy, so even in Jacksonville, where he held lieutenant's rank, I called him "Chief." He knew what illness and injury looked like, smelled like, and felt like on the street. Voluminous textbooks on pathophysiology and pharmacology that we had to read to prepare for the state paramedic exam couldn't capture that experience. "But that's just me," Chief would say whenever we disagreed about the diagnosis, and, as far as I know, he was always right.

When we arrived on scene, whether it was in Micanopy or in Jacksonville, my companions would tell patients that they were "in good hands." "She's a doc," they'd say, pointing to me as I prepared to take their vital signs. "Not that kind of doc," I would clarify. People I knew laughed at the fact that I got my PhD and became an EMT only days apart. But it took me a while to accept that I could combine my work as an emergency responder with anthropology. Though I recognized the links between these modes of knowledge and practice and felt them strengthen over time, for years I tried to keep these two fields of my life separate. I knew I could not do ethnography in the fire departments I was affiliated with in Florida—not because I feared losing objectivity, though that could have happened, but because I did not want to risk severing ties with those who had become my family. Four years in a row I spent Thanksgiving at the fire station; twice I made the turkey. The firehouse was where I felt at home.

It was serendipity. I wrote my first book about borders and security in northeastern Argentina, and these topics continued to be central to my academic work. But when I went to my fieldsite in 2014, looking for ideas to start a new research project in Puerto Iguazú, I returned empty-handed. It was then that I stumbled upon an article in the *New York Times,* with the title "Border Cities Are Burdened with Calls for Help."[2] The author interviewed fire officials in California and Arizona who told the reporter about the increased number of calls for medical assistance at the US-Mexico border and how, without support from the federal government, these were becoming "a growing burden" on the resources of local fire departments and the communities they served. As an anthropologist studying borders and as an emergency responder, I was curious about this situation, so I immediately began looking for more information. In a November 2013 article in the *Washington Times,* reprinted in *JEMS: Journal of Emergency Medical Services,* another journalist wrote that after the government doubled the height of the border fence in Nogales, ambulance calls for injured crossers spiked.[3] City officials quoted in the article said that the fire department provides emergency care to everyone, regardless of whether the injured person is in the country illegally, and the city absorbs the costs. That was how I found my research topic. I wanted to know what it was like to be part of fire and emergency medical services on both sides of the militarized border. Though I initially approached it through questions of law and ethics, it was only a matter of time before I stumbled upon the significance of terrain.

Between May 2015 and May 2017, for varied periods of time, I lived in Nogales, Arivaca, and Rio Rico and did ethnographic fieldwork in fire departments along the Arizona-Sonora border, both north and south of the line. In my research, I used qualitative methods common to social anthropology. Interviews with chiefs and firefighters in Arizona and Sonora were conducted in English or in Spanish, depending on the choice of my respondents, and code-switching was ordinary. I spent at least one day a week at Station 2 of the Nogales Fire Department, accompanying Shift A through their daily routine at the firehouse and responding to emergency calls. My observations were jotted in a pocket notebook and typed up in the fieldwork journal the following morning. In addition to NFD, I was involved in the activities of the Arivaca Fire District and the bomberos of Nogales, Sonora, going on runs, hanging out at the station, participating in training, attending commemorative ceremonies, campaigns, parades, family events, and retirement parties. Wearing a helmet and a turnout coat, I marched with the bomberos in the Virgen de Guadalupe procession through Nogales, and attended a Mass that was punctuated by drums and trumpets of the banda de guerra. Sometimes I was the liaison for the Mexican firefighters in Arizona: I'd pick them up at the port of entry and drive them to meetings at the emergency manager's office or at one of the fire stations on the US side of the border. I translated and I took many pictures.

Former and present Santa Cruz County emergency managers invited me to local emergency planning committee meetings in Nogales; trainings, drills, and Border 2020 task force meetings in Agua Prieta and Puerto Peñasco; and the Integrated Emergency Management Course at the FEMA National Emergency Training Center in Maryland. Whenever my schedule permitted, I also sat in on the Arivaca Fire District Board and the Nogales City Council meetings. To get information about the types and frequency of emergency calls, I requested public records from the Santa Cruz County Sherriff's Office and the Arivaca Fire District. The Freedom of Information Act (FOIA) request that I filed with the US Border Patrol on February 27, 2017, to obtain the numbers of injured "illegal aliens" in the Tucson Sector is still pending. For original news reports on vehicle accidents involving unauthorized migrants I conducted archival research at Joel D Valdez Public Library in Tucson, where the *Tucson Citizen,* the historic area newspaper founded in 1870 and discontinued in 2014, is available on microfilm. I also regularly consulted online archives of *Tucson Citizen,* the *Arizona Daily Star,* and *Nogales International.*

Determined to practice engaged and public anthropology, I worked closely with research partners from the emergency responder community. Tangye Beckham, at the time the acting fire chief and paramedic in the Arivaca Fire District, and Victor Garay, lieutenant firefighter and hazardous materials technician at the Honorable Cuerpo de Bomberos Voluntarios "Gustavo L. Manriquez" in Nogales, Sonora, were my field assistants. The two of them helped with the logistics, arranged interviews, and obtained records and permissions, but they also contributed ideas and questions to the project, and we discussed this research every step of the way. Four members of the Nogales Fire Department in Arizona read the first draft of this manuscript and gave me feedback. My student assistants at the University of Florida and at Harvard University scoured media archives and analyzed legal documents to fill in the gaps.

During my time on the US-Mexico border I also volunteered as a wildland firefighter and EMT/paramedic at the Nogales Suburban Fire District in Arizona and, with the Tucson Samaritans, at the Kino Border Initiative's migrant aid center, known as "el comedor," in Nogales, Sonora. With both organizations my responsibility was to provide prehospital medical care to the sick and the injured, not to do ethnography, so my notes from those days are scarce. Since there was only one paid firefighter on duty in each of the two fire stations in Nogales Suburban, as often as I could I stayed on shifts as a volunteer. I also served as the instructor for medical training: few of the firefighters in the district were EMTs; most had no more than basic CPR certification. At el comedor, more than anything I rationed ibuprofen pills and cough drops that could be spared for each migrant who came asking for something to soothe their chronic and acute conditions and prepare them for the pains they were yet to endure when they attempted to cross the border; I often worked alongside a nurse, helping to clean infected wounds on their feet.

But even when I was not volunteering, being a first responder was an asset conducting ethnographic research in fire stations on both sides of the border. I knew how to stay out of the way and not become a burden. On scene, whether it was a fire or a medical call, nobody had to warn me about potential hazards. And, when I could, I helped, in small ways, dropping my notebook to hold an IV bag, position a trauma patient onto a backboard, do chest compressions, or guard the perimeter of a brush fire. These interventions were minimal, and usually I had time to do the typical ethnographic work—scribbling notes, taking pictures. In Nogales, I was allowed to participate in performing firehouse duties, which included cooking meals and washing dishes, and cleaning the floors and the bathrooms. For twenty-four hours every three days, the station was their home. That I, too, was an emergency responder, made these firefighters feel a bit more comfortable with my presence. This was all the more significant since most of the time I was the only female in their company.

Putting this embedded and embodied fieldwork on the page was not an easy task. Stories I heard and situations I witnessed in Nogales, Arivaca, and elsewhere were refracted through my own earlier experiences of rescue and death, accrued while learning life-saving skills in the back of an ambulance and running calls on a fire engine before I ever set foot in the Arizona-Sonora borderlands. There were moments, many of them, when my background as a paramedic and a volunteer firefighter helped me notice and understand. But there were also times when it may have blinded me. My reactions to injury have been blunted, lacking the shock and outrage that witnessing situations described in this book should provoke. That's part of the coping mechanism that we, as first responders, develop in order to survive in a profession where emergency is the routine. Perhaps this book is a form of coping too. I started writing it the morning after I handed in my turnout gear and said farewell to my chief, leaving Micanopy and the fire service. He let me keep my helmet, which now hangs on the wall in my apartment in Cambridge, as a reminder that those experiences were real.

But this book is also a call to action. The sun that sucks life out of displaced migrant bodies, the fires, the floods, the environmental contamination—they don't respect the boundaries drawn in the sand by sovereign states. Industry and crime have found ways around them, as do those on the move because they are drawn by the opportunities of the former or pushed away from home by the latter. The US-Mexico borderlands is a space of entanglement. Instead of talking about how to reinforce it with another wall, we should make the border more pervious for firefighters, paramedics, and hazardous materials specialists, who are ready to cross the line to help in an emergency on either side.

I hope it changes our conversations about security.

ACKNOWLEDGMENTS

This book is dedicated to the firefighters on both sides of the border, in Mexico and in the United States. They took me in as one of their own and showed me what it was like to work on the frontlines, rescuing people for a living. They were kind and patient, and brutally honest. They put up with my questions and my camera— as well as my cravings for tamales. Above all, I thank Ricardo Bojorquez for answering a call from a stranger and everything that followed; Alex Flores, for standing up for me; Leo Lopez, for offering me a seat at the table and a mop; César Vélez, for coyotas de nieve; and Eduardo Canizales, for not letting me forget las puras pendejadas. Tangye Beckham and Victor Garay were my research assistants; they accompanied me in Arizona and in Sonora and found the answers that made this book possible. These firefighters proved to me that, despite the monstrous border wall, there is a brotherhood that has never recognized such a divide.

But first things first.

I would have never set out on this journey were it not for those who took my wish to become an emergency responder seriously and for those who persuaded me that my experiences in the fire department had a place in my scholarship. I did not take either for granted.

Jesse Modican, my chief at Micanopy Fire Department and preceptor during my paramedic internship with Jacksonville Fire and Rescue in Florida, taught me most of what I know about being an emergency responder. He gave me a chance and had my back when I made mistakes. He didn't offer me exceptions. An outstanding medic, he ingrained in me not only the skills but also the ethics of care. During my years on rescue units I've seen some emergency responders treat patients with apathy or contempt, either out of disapproval for what they'd done or who they were, or simply because of fatigue at the end of a 24-hour shift. But not chief. He took no bullshit from anyone, but whether we were helping a little old lady having difficulty breathing or a homeless man faking a seizure to be able to spend a night at the hospital, he acted with kindness and respect. He kept my bunker gear at the station awaiting my return from the desert and listened to my stories about the borderlands.

Henry Rivera showed me what to do on "truck days" and trusted me to make firehouse turkey on Thanksgiving. He also moved me from apartment to apartment too many times and took care of my lemon tree while I was away. Jeshua Kavanaugh, Michael Lawrence, and Brett Thomas gave their support when I needed it.

My journey into the world of firefighting and emergency medicine began in earnest in Cambridge and Waltham, Massachusetts, where Richie Thorne, CJ Roberts, Kenny Albert, Billy Dusablon, Mike Donovan, Danny Lewicki, Miguel Torres, and others let me ride on the trucks and practice sliding down the poles, in exchange for home-baked cookies. They shared their advice, their company, and the uncomfortable wooden bench at the station. John Hathaway gave me a leather helmet with a Lithuanian flag and told me about fires, both old and new. I thank my peers in the auxiliary for accepting me into their ranks and in particular Pete Davekos for the toolbox and for always doing more than he had to.

Some of the people who contributed to this project cannot be named, either because what they told me could jeopardize their jobs or because their identities are not legal in this country. Others, however, cannot escape public acknowledgment. On the border, I am grateful to the fire officials and emergency managers who recognized the importance of this research and gave me their permission to do it: Manuel Hernández, William Sanchez, Anthony Gonzales, Mario Novoa, Les Caid, Rod Lopez, Sergio Díaz, Joseph DeWolf. Carlos Parra enlisted me as volunteer no. 656 and for a while I called him "chief." Louie Chaboya warned me that I would have to write more than one book, and brought tequila. Ray Sayre invited me to FEMA. Strong support from administrators was crucial: their trust allowed me to partake in activities that were happening behind closed doors and that I would otherwise be excluded from. Yet I spent most of my time with shift workers, and it is to them that I am indebted for letting me stick around. Jorge Lopez, Carlos Rivas, Angel Taddei, William Beyerle, Pete Ashcraft, Frank Teran, Gerardo Romo, Jorge Alba, Pete Mendoza, Carmen Hernández, Cuauhtémoc Durazo, Daniel Osuna, Pablo Domínguez, Armando Reyes, and so many others—thank you. Chucky Parra—rest in peace brother.

Bob Kee and Norma Price of the Tucson Samaritans showed me how to provide first aid to those who needed it most. Teresa Small, from US Customs and Border Protection in Tucson, gave me a rare opportunity to hear the federal government's point of view. Javier de la Ossa handled my public records request at the Santa Cruz County Sheriff's Office. On different sides of the border doctors Carlos Sodi and Brian Kniff fixed me up when I was falling apart for nothing more than a thank you. I am grateful to Don Fito Monroy for huevos con nopales, Jill Farrell for introducing me to vermillion flycatchers, Janeth Valdez for a bag of cloves to share with migrants suffering from toothache, Mary and Rob Kasulaitis for stories and poems, Chad for the frog legs, Santiago for the last resort, and Brad Knaub for the coffee, which still keeps me up as I write the last words of the book. My favorite Arivaca blend arrived by mail just in time.

I have been fortunate to be able to count on colleagues who thought that writing this book was a good idea and who supported me from the very beginning, particularly Jason de León, Daniel M. Goldstein, Sharon Abramowitz, Ruth Goldstein, Susan Ellison, Winifred Tate, and Charles Wood. Elizabeth Ferry, Josiah Heyman, Shaylih Muehlmann, Joseph Masco, and Gastón Gordillo read an early draft of the manuscript and provided generous comments. My writing group—Kirsten Weld, Sergio Delgado, and Ana Villarreal—helped me find the right words to say what I wanted to say. Conversations with John Comaroff, Diane Davis, Ajantha Subramanian, and Jon Carter shaped and sharpened the arguments. June Erlick gave me confidence to write. Students in my Law and Violence in Latin America seminar read part of the manuscript and met with firefighters from Nogales to discuss it during their visit to Cambridge.

Several students assisted me during various stages of this project: Jose Abastida, Ed Haning, and Iliana Villegas at the University of Florida, and Michelle Borbon and Juana Davila at Harvard University. Without their help chasing the leads through the archives, public records, and legal documents, this book would not have been ready on time. If it weren't for Michelle, I would not have known to look for the first edition of the boundary survey report at the Widener Library; I spent hours flipping through its stained, fragile pages.

Though this project started while I was at the University of Florida, it is at Harvard that I found my academic home and the intellectual community that allowed me to turn it into a book. The chair of the Anthropology Department, Gary Urton, provided unwavering support during my first two years here; Monica Munson, Andrew Cepeda, Karen Crabtree, and Cris Paul handled administration and logistics that made this project possible.

Research in Arizona and Sonora was supported by a Senior Research Award from the National Science Foundation, a postdoctoral grant from the Wenner-Gren Foundation, and the Humanities Scholarship Enhancement Fund from the University of Florida. The Weatherhead Center for International Affairs and the Faculty of Arts and Sciences at Harvard University funded a book manuscript workshop. I made the final revisions as an academic writing fellow at the Rockefeller Foundation Bellagio Center in Italy.

Some ethnographic material has been previously presented in public talks I gave at the Peabody Museum of Archaeology and Ethnology and David Rockefeller Center for Latin American Studies at Harvard University, at the "Security Aesthetics and the Urban Imaginary" conference at Rutgers University, and at the Center for Research in the Arts, Social Sciences and Humanities at the University of Cambridge. The book further develops ideas first briefly introduced in "Called to 'Ankle Alley': Migrant Injuries and Emergency Medical Services on the U.S.-Mexico Border" (*American Anthropologist* 120[1], 2018) and "The Wall and the Wash: Security, Infrastructure and Rescue on the US-Mexico Border" (*Anthropology Today* 33[3], 2017). A short section of part 3, "Some Pill to Help Us Walk," appeared in *ReVista: Harvard Review of Latin America* 16(1) (2017) as "Pain on the Border: Fieldnotes from a Migrant Aid Center in Nogales, Mexico."

Working with my editor, Kate Marshall, has been one of the most rewarding experiences I've had as an author. She believed in the idea for this book even before I did, steered the early drafts in the right direction, and made sure I did not wait until the end to tell the reader that I was a first responder. She made me a better, bolder writer. At the University of California Press, I am also grateful to Bradley Depew and Kate Hoffman for seeing the manuscript through to completion; Sue Carter for patiently editing medical terminology and Mexican slang; and Tom Sullivan and Alex Dahne for presenting the book to its publics.

Bryce Davenport drew the maps. Six years earlier, he also agreed to be placed on a backboard for my EMT skills test.

Rachana and Sachin Agarwal, Mary Risner, Anna Jaysanne-Darr, Casey Golomski, Mrinalini Tankha, Sylvia Chen, Arto Suren, and Burcu Yucesoy were amused by my pursuits and did not allow the fire alarms that interrupted our time together stand in the way of our friendship.

My parents, who have admired firefighters ever since they put out the flames on the roof of our house, have persistently wished that I would stop rushing toward danger and start running away from it. Unfortunately, I can't promise them that. They raised me to chase my dreams.

My nephew Liudvikas has several fire trucks, an ambulance, and a helicopter—all equipped to rescue toys in peril. I look forward to the day when he meets my friends on the line.

ABBREVIATIONS

A&O	Alert and oriented (x4: to four elements—person, place, time, event)
ABC	Airway, breathing, circulation
AC	Antecubital (front surface of the forearm)
AED	Automated external defibrillator
ALS	Advanced life support
BANWR	Buenos Aires National Wildlife Refuge
BLM	US Bureau of Land Management
BORSTAR	Border Patrol's Search, Trauma, and Rescue team/unit
BP	Blood pressure
C4	Centro de Control, Comando, Comunicación y Cómputo
CBP	US Customs and Border Protection
CBRNE	Chemical, biological, radiological, nuclear, and explosive
CONAFOR	Comisión Nacional Forestal (National Forestry Commission)
CPR	Cardiopulmonary resuscitation
DHS	US Department of Homeland Security
DPS	Department of Public Safety
ECG	Electrocardiogram
EHS	Extremely hazardous substances
EMS	Emergency medical services
EMT	Emergency medical technician
EPA	US Environmental Protection Agency
ERG	Emergency Response Guidebook
ETA	Estimated time of arrival

FEMA	Federal Emergency Management Agency
FOIA	Freedom of Information Act
FWS	US Fish and Wildlife Service
GAO	US Government Accountability Office
GCS	Glasgow Coma Scale
GIS	Geographic information system
HEPA	High efficiency particulate air
HIPAA	Health Insurance Portability and Accountability Act of 1996
IAFF	International Association of Fire Fighters
ICE	US Immigration and Customs Enforcement
INM	Instituto Nacional de Migración (National Migration Institute)
INS	US Immigration and Naturalization Service
IOI	International Outfall Interceptor
LR	Lactated ringer's [solution]
MCI	Mass casualty incident
MOI	Mechanism of injury
MSDS	Material Safety Data Sheet
MVA	Motor vehicle accident
NAFTA	North American Free Trade Agreement
NFD	Nogales Fire Department
NFPA	US National Fire Protection Association
NORTHCOM	US Department of Defense Northern Command
NSAID	Nonsteroidal anti-inflammatory drug
NSFD	Nogales Suburban Fire District
OSHA	US Occupational Safety and Health Administration
PACE	Programa de Actualizaciones, Capacitación y Equipamiento (Program for Upgrades, Training, and Equipment)
PASS	Personal Alert Safety System
PPE	Personal protective equipment
PRD	Personal radiation detector/device
PROFEPA	Procuraduría Federal de Protección al Ambiente (Federal Attorney for Environmental Protection)
RIT	Rapid intervention team
RRFD	Rio Rico Fire District
SAEMS	Southern Arizona Emergency Medical Services

SCBA	Self-contained breathing apparatus
SEMARNAT	Secretaría del Medio Ambiente y Recursos Naturales (Secretariat of Environment and Natural Resources)
TAR	Transport authorization request
TKO	To keep [vein] open
TTX	Tabletop exercise
UAV	Unmanned aerial vehicle
UDA	Undocumented alien
UMC	University Medical Center (Tucson)
USBP	US Border Patrol
USCIS	US Citizenship and Immigration Services

NOTES

INTRODUCTION

1. In Nogales, where most residents are bilingual, code-switching is very common. Throughout the book, popular Spanish words and phrases appear in roman and are generally not translated. This narrative style best conveys the tone of local conversations.

2. Some of the names in this book are real; others have been changed. It is a standard practice in anthropology to change people's names and other identifying characteristics to protect the identity of the research participants. However, acknowledging the fact that some emergency responders I interviewed wanted to go on the record and specifically asked me to use their names, while others were public figures and spoke as official representatives of their institutions, I let each individual make an informed decision. The default option on the consent forms stated that the names of research participants would be changed unless they checked a box indicating their preference to reveal their names. I will not indicate which names have been altered—this should not matter from the reader's perspective.

3. Kenward et al. 2016.

4. Following President Trump's executive order calling for the construction of a wall along the entirety of the US-Mexico border, issued on January 25, a report by the Center for Biological Diversity analyzed data from the US Fish and Wildlife Service and identified ninety-three threatened, endangered, and candidate species that would be harmed by the construction of a wall. See Greenwald et al. (2017).

5. Blust 2016b.

6. Rosas (2012) claims that "warfare and policing have transformed it [the Sonoran Desert] into a neoliberal oven, a killing desert." He also writes about migrants crossing "neoliberal ovens of the killing deserts." De León (2015) describes the federal "prevention through deterrence" policy as "killing machine."

7. Urrea 2004.

8. Jimenez 2009.

9. Border Patrol Overview, US Customs and Border Protection, https://www
.cbp.gov/border-security/along-us-borders/overview.

10. See my article (Jusionyte 2015b) about former firefighters who used an ambulance to transport drugs in northeastern Argentina.

11. Smith 2016; *Nogales International* 2015a.

12. See Vélez-Ibáñez (1996) for an account of population shifts in the region since the Spanish expansion in the sixteenth century.

13. Emory 1987 [1857]:118.

14. According to St John, "The boundary commission's experiences revealed the limits of the nation-state's ability to force land and people to conform to their presumptions of sovereignty and divisions of national space" (2011:28).

15. According to Kenward et al. (2016), the average spring and summer temperatures in Arizona have increased 2.3°F since the 1970s, the second largest increase among the western states. Higher temperatures have been associated with increased frequency and severity of wildfires. By 2050, Arizona is expected to see more than a month of additional "high-risk fire days." For more on intensifying wildland fires see Kramer (2013). Arizona monsoons have also become more intense in the last twenty years; see Luong et al. (2017).

16. See Schlyer (2017). In addition, Mumme and Ibáñez (2009) note that the unilateral initiative to rapidly construct security infrastructure along the border overlooked international environmental agreements, such as the 1944 Water Treaty and the 1983 La Paz Agreement, which require the US federal government to coordinate actions that might impact Mexico with the neighboring country's authorities.

17. McCombs 2008.

18. Although the idea that territory is a historically specific articulation of place and power, used as a political technology, is not new (see, for example, Elden 2013), the focus on the materiality of terrain is rather recent. Elden (2017) suggests seeing terrain as a fusion of geopolitics and geophysics. Gordillo (2018:55) defines terrain as "a non-representable multiplicity of forms and objects that includes human bodies within it yet is also irreducible to human experiences." Gordillo proposes "affective geometry" as a theoretical lens to examine how, in Afghanistan's Korengal Valley, where American soldiers and local fighters were differently affected by the opacity, temporality, and verticality of the mountains, terrain served as an insurgent weapon.

19. "tactical," Merriam-Webster.com, www.merriam-webster.com/dictionary
/tactical.

20. Mbembe 2003:26.

21. In his 1977–1978 lectures at the Collège de France, Foucault argued that security differs from sovereignty and discipline in how it treats space. Security relies on "material givens"—both natural (such as rivers, marshes, hills) and artificial (houses)—in the type of space Foucault calls "milieu" (2007:20–21). He writes: "It will, of course, work on site with the flows of water, islands, air, and so forth. Thus it works on a given. This given will not be reconstructed to arrive at a point of perfection, as in a disciplinary town. It is simply a matter of maximizing the positive elements, for which one provides the best possible circulation, and of minimizing what

is risky and inconvenient, like theft and disease, while knowing that they will never be completely suppressed" (19). For Foucault, security works with reality "by getting the components of reality to work in relation to each other" (47).

22. Feldman 1991:27.

23. American College of Surgeons Committee on Trauma 2011:64–65.

24. Weizman 2017:119.

25. Anthropologists have called this form of indirect violence "structural violence," "systemic violence," or "everyday violence." What is common to all these concepts is the difficulty of establishing a clear link between perpetrators and the victim. It also entails a different temporality.

26. Weizman (2014:16) defines "built environment" as "composite assemblies of structures, spaces, infrastructure, services, and technologies" that "structure and condition [. . .] human action."

27. Weizman 2014:27.

28. In the field of emergency medical services (EMS), there are different levels of certifications for providers of care. Emergency medical technicians (EMTs), sometimes referred to as EMT-Basics, are the most common entry-level providers of out-of-hospital emergency medical care and transportation for critical patients. After completing a course that is about 120–150 hours in length and passing state or national exams they can give CPR, administer oxygen and glucose, or help patients with asthma attacks or allergic reactions (scope of practice varies by state). Paramedics are more advanced providers of emergency medical care. Their training requires 1,200–1,800 hours of work, and they are allowed to start IV lines, interpret 12-lead ECGs, provide advanced airway management, such as endotracheal intubation and chest decompression, as well as administer a wide variety of cardiac and other medications. Most paramedics begin as EMTs and then build on this basic education. An "EMT" is therefore a more encompassing category—it applies to both EMT-Basics and paramedics.

29. Tebeau 2003:287.

30. See Desmond 2007.

31. GAO-12–73.

32. Smith and Shearer 2017.

33. Doty (2011:607) argues that natural topography provides the government with a convenient "moral alibi" when locating responsibility for migrant deaths. See also Infante et al. 2012; Rubio-Goldsmith et al. 2006; Slack and Whiteford 2011; among others.

34. USBP 1994:7.

35. Anthropologists working with refugees in Europe and the Middle East have shown how bodily evidence of physical and psychological trauma have been mobilized to make claims for asylum. See, for example, Ticktin 2011; Fassin and D'Halluin 2005; Dewachi 2015.

36. In her analysis of car accidents in post-apartheid South Africa, Morris (2010:612) argues that "the state opens a space to exercise force" not by making crimes look like mere accidents, but by representing the accident as a possible crime.

37. In the speech launching his presidential campaign in June 2015, Donald Trump accused Mexican people of "bringing drugs" and "bringing crime" and called them "rapists." During interviews he also talked about immigrants being "killers" and "murderers."

38. Dewachi 2015:77.

39. For more on the intermixing of care and control at Europe's borders see Andersson (2017). The issue of humanitarian justification of border enforcement is also addressed in Fassin and Pandolfi (2010), Fassin (2012), and Ticktin (2011).

40. Redfield (2005:329) describes this form of intervention as "minimalist biopolitics."

41. CBP has been running its own EMT-Basic courses for its agents since 2008, when the program was first initiated in El Paso, Texas. The Tucson Sector now offers two EMT courses per year.

42. Gaynor 2007.

43. Among numerous reports that document how CBP violates the rights of unauthorized migrants are these two: *Border Security and Migration: A Report from Arizona* (Isacson et al. 2013) and "Our Values on the Line: Migrant Abuse and Family Separation at the Border" (Danielson 2015).

44. For more on the formation of military and civilian emergency medicine see van Stralen (2008) and Goniewicz (2013). For more on the history of prehospital and emergency medicine see Haller (1992), Hutchinson (1996), and Zink (2006).

45. In some countries, including Mexico, Red Cross societies, as nongovernmental humanitarian assistance groups, take on the first responder role within the national health care system. In Nogales and other towns in northern Sonora, the Sonoran delegation of the Cruz Roja Mexicana offers training to emergency medical technicians and provides ambulance service to the community.

46. Fire departments have never been impervious to politics: as municipal service providers, firefighter unions have long played an important role in local governance, supporting candidates in mayoral and city council elections. But until the second half of the twentieth century they were not integrated into the federal emergency management structures to the extent that they are now.

47. Several notable anthropological studies on emergency preparedness in the United States include Fosher (2009), Masco (2014), and Lakoff (2007).

48. Donahue 2011; Rothenbuhler 2005.

49. The industrial zone in Nogales, Sonora, is about 7 kilometers (4 miles) away from the US-Mexico border and 91 meters (almost 300 feet) above Nogales, Arizona.

50. St John 2011.

51. In his ethnographic study on risk management in Colombia, Zeiderman (2016:16) noted a similar shift in how the definition of threat changed from "disorder, criminality, and insurgency to floods, landslides, and earthquakes," precipitating the creation of new forms of governing the city, organized around the anticipation of future harm.

52. Dorsey and Díaz-Barriga (2015) show that citizens who live in the Rio Grande Valley of Texas do not have the right "to be secure in their persons, houses,

papers and effects," which is a violation of the Fourth Amendment. Border Patrol and Texas DPS (who now act as the Border Patrol due to 287(g) legislation) can pull citizens over and search cars without probable cause.

53. According to the CBP, the authority for this is based on the Immigration and Nationality Act 287(a)(3) and copied in 8 Code of Federal Regulations (CFR) 287 (a)(3), https://help.cbp.gov/app/answers/detail/a_id/1084/~/legal-authority-for-the-border-patrol.

54. For Bourdieu (2014:20) "the left hand" of the state consists of spending or social ministries, in charge of public education, health, housing, and welfare, whereas "the right hand" refers primarily to financial ministries. Wacquant (2010) later expanded the latter category to include the police, the courts, and the prison as the core constituents of the "right hand" of the penal state. Here, I use "the right hand" in reference to government institutions responsible for enforcing economic discipline and social order. For more on Bourdieu's definition of the state's two hands see Bourdieu (1994, 2006).

55. Herzfeld (1997) called them "disemic" processes. Heyman's (2000, 2002) studies show how these tensions unfolded on the US-Mexico border.

56. Fassin 2012.

57. Weber 2012:101–2.

58. Fassin 2015:ix.

59. Bourdieu 1999:184.

60. See Heyman 2002. Heyman studied Mexican and Mexican American officers at the US Immigration and Naturalization Service (INS). This agency ceased to exist in 2003, when its functions were transferred to three new entities: US Citizenship and Immigration Services (USCIS), US Immigration and Customs Enforcement (ICE), and US Customs and Border Protection (CBP). Officers that Heyman interviewed were likely reassigned to either CBP or ICE, so his findings are relevant to understanding the dynamics of these new agencies. Heyman argues that the case of Mexican American officers is "intriguing because their development as citizens motivated them to join a law enforcement agency openly and overwhelmingly directed at people of their own national origin" (483). After reviewing study data, he contends that "internal struggles to achieve substantive citizenship result in institutionally delivered rights and redistributions that shape external politics of inclusion and exclusion of new immigrants from such rights and redistributions" (483).

61. "thrash | thresh, v," OED Online, www.oed.com.ezp-prod1.hul.harvard .edu/view/Entry/201108.

62. "threshold, n." OED Online. www.oed.com.ezp-prod1.hul.harvard.edu /view/Entry/201234.

63. Research for the genealogy of *umbral* was conducted by Michelle Borbon, a junior at Harvard College.

64. Although the English term "threshold" also has negative connotations that link it to beating and stumbling, the interpretation of *umbral* as a spatial figure constituted by an interplay of light and shadow exists only in Spanish.

65. "threshold," 2. C. (b), www.oed.com.ezp-prod1.hul.harvard.edu/view/Entry /201234.

66. Hazmat Glossary of Terms and Definitions of Acronyms, www.newenv .com/Downloads/definitions.pdf.

67. Das and Poole (2004) show that the view from the margins requires a radical rethinking of the state as an unfinished project. They write that "margins are a necessary entailment of the state, much as the exception is a necessary component of the rule" (4). Taussig (1992:132) also notes the significance of the margins: what is most politically important to the state idea and state fetishism is not "the ideologies of the center, but the fantasies of the marginated concerning the secret of the center."

68. Aretxaga 2003:396.

69. Trouillot (2001:131) called the state "a set of practices and processes and their effects."

70. Derrida 1992:35.

71. Augustine and Spirato 2011.

72. Ralph (2014) writes that the injuries he studied in the community on Chicago's West Side were not just physical. They overlapped with social abandonment, were intensified by government policies, and intertwined with historical emotions and philosophical sentiments. I witnessed similar patterns in this Jacksonville neighborhood.

73. This methodical tone is not unique to emergency responders. For example, writing about diagnostic terminology used to describe blast injuries in military medicine, Terry (2017:59–64) notes the impersonal, dispassionate, and alienating character of expert discourse on explosion-caused injuries during the wars in Afghanistan and Iraq.

74. During rapid trauma assessment, EMTs check the patient for DCAP-BTLS—deformities, contusions, abrasions, punctures/penetrations, burns, tenderness, lacerations, and swelling. The mnemonic OPQRST, used for assessing patient's pain during the focused exam, stands for onset, provocation/palliation, quality, region/radiation, severity, and time. Symptoms of organophosphate poisoning can be remembered by using the mnemonic SLUDGE: salivation, lacrimation, urination, diarrhea, gastrointestinal issues, emesis.

75. An International Association of Fire Fighters' report released in September 2016 found that firefighters exhibit levels of PTSD rivaling that of combat veterans. See Pao and Tran 2017.

76. The Moral Injury Project at Syracuse University provides this definition: within the context of military service, particularly regarding the experience of war, "moral injury" refers to the emotional and spiritual impact of participating in, witnessing, and/or being victimized by actions and behaviors that violate a service member's core moral values and behavioral expectations of self or others" (http:// moralinjuryproject.syr.edu/about-moral-injury/). Mental health diagnoses, such as PTSD, cannot fully account for the symptoms caused by moral wounds—high levels of anguish, anger, and alienation that result from following illegal orders or causing harm to civilians. Returning veterans wrestle with how to justify what they

saw and what they did with their sense of morality and identity. But moral injury is not limited to soldiers. Cantú (2018:150–51) writes about moral injury in the context of his service as a Border Patrol agent.

77. Discussing gender and sexuality, however, is not off limits and, from my experience, women as well as LGBTQ people remain acceptable targets of ridicule.

78. Dunn 1996.

79. Emergency responders follow regulations established by the Health Insurance Portability and Accountability Act (HIPAA) of 1996. As an EMT, I had an obligation to safeguard patient confidentiality and to not disclose protected health information. Therefore, I decided against writing about any patient encounter where the narrative would have made it even remotely possible to identify the individual. This significantly limited what I could tell. For example, I could not describe a tragic incident in which a firefighter died because a quick search on the internet would have revealed his identity. While I include several accounts of my own experiences with patients (which are so typical that their repetitiveness helps protect particular individuals involved), I draw heavily on narratives shared with me by emergency responders and incident descriptions that appeared in the press. Stitching the story from multiple sources was the only way to tell it.

PART ONE. ANKLE ALLEY

1. Ziegler 2015.
2. *Nogales International* 2016b.
3. *Nogales International* 2016a.
4. Boyd 1981.
5. *Arizona Highways* 1964:47.
6. Lewis 2004.
7. Johnson 2017.
8. Montoya 2015. However, this opposition does not mean that law enforcement officers in southern Arizona reject any involvement in border security. Both the Santa Cruz County's Sheriff's Office and the Nogales Police Department have received funding from Operation Stonegarden, a Department of Homeland Security grant program that supports enhanced coordination between local, state, federal, and tribal law enforcement agencies to combat "transnational threats" (https://azdohs.gov/opsg).
9. Johnson 2017.
10. Johnson 2017.
11. Andreas (2000:12) writes: "Feedback effects of state practices on both sides of the border helped to create the very problems for which increased law enforcement has been promoted as the solution."
12. Coppola 2015b.
13. Woodhouse 2016.
14. The Emergency Planning and Community Right-to-Know Act (EPCRA) of 1986 was created to help communities plan for chemical emergencies. It requires

industry to report on the storage, use, and release of hazardous substances to federal, state, and local governments. EPCRA also requires state and local governments, as well as Native American tribes, to use this information to protect their community from potential risks. Chapter 116—Emergency Planning and Community Right-to-Know 2011, www.gpo.gov/fdsys/pkg/USCODE-2011-title42/html/USCODE-2011-title42-chap116.htm.

15. The List of Extremely Hazardous Substances and Their Threshold Planning Quantities can be found in the Code of Federal Regulations, Title 40–Protection of Environment, part 355, appendix A. www.ecfr.gov/cgi-bin/text-idx?SID=2b4d2d375e73ebc5c93d8b2fe632cb6f&mc=true&node=pt40.28.355&rgn=div5#ap40.30.355_161.a.

16. The National Institute for Occupational Safety and Health (NIOSH) determines the thresholds that are Immediately Dangerous to Life and Health (IDLH). For sulphuric acid, IDLH is 15 mg/m³ based on acute inhalation toxicity.

17. Hartman 1999.

18. Woodhouse 2015b.

19. Coppola 2015a.

20. Presentation by Jose Arriola, public health specialist for Santa Cruz County, at the Integrated Emergency Management Course, National Emergency Training Center, Emmitsburg, MD, August 11, 2016.

21. Coppola 2016.

22. Rosas (2012: Loc 839) describes the rise of maquiladoras in Mexico "as novel stratagems of global capital." In the mid-1960s, through the Border Industrialization Program, the Mexican government allowed foreigners to own assembly plants in the border region, exempting them from laws requiring majority-Mexican ownership of private companies. The industry developed slowly at first, but by 1979 maquiladora production accounted for a quarter of the country's manufacturing exports.

23. Montoya 2016. Other southwest border sectors, such as the Yuma Sector, reported only 7,142 apprehensions and 3,297 "Other Than Mexican" (OTM) apprehensions. With nearly 150,000 apprehensions, the Rio Grande Valley was the busiest sector in the country in 2015. But the total number of arrests nationwide, 331,000, was the lowest since 1972 (Trevizo 2016b).

24. For a detailed analysis of Operation Blockade, including extensive interviews with Chief Reyes, see Dunn (2009).

25. Nevins 2010.

26. Hartman 1994.

27. USBP 1994:4.

28. USBP 1994:6.

29. Meissner 1995:28.

30. USBP 1994:7.

31. Stevens 2006:28.

32. Stevens 2006:30.

33. Hartman 1995.

34. GAO-01–842:19.

35. GAO-01–842.

36. USBP 1994:2.

37. Since there is no federal registry of border crosser fatalities, the exact number of deaths is not known. According to different estimates, between 3,861 and 5,607 migrants died on the border between 1994 and 2009 (Jimenez 2009).

38. USBP 1994:10.

39. Hunter 2006:15.

40. The Illegal Immigration Reform and Immigration Responsibility Act (IIRIRA) was passed in 1996. Section 102 of IIRIRA concerns the improvement and construction of barriers at international borders. It gives the attorney general broad authority to install additional physical barriers and roads "in the vicinity of the United States border to deter illegal crossings in areas of high illegal entry into the United States." Section 102(b) mandates the construction of a three-tiered barrier along the 14 miles of land border near San Diego. Section 102(c) waives the Endangered Species Act (ESA) of 1973 and the National Environmental Policy Act (NEPA) of 1969, to the extent that the AG determined necessary, in order to ensure expeditious construction of the barriers (see Nuñez-Neto and Viña 2005). H.R. 4437, the Border Protection, Antiterrorism, and Illegal Immigration Control Act of 2005, contains a number of border fence measures, including amending §102(b) of IIRIRA to require the construction of at least two layers of reinforced fencing and the implementation of surveillance measures (lighting, sensors, cameras) along vast portions of the southwest international land border. The REAL ID Act of 2005 amended §102(c) of IIRIRA to, among other things, authorize the waiver of all legal requirements determined necessary for the construction of the barriers and roads authorized by §102 of IIRIRA.

41. H.R. 6061 (109th): Secure Fence Act of 2006. www.gpo.gov/fdsys/pkg /BILLS-109hr6061enr/pdf/BILLS-109hr6061enr.pdf. Among other areas, reinforced fencing would extend "from 10 miles west of the Calexico, California, port of entry to 5 miles east of the Douglas, Arizona, port of entry."

42. Trevizo 2015a.

43. From CBP website: www.cbp.gov/border-security/air-sea/oam-operating-locations.

44. Coleman 2007, 2009; Stuesse and Coleman 2014.

45. Slack and Campbell 2016.

46. Katherine Goodshall, presentation at the Integrated Emergency Management Course, National Emergency Training Center, Emmitsburg, MD, August 10, 2016.

47. An important step in the fortification of the border was the Secure Border Initiative (SBI), announced in November 2005. It consisted of expanding "tactical infrastructure" along more than 600 miles of the US-Mexico border and the creation of a technology barrier—surveillance towers that monitor activity and look for incursions using radar, high-resolution cameras, and wireless networking, known as a "virtual fence." A three-year contract to implement SBInet was awarded to Boeing. But project delays, high costs, and the lack of evidence that the deployment of infrastructure and technology augmented border security led to heavy criticism from the Government Accountability Office. In 2011, Homeland Security Secretary Janet

Napolitano canceled the program, redirecting the remainder of the funds to the construction of the see-through steel wall.

48. Trevizo 2015c.

49. Miller and Schivone 2015.

50. Trevizo 2015c.

51. "Wetback" is a derogatory term that has been used to refer to unauthorized Mexican migrants by invoking their actual or metaphorical crossing of the Rio Grande to reach the US.

52. The term "tactical infrastructure" is used extensively in DHS documents concerning CBP (see GAO-10–651T). Tactical infrastructure includes roads, fencing, lights, electrical components, and drainage structures. www.dhs.gov/xlibrary /assets/mgmt/cbp-fmetacticalinfrastructure2012.pdf.

53. Exhibit 300 BY13 (Form)/CBP—Facilities Management & Engineering (FM&E) Tactical Infrastructure, February 29, 2012, www.dhs.gov/xlibrary/assets /mgmt/cbp-fmetacticalinfrastructure2012.pdf. See also: Tactical Infrastructure Maintenance and Repair (TIMR) Environmental Assessments, www.cbp.gov /document/environmental-assessments/tactical-infrastructure-maintenance-and-repair-timr-environmental.

54. Haddal et al. 2009. Emphasis added.

55. The chart appears in the Prepared Joint Statement of Deborah J. Spero and Gregory Giddens before the US House of Representatives Committee on Homeland Security (Secure Border Initiative 2006:13). Although the image could not be reproduced here due to low resolution, it can be found online at www.gpo.gov/fdsys /pkg/CHRG-109hhrg35630/pdf/CHRG-109hhrg35630.pdf.

56. Anthropologists have joined the recent "volumetric turn" in political geography and architecture theory for a new perspective to examine border processes. For example, see the "Speaking Volumes" series published by *Cultural Anthropology* in October 2017, https://culanth.org/fieldsights/1247-speaking-volumes.

57. Weizman (2017) introduced the concept "politics of verticality" when writing about the governance and experience of territory in the West Bank. Gordillo (2018b:59) built on this three-dimensional rendering of relations between power and violence to discuss how soldiers and insurgents in Afghanistan competed to control the verticality of terrain in the Korengal Valley. US drones and helicopters gave them an aerial advantage; the steep mountain slopes were difficult for American soldiers carrying heavy weapons and gear, who regularly broke their ankles, but facilitated the swift mobility of guerilla fighters.

58. Becker 2013.

59. According to the ACLU, 8 USC § 1357(a)(3), CBP officials have authority to stop and conduct searches on vessels, trains, aircraft, or other vehicles anywhere within "a reasonable distance from any external boundary of the United States." Without further statutory guidance, regulations alone expansively define this "reasonable distance" as 100 air miles from any external boundary of the US, including coastal boundaries, unless an agency official sets a shorter distance. See "Customs and

Border Protection's 100-Mile Rule" fact sheet, www.aclu.org/other/aclu-factsheet-customs-and-border-protections-100-mile-zone?redirect=immigrants-rights/aclu-fact-sheet-customs-and-border-protections-100-mile-zone.

60. Lieberman 2014. Also see Wagner 2009; Trevizo 2016a.

61. The Border Crossing Card is an identity document accompanying the B1/B2 visitor visa that allows Mexican citizens to enter the US temporarily for business, tourism, pleasure, or visiting. https://travel.state.gov/content/travel/en/us-visas/tourism-visit/border-crossing-card.html.

62. Ingram 2016.

63. Rowley 2008.

64. Trevizo 2015b.

65. Data provided by the Mexican Consulate in Tucson, February 16, 2017.

66. Echavarri 2015; Trevizo 2015b.

67. Echavarri 2015.

68. Trevizo 2015b; also Echavarri 2015.

69. Emory 1987 [1857]:118.

70. When the border was resurveyed in 1891–1894, it was replaced by Boundary Monument 122. See Eppinga 2002.

71. St John 2011:145.

72. McGuire 2013.

73. Haddal et al. 2009.

74. Hattam 2016.

75. Although other types of matting were returned to Davis-Monthan Airforce Base in Tucson, Arizona, following the cessation of the war, shipping records for retrograded M8A1 mats have been lost. Therefore, it is unclear if M8A1 mats were returned to the US or abandoned in Vietnam, in which case the supply for the fence may have been undeployed stock left in the US.

76. Marsh et al. 1999:14.

77. Meissner 1995:71.

78. Stevens 2006:31.

79. Stephenson 2011.

80. Goth 2012.

81. Goth 2012.

82. Iglesias-Prieto 2017:23.

83. Pineda 2015.

84. Pineda 2015.

85. Degloving (or avulsion) happens when the skin is pulled off from the muscles and bones, usually of a hand or fingers.

86. Stevens 2006:31.

87. Pineda 2016.

88. SAEMS Prehospital Protocols, Trauma Triage Decision Scheme. http://saemscouncil.com/wp-content/uploads/2014/12/TRAUMATRIAGEDECI-SIONSCHEME.pdf.

89. The trial in US District Court in Tucson started on March 20, 2018, at the time this book was going into production. Swartz is facing charges for second-degree murder.

90. Binelli 2016.

91. Nogales Fire Department, Incident Type Report, Alarm Date between January 1, 2015, and December 31, 2015.

92. Interview with Teresa Small, chief public affairs liaison at the U.S. Customs and Border Protection's Office of Field Operations. Tucson, Arizona, September 3, 2015.

93. More than 140 children were at the day care center when the fire erupted; 49 lost their lives. In the days following the fire, medical teams from the northern California and Los Angeles Shriners Hospitals traveled to Hermosillo to assist local health care providers. See "Mexican Government Thanks Shriners Hospitals for Children°," August 13, 2010.

94. Flores and Muñoz 2015.

95. For an informative and insightful historical account of state-making, boundary negotiations, and sovereignty along the US-Mexico border, see St John (2011). Brown (2014) argues that wall building is a sign of weakening nation-state sovereignty. She suggests that "the US-Mexico barrier stages a sovereign power and control that it does not exercise, is built from the fabric of a suspended rule of law and fiscal nonaccountability, has multiplied and intensified criminal industries, and is an icon of the combination of sovereign erosion and heightened xenophobia and nationalism" (38). Anthropologists studying borders ethnographically have also shown them to be sites where state power is continuously reenacted. For example, Reeves (2014) examines borders through their *eventfulness*—they materialize in response to political dynamics occurring far from where they are located—and *multiplicity:* the border of the map, the border guard, the state official, the trader is not one and the same. Reeves explores how and when borders acquire social salience, attending to "the diverse practices—of provisioning and the cutting-off of provisioning, of incorporating and deporting, of legalizing and illegalizing—through which limits were and are produced and erased" (104).

96. C4 stands for Centro de Control, Comando, Comunicación y Cómputo (Center of Control, Command, Communication, and Computation). It is Mexico's emergency services operator, equivalent to 911 in the United States.

97. Ley 161 de Protección Civil para el Estado de Sonora, book 176, no. 27, sec. 2, October 3, 2005.

98. Estatutos del Cuerpo de Bomberos Voluntarios "Gustavo L. Manriquez" de Nogales, Sonora, México, December 20, 1945.

99. The Occupational Safety and Health Administration (OSHA) is an agency at the US Department of Labor that sets and enforces standards to ensure safe and healthful working conditions.

100. US Army Corps of Engineers Los Angeles District and the International Boundary and Water Commission 2004.

101. The National Border Program (Programa Nacional Fronterizo), announced on January 10, 1961, promoted economic, social, and cultural development along the border. The program had an important urban planning component with an aim to modernize border towns (see Rodriguez and Rivero 2011). PRONAF preceded the Border Industrialization Program (BIP), launched in 1965, which opened the doors for the maquiladoras.

102. Data presented at the citizens' forum held by the US-Mexico International Boundary and Water Commission's Mexico Section.

103. *Nogales International* 2015b.

104. When the Mexican Navy killed Arturo Beltrán-Leyva in December 2009, the associates of Joaquín "El Chapo" Guzmán Loera moved to retake the smuggling routes in Sonora, causing bloodshed. In July 2010, in a shootout in Tubutama, about 30 miles southwest of Nogales, at least twenty-one people died when El Chapo's hitmen confronted members of the Beltrán-Leyva Cartel. In Nogales, Sonora, murders jumped from 130 in 2009 to 226 in 2010. See Clark 2014.

105. Prendergast 2014.

106. In fiscal year 2014 (October 1, 2013–September 30, 2014), CBP apprehended 68,541 unaccompanied alien children (birth to seventeen years old) from Honduras, Guatemala, El Salvador, and Mexico along the southwest border. The majority of them, 49,959, were apprehended in Rio Grande Sector, and sent to facilities around the country, including Nogales, for processing. In Tucson Sector, CBP apprehended 8,262 minors on the border that year. Statistics published by CBP on November 24, 2015. www.cbp.gov/newsroom/stats/southwest-border-unaccompanied-children /fy-2014.

107. Nogales Fire Department, Incident Type Report, Alarm Date between January 1, 2015, and December 31, 2015.

108. National Academy of Sciences 1966.

109. "accident, n," OED Online, www.oed.com.ezp-prod1.hul.harvard.edu /view/Entry/1051.

110. Virilio 2011:10.

111. Siegel 2014:20.

112. Mbembe 2003:21.

113. De León 2015:39.

114. The same way that burglary is, according to Manaugh (2016), a function of architecture.

PART TWO. DOWNWIND, DOWNHILL, DOWNSTREAM

1. Eppinga 2002:119.

2. Romero 2005.

3. Incident report, Nogales Fire Department, April 13, 2010.

4. Coppola 2010.

5. Pablo Domínguez González, "Remembranza 13 abril 2010," Facebook page, April 13, 2012, www.facebook.com/notes/bomberos-nogales/remembranza-13-abril -2010/406131506083323/?hc_ref=PAGES_TIMELINE.

6. Incident report, Nogales Fire Department, May 10, 2012.

7. Hillinger 1986.

8. Woodhouse 2015a.

9. Coppola 2012.

10. While CBP is a federal agency, NFD works under the city government. If there is an incident in a federal building or at the port of entry, CBP's backup is an hour away, in Tucson. Therefore, CBP's protocols instruct them to call NFD as their first line of response and follow their recommended course of action, whether it's a medical emergency, a flood, or a hazardous materials incident. The fence is also federal property, so firefighters need permission from CBP to open the gates and throw lines to help the bomberos fighting a fire on the other side. Authorization to shut down the port of entry comes from Washington, DC, and it is not granted easily.

11. US EPA and SEMARNAT 2012.

12. The Joint Contingency Plan is available at https://www.epa.gov/sites /production/files/2016-01/documents/us_mexico_joint_contingency_plan.pdf. Signed on November 17, 2017, under the full title of Mexico–United States Joint Contingencies and Emergencies Plan for Preparedness and Response to Events Associated with Chemical Hazardous Substances in the Inland Border Area, the current plan is the fourth iteration of a document first written in 1988 and revised in 1999 and 2008.

13. US EPA 1983.

14. Binational Prevention and Emergency Response Plan 2005:3.

15. Binational Prevention and Emergency Response Plan 2005:8.

16. The Douglas Fire Department gets insurance from Global Companion, which also covers US companies abroad (e.g., insurance for oil rigs). In 2016, the city paid a $7,000 premium to insure the five units.

17. Morris 2016.

18. In 2014, the more than one hundred maquiladoras in Nogales, Sonora, pro-vided about thirty-four thousand jobs. The biggest manufacturing sectors (measured by percentages of employment) were computer and electronic products (23%), apparel (15%), transportation equipment including components and parts for the aerospace industry (14.1%), and electrical equipment (13.7%). Other sectors included manufacturing of plastics, rubber, and paper products. See Pavlakovich-Kochi 2014.

19. Firefighters carry these monitors inside the buildings when they are called for gas leaks, strange odors, or carbon monoxide alarms. The device shows elevated concentrations of these gases and helps emergency responders identify potentially explosive or otherwise hazardous environments.

20. Burke 2006; Rochford 2009.

21. US DOT, PHMSA 2016.

22. OSHA guidelines mandate the wearing of level A suits in situations where the greatest degree of skin, respiratory, and eye protection is required, for example, containing leaks of poisonous gases. The Thermal Heat Stress Protocol for Fire Fighters and Hazmat Responders establishes that any personnel with a pulse above 100, blood pressure outside the range of 90/60–150/90, or a temperature above 99°F should not be allowed to enter the site.

23. That same year the bomberos fought 181 structure fires in residential and commercial buildings and about twice as many brushfires or wildland fires, according to Estadistica Anual de Servicios, Enero–Diciembre 2015, compiled by Pablo Domínguez González, Cuerpo de Bomberos Voluntarios "Carlitos L. Manriquez."

24. Rotstein 2003.

25. Through the PACE program, the US organized meetings for Mexican fire chiefs and other officials, offered "train the trainer" courses (seeking to multiply the effects throughout Mexico), and taught the bomberos how to develop standard operating procedures (SOPs).

26. In Mexico, *gabacho* is a pejorative term used for English-speaking, non-Hispanic people, generally white Americans.

27. In her ethnography of the homeland security community in Boston, Fosher (2009) notes that 9/11 boosted the cultural capital of fire and police services. She criticizes what she calls the "romance with response" because it "leaches attention away from the critical preparedness tasks, such as planning, mitigation, public education, and system building, each of which is necessary for response activities to be successful" (Loc 3066). She further notes that the valorization of first responders in the media "as authorities on all aspects of security" (Loc 3069) leads them to be given jobs that require them to write policy and craft plans, for which they have no training. In the emergency responder community of southern Arizona, opinions differed about whether it is better to have emergency managers that have a background in fire or EMS service or professionals in incident management and administration who are outsiders to the fire service. The former understand the operational logics and the needs of first responders better because they have that experience of being on the frontlines, but there is a risk that they might abandon their position to join the teams on the ground. The latter can be more "objective" and think on the larger scale, considering the multiple scales of action and actors involved.

28. Simpson 2013.

29. Castillo 2016.

30. Secretaría de Gobernación 2016.

31. Pestano 2016.

32. Standards—29 CFR, Part 1910 (Occupational Safety and Health Standards) Subpart Z (Toxic and Hazardous Substances), 1910.1096 (Ionizing Radiation), www.osha.gov/pls/oshaweb/owadisp.show_document?p_table= STANDARDS&p_id=10098. REM stands for "Roentgen equivalent in man" and measures the amount of energy from any type of ionizing radiation deposited in human tissue along with the medical effects of the given type of radiation. Beta and

gamma radiation is less damaging to the human body than alpha or neutron radiation.

33. Hitti 2005.

34. *Nogales International* 2016c.

35. McCain and Flake 2014.

36. www.simtable.com/about/.

37. Tabletop exercise, Santa Cruz County; Weather Event, Situation Manual. Thursday, August 11, 2016.

38. Masco 2014:165.

39. In my first book (Jusionyte 2015a), I wrote about a similar criminalization of the tri-border region between Argentina, Brazil, and Paraguay.

40. Massumi 2016:201.

41. Masco 2014:197.

42. Distributed preparedness consists of a spatial understanding of vulnerability grafted onto the structure of territorial administration. See Collier and Lakoff 2008.

43. *Nogales International* 2017.

44. A talk by Gastón Gordillo, "Ambient Thickness: On the Atmospheric Materiality of the Anthropocene," at the History of Science Seminar, Harvard University, February 8, 2018.

45. McKinnon 2011.

46. The practice of outsourcing US government functions to Mexico is not new: the Mérida Initiative, a security cooperation agreement signed in 2008, has allowed the US government to outsource the "war on drugs," while Plan Frontera Sur, announced in 2014, delegated to the Mexican government an important role in immigration control and border enforcement.

47. Masco 2014:199.

PART THREE. WILDLAND

1. For a detailed history of mining ventures in the Arizona-Sonora border region see Truett (2006).

2. Kasulaitis 2002:121.

3. Pruitt (2014:208) argues, "By articulating the rural as inaccessible, as enhancing vulnerability, and as self-reliant, legal actors and institutions constitute rurality as all of these things, endowing it with these characteristics as surely as material spatiality does the same work."

4. Bowden 2006.

5. Preliminary History of the Arivaca Volunteer Fire Department up to the Formation of the Arivaca Fire District. www.arivacafiredistrict.org/home/history.

6. *Tucson Citizen* 1998.

7. *Sahuarita Sun* 2000.

8. *Green Valley News* 2002.

9. Everett-Haynes and Carroll 2002.

10. Everett-Haynes and Carroll, 2002.

11. Teibel 2003.

12. Pallack 2005.

13. Monica Aviles, DPS, e-mail communication, June 18, 2015.

14. Pallack 2005.

15. Caesar 2009.

16. The informal agreement between No More Deaths and the Border Patrol no longer guarantees injured migrants a temporary shelter. It did not prevent federal agents from using a search warrant to enter the camp in June 2017 and arrest four men suspected of being in the country illegally.

17. Lomonaco 2006; Bishop 2006.

18. Information obtained from the Arivaca Fire District through a public records request, May 9, 2017.

19. Department of Health and Human Services 2014.

20. Both Sonoita and Three Points are census-designated places (CDPs)—small unincorporated communities and surrounding inhabited countryside that exist for gathering statistical data only.

21. Banks 2004.

22. One of the agency's elite special operations units, Border Patrol's Search, Trauma, and Rescue (BORSTAR) was created in 1998 with the mission of providing emergency care and evacuation to injured Border Patrol agents in remote areas, and to help prevent more migrant deaths. In southern Arizona, BORSTAR operates UH-60 Black Hawk helicopters that have been used to transport injured border crossers and stranded or lost hikers to the UMC in Tucson. In fiscal year 2015, Border Patrol in the Tucson Sector reported 790 rescues, though it is unclear how many of them were by BORSTAR.

23. Williams 2015:16.

24. Caid 2016.

25. See chap. 5, "Learning and Burning," in Desmond (2007).

26. GAO-12–73.

27. GAO-12–73.

28. *Nogales International* 2011.

29. Clark 2012.

30. Interview with Joe Agosttini, assistant port director, US Customs and Border Protection, November 4, 2015, Nogales, Arizona.

31. Gerber 2012.

32. Believing that it would make them less visible to the Border Patrol, migrants purchase one-gallon water jugs made of black instead of white plastic. Not everyone is aware that the water inside black bottles heats up much faster and in summer can reach 126.3°F (de León 2012:486). Drinking such hot water further raises a person's core temperature and risk of developing heatstroke.

33. For more on humanitarian organizations that help migrants see Jimenez (2009).

34. www.tucsonsamaritans.org/about-samaritans.html.

35. Operation Streamline is an initiative of the Department of Homeland Security and the Department of Justice that began in 2005 with the intention of establishing "zero-tolerance" immigration enforcement zones along the US-Mexico border. Through this fast-track prosecution program, which critics have called "assembly-line justice," magistrate judges conduct en masse hearings, trying as many as seventy people simultaneously. In addition to formal deportation and removal from the United States, unauthorized migrants face criminal prosecution and potential prison sentences. See Lydgate 2010.

36. Cook 2011:577.

37. Lacey 2010.

38. Such articulation of militarized campaigns against drug smuggling and unauthorized migration, on the one hand, and conservation efforts, on the other, is not unique to southern Arizona. Megan Ybarra writes about a similar phenomenon—she calls it "the logics of green security" (2017:20)—in the Maya Forest near the Guatemala-Mexico border, where people are doubly criminalized as dangerous narcos and as threats to the protected environment.

39. Frey 2012.

40. Founded in 2000, Humane Borders is a nonprofit organization that provides humanitarian assistance to migrants crossing the Sonoran Desert. It maintains a system of forty-eight water stations throughout southern Arizona and in Nogales and El Sásabe in Sonora, Mexico. For details on the vandalism incident see Blust 2016a.

41. For an overview of how US laws enacted a revolving door policy for Mexican migrant labor, see DeGenova (2004).

42. Coutin 1993.

43. 8 U.S.C. §§1324(a)(1)(A)(ii) established penalties for any person who "knowing or in reckless disregard of the fact that an alien has come to, entered, or remains in the United States in violation of law, transports, or moves or attempts to transport or move such alien within the United States by means of transportation or otherwise, in furtherance of such violation of law." www.gpo.gov/fdsys/pkg/USCODE-2011 -title8/pdf/USCODE-2011-title8-chap12-subchapII-partVIII-sec1324.pdf.

44. Bowden 2006.

45. See Magahern 2013; González 2011b.

46. Border Crossing Data for 2015 from the Bureau of Transportation Statistics. www.bts.gov/content/border-crossingentry-data.

47. Border Crossing Data for 2015 from the Bureau of Transportation Statistics.

48. González 2011a.

49. Martínez 2014:176–77.

50. Ingram 2015.

51. Blust 2016b.

52. McIntyre 2014.

53. Fisher 2011.

54. Jiménez 2015.

55. Holley 2014.

EPILOGUE

1. US CBP 2017.
2. Ross et al. 2017.
3. Galvan 2017.
4. NPR 2017.
5. Rael 2017.
6. The Deferred Action for Childhood Arrivals (DACA) program, announced in 2012, granted temporary protection from deportation to undocumented migrants brought to the US as children. Schwartz 2017; Alter 2017.
7. Michael Evangelista Ysasaga speaking on *Morning Edition,* NPR, March 29, 2017.
8. Building on Schmitt (2005), who claims that the sovereign is both inside and outside of the law and that he decides on the state of exception, Agamben and Mbembe argue that sovereignty and biopower are fundamentally integrated. For Agamben, "In modern biopolitics, sovereign is he who decides on the value or the nonvalue of life as such" (1998:142); Mbembe, who defines sovereignty as the right to kill (or "control over mortality"), shows how slain or wounded human bodies are inscribed in the order of power (2003:12).
9. See Sessions 2017. "It is here, on this sliver of land, where we first take our stand against this filth," was written in his remarks, even though Sessions did not read the sentence to the end.
10. Corey and Becker 2017. According to the Center for Investigative Reporting, which used open-source mapping and information obtained through public records requests, there were about 700 miles of fence along the US-Mexico border in 2017. Since some areas have more than one layer of fencing, reporters suggest that somewhere between 652 and 690 miles of the border is actually covered by fence. They further estimate that this includes at least 385 miles of pedestrian fence and 301 miles of vehicle fence. In Arizona, where the border stretches for 376 miles, 142 miles have various types of pedestrian fencing, 183 miles are lined with vehicle barriers, and 51 miles have no barrier (see Janetsky 2018).
11. "CBP's top priority," the agency's official website claims, "is to keep terrorists and their weapons from entering the US. Border Security." US Customs and Border Protection, www.cbp.gov/border-security.
12. Kafka 1931.

ABOUT THIS PROJECT

1. Fahy 2012.
2. Lovett 2012:A16.
3. Dinan 2013.

REFERENCES

Agamben, Giorgio
  1998 *Homo Sacer: Sovereign Power and Bare Life.* Stanford: Stanford University Press.
Alter, Charlotte
  2017 "A Picnic at the Border." *Time,* October 12. http://time.com/4979252 /lightbox-picnic-at-the-border/.
American College of Surgeons Committee on Trauma
  2011 *PHTLS: Prehospital Trauma Life Support.* 7th ed. St. Louis: Mosby JEMS, Elsevier.
Andersson, Ruben
  2017 "Rescued and Caught: The Humanitarian-Security Nexus at Europe's Frontiers." In *The Borders of "Europe": Autonomy of Migration, Tactics of Bordering.* Nicholas de Genova, ed. Durham: Duke University Press.
Andreas, Peter
  2000 *Border Games: Policing the U.S.-Mexico Divide.* Ithaca: Cornell University Press.
Anzaldúa, Gloria
  1987 *Borderlands/La Frontera: The New Mestiza.* San Francisco: Spinsters/Aunt Lute.
Aretxaga, Begoña
  2003 "Maddening States." *Annual Review of Anthropology* 32:393–410.
Arizona Highways
  1964 "Progress Born of Blueprints, Dreams and Concrete." November.
Augustine, Matt, and Alyssa Spirato
  2011 "Study: Jacksonville Still Murder Capital of Florida." WOKV, December 2. www.wokv.com/news/news/local/study-jacksonville-still-murder-capital- florida/nFsNT/.
Banks, Leo W.
  2004 "The Saga of Three Points." *Tucson Weekly,* March 18.

Becker, Andrew

2013   "New Drone Radar Reveals Border Patrol 'Gotaways' in High Numbers."
        Center for Investigative Reporting. April 4. https://www.revealnews.org
        /article/new-drone-radar-reveals-border-patrol-gotaways-in-high-numbers/

Binelli, Mark

2016   "10 Shots across the Border." *New York Times,* March 3. www.nytimes
        .com/2016/03/06/magazine/10-shots-across-the-border.html.

Bishop, Julia

2006   "91 Illegal Immigrants Apprehended in Truck." *Nogales International,* May
        21. www.nogalesinternational.com/news/illegal-immigrants-apprehended-
        in-truck/article_87a43dcf-e0c7-5452-ba83-695bb60b63d3.html.

Blust, Kendal

2016a   "Border Volunteers Find 'Gory' Vandalism at Water Stations." *Arizona
        Daily Star,* February 10. http://tucson.com/news/local/border/border-
        volunteers-find-gory-vandalism-at-water-stations/article_66600352-
        b0d0-5df4-8727-49533f4ec55b.html.

2016b   "Deaths per 10,000 Border Crossers Are up 5 Times from a Decade Ago."
        Arizona Daily Star, May 21. http://tucson.com/news/local/border
        /deaths-per-border-crossers-are-up-times-from-a-decade/article_c1279aaf-
        4ad8-51c9-82d8-3143b836f52e.html.

Bourdieu, Pierre

1994   "Rethinking the State: On the Genesis and Structure of the Bureaucratic
        Field." *Sociological Theory* 12(1):1–19.

1999   "The Abdication of the State." In *The Weight of the World: Social Suffering
        in Contemporary Society.* P. Bourdieu et al., eds. Pp. 181–88. Cambridge,
        UK: Polity Press.

2006   *Acts of Resistance: Against the Tyranny of the Market.* New York: New Press.

2014   *On the State: Lectures at the Collège de France, 1989–1992.* Cambridge, UK:
        Polity Press.

Bowden, Charles

2006   "Exodus: Border-Crossers Forge a New America." *Mother Jones,*
        September/October. www.motherjones.com/politics/2006/09/exodus-
        border-crossers-forge-new-america/.

Boyd, Consuelo

1981   "Twenty Years to Nogales: The Building of the Guaymas-Nogales Rail-
        road." *Journal of Arizona History* 22(3): 295–324.

Brown, Wendy

2014   *Walled States, Waning Sovereignty.* Brooklyn, NY: Zone Books.

Burke, Robert

2006   "Hydrogen Cyanide: The Real Killer among Fire Gases." *Firehouse,* Decem-
        ber 31. www.firehouse.com/rescue/article/10502165/hydrogen-cyanide-the-
        real-killer-among-fire-gases.

Caesar, Stephen

2009   "Rollover Kills 8 in SUV near Sonoita." *Arizona Daily Star,* June 8.

Caid, Les P.

2016 "The Shift toward Community Integrated Paramedicine." *Firehouse,* May 1. www.firehouse.com/article/12189548/fire-based-ems-the-shift-toward-community-integrated-paramedicine.

Cantú, Francisco

2018 *The Line Becomes a River: Dispatches from the Border.* New York: Riverhead Books.

Castillo, Mariano

2016 "Stolen Radioactive Material Found in Mexico." CNN, March 9. www.cnn.com/2016/03/09/us/mexico-radioactive-device-recovered/.

Clark, Jonathan

2012 "An Alternative Reality." *Nogales International,* September 28. www.nogalesinternational.com/opinion/editorial/an-alternative-reality/article_8bfadf78-0984-11e2-865d-0019bb2963f4.html.

2014 "After 'El Chapo' Guzman Captured in Mexico, What's Next for Sonora?" *Nogales International,* February 22. www.nogalesinternational.com/news/after-el-chapo-guzman-captured-in-mexico-what-s-next/article_ac367384-9bfe-11e3-b5dc-0014bcf887a.html.

Coleman, Mathew

2007 "Immigration Geopolitics beyond the Mexico-US Border." *Antipode* 39(1):54–76.

2009 "What Counts as the Politics and Practices of Security, and Where? Devolution and Immigrant Insecurity after 9/11." *Annals of the Association of American Geographers* 99(5):904–13.

Collier, Stephen, and Andrew Lakoff

2008 "Distributed Preparedness: The Spatial Logic of Domestic Security in the United States." *Environment and Planning D* 26(1):7–28.

Cook, Maria Lorena

2011 "'Humanitarian Aid Is Never a Crime': Humanitarianism and Illegality in Migrant Advocacy." *Law and Society Review* 45(3):561–91.

Coppola, Manuel C.

2010 "2nd Fire Jolts NFD after Ellis St. Blaze." *Nogales International,* April 15. www.nogalesinternational.com/news/nd-fire-jolts-nfd-after-ellis-st-blaze/article_7c6e0345-7837-58a2-9fe0-08e869a9cdd1.html.

2012 "Binational Plan Put to Test by Hotel Fire." *Nogales International,* May 15. www.nogalesinternational.com/news/binational-plan-put-to-test-by-hotel-fire/article_143e334a-9ea4-11e1-b220-0014bcf887a.html.

2015a "Dille: Video Shows Drug Bundles Blocking Sewer Line." *Nogales International,* July 7. www.nogalesinternational.com/news/dille-video-shows-drug-bundles-blocking-sewer-line/article_fff50140-24ef-11e5-b566-2f421c1edff3.html.

2015b "Efforts under Way to Mitigate Peso Slump." *Nogales International,* September 8. www.nogalesinternational.com/news/efforts-under-way-to-mitigate-peso-slump/article_a4a5645e-5363-11e5-916e-ef64c57c3e27.html.

2016 "Fetus Found among Sewage at Plant in Rio Rico." *Nogales International,*
March 6. www.nogalesinternational.com/news/fetus-found-among-sewage-at-plant-in-rio-rico/article_c32032e0-e3ca-11e5-a6e6-ffdc452328e9
.html.

Corey, Michael, and Andrew Becker
2017 "The Wall: Building a Continuous US-Mexico Barrier Would Be a Tall
Order." *Reveal.* Center for Investigative Reporting, January 22. www
.revealnews.org/article/the-wall-building-a-continuous-u-s-mexico-barrier-
would-be-a-tall-order/.

Coutin, Susan Bibler
1993 *The Culture of Protest: Religious Activism and the U.S. Sanctuary Movement.*
Boulder, CO: Westview Press.

Danielson, Michael S.
2015 "Our Values on the Line: Migrant Abuse and Family Separation at the
Border." Jesuit Conference of Canada and the United States and Kino
Border Initiative. https://jesuits.org/Assets/Publications/File/REPORT_
2015_Our_Values_on_the_Line1.pdf

Das, Veena, and Deborah Poole
2004 *Anthropology in the Margins of the State.* Santa Fe, NM: School of American Research Press.

DeGenova, Nicholas
2004 "The Legal Production of Mexican Migrant 'Illegality.'" *Latino Studies*
2(2):160–85.

de León, Jason
2012 "'Better to Be Hot than Caught': Excavating the Conflicting Roles of
Migrant Material Culture." *American Anthropologist* 114(3):477–95.
2015 *The Land of Open Graves: Living and Dying on the Migrant Trail.* Oakland:
University of California Press.

Department of Health and Human Services
2014 Section 1011: Federal Reimbursement of Emergency Health Services Furnished to Undocumented Aliens. Factsheet prepared by Medicare Learning Network. November.

Derrida, Jacques
1992 "Force of Law: The 'Mystical Foundation of Authority.'" In *Deconstruction
and the Possibility of Justice.* Drucilla Cornell, Michel Rosenfeld, and David
Gray Carlson, eds. Pp. 3–67. New York: Routledge.

Desmond, Matthew
2007 *On the Fireline: Living and Dying with Wildland Firefighters.* Chicago:
University of Chicago Press.

Dewachi, Omar
2015 "When Wounds Travel." *Medicine Anthropology Theory* 2(3):61–82.

Dinan, Stephen
2013 "Federal Government Leaves Border Towns with Unpaid Ambulance
Bills." *Washington Times,* November 12.

Donahue, Katherine C.

2011   "What Are Heroes For? Commemoration and the Creation of Heroes after September 11." *Anthropology News* 52(6):6.

Dorsey, Margaret, and Miguel Díaz-Barriga

2015   "The Constitution Free Zone in the United States: Law and Life in a State of Carcelment." *PoLAR: Political and Legal Anthropology Review* 38(2):204–25.

Doty, Roxanne Lynn

2011   "Bare Life: Border-Crossing Deaths and Spaces of Moral Alibi." *Environment and Planning D: Society and Space* 29(4):599–612.

Dunn, Timothy J.

1996   *The Militarization of the U.S.-Mexico Border, 1978–1992: Low-Intensity Conflict Doctrine Comes Home.* Austin: University of Texas at Austin.

2009   *Blockading the Border and Human Rights: The El Paso Operation That Remade Immigration Enforcement.* Austin: University of Texas Press.

Echavarri, Fernanda

2015   "More Immigrants Injured Falling from Border Fence." Arizona Public Media, June 30. https://news.azpm.org/p/news-spots/2015/7/1/67312-more-immigrants-injured-falling-from-border-fence/.

Elden, Stuart

2013   *The Birth of Territory.* Chicago: University of Chicago Press.

2017   "Legal Terrain—The Political Materiality of Territory." *London Review of International Law* 5(2):199–224.

Emory, William H.

1987
[1857]   *Report on the United States and Mexican Boundary Survey.* Austin: Texas State Historical Association.

Eppinga, Jane

2002   *Nogales: Life and Times on the Frontier.* Charleston, SC: Arcadia.

Everett-Haynes, La Monica, and Susan Carroll

2002   "Fatal Rollovers." *Tucson Citizen,* August 9.

Fahy, Rita F.

2012   "US Firefighter Deaths Related to Training, 2001–2010." National Fire Protection Association. January. www.nfpa.org/News-and-Research/Fire-statistics-and-reports/Fire-statistics/The-fire-service/Fatalities-and-injuries/US-firefighter-deaths-related-to-training-2001-to-2010.

Fassin, Didier

2012   *Humanitarian Reason: A Moral History of the Present Times.* Berkeley: University of California Press.

2015   *At the Heart of the State: The Moral World of Institutions.* London: Pluto.

Fassin, Didier, and Estelle D'Halluin

2005   "The Truth from the Body: Medical Certificates as Ultimate Evidence for Asylum Seekers." *American Anthropologist* 107(4):597–608.

Fassin, Didier, and Mariella Pandolfi

    2010   *Contemporary States of Emergency: The Politics of Military and Humanitarian Interventions.* New York: Zone Books.

Feldman, Allen

    1991   *Formations of Violence: The Narrative of the Body and Political Terror in Northern Ireland.* Chicago: University of Chicago Press.

Fisher, Michael J.

    2011   Testimony before House Committee on Homeland Security, Subcommittee on Border and Maritime Security on "Securing our Borders—Operational Control and the Path Forward." Released February 15. https://www.dhs.gov/news/2011/02/15/us-customs-and-border-protection-border-patrol-chief-michael-fishers-testimony

Flores, Marco A., and Rosalía Muñoz

    2015   "Regresaron a la vida a la niña de 9 años." *El Diario de Sonora,* July 2. www.eldiariodesonora.com.mx/diarioson/archivo/02072015/pdf/5a02072015.pdf.

Fosher, Kerry B.

    2009   *Under Construction: Making Homeland Security at the Local Level.* Chicago: University of Chicago Press.

Foucault, Michel

    2007   *Security, Territory, Population: Lectures at the Collège de France, 1977–78.* New York: Palgrave Macmillan.

Frey, John Carlos

    2012   "Cruelty on the Border." *Salon,* July 20. www.salon.com/2012/07/20/cruelty_on_the_border/.

Galvan, Astrid

    2017   "Grijalva, Wildlife Group File Lawsuit over Trump's Proposed Border Wall." Associated Press, April 12. http://tucson.com/news/local/border/grijalva-wildlife-group-file-lawsuit-over-trump-s-proposed-border/article_e90aa99c-9946-5fe9-99c6-59d8ea872249.html.

GAO-01–842. United States Government Accountability Office. Report to Congressional Committees.

    2001   *INS' Southwest Border Strategy: Resource and Impact Issues Remain after Seven Years.* August 2. www.gao.gov/assets/240/231964.pdf.

GAO-10–651T. United States Government Accountability Office. Statement for the Record to the Committee on Homeland Security and Governmental Affairs, US Senate.

    2010   *Secure Border Initiative: DHS Has Faced Challenges Deploying Technology and Fencing along the Southwest Border.* May 4. www.gao.gov/assets/90/82411.pdf.

GAO-12–73. United States Government Accountability Office. Report to Congressional Requesters.

    2011   *Arizona Border Region: Federal Agencies Could Better Utilize Law Enforcement Resources in Support of Wildland Fire Management Activities.* November 22. www.gao.gov/assets/590/586139.pdf.

Gaynor, Tim
    2007   "Bullet-Proof Helicopters Play Key U.S. Border Role." Reuters. September 9. www.reuters.com/article/us-usa-immigration-blackhawk/bullet-proof-helicopters-play-key-u-s-border-role-idUSN0731398720070910.

Gerber, Marisa
    2012   "Sonoran Firefighters Get U.S. Training." *Nogales International,* January 27. www.nogalesinternational.com/news/sonoran-firefighters-get-u-s-training /article_24deb39e-48fc-11e1-97cf-0019bb2963f4.html.

Goniewicz, Mariusz
    2013   "Effect of Military Conflicts on the Formation of Emergency Medical Services Systems Worldwide." *Academic Emergency Medicine* 20:507–13.

González, Daniel
    2011a   "Arizona Border Outpost One of the Quietest in U.S." *Arizona Republic,* November 27. http://archive.azcentral.com/news/articles/20111115arizona-border-outpost-sasabe.html.
    2011b   "Tiny Arizona Border Town Full of Strange Stories." *Arizona Republic,* November 13. http://archive.azcentral.com/arizonarepublic/news/articles /20111112arizona-border-town-sasabe.html.

Gordillo, Gastón
    2018   "Terrain as Insurgent Weapon: An Affective Geometry of Warfare in the Mountains of Afghanistan." *Political Geography* 64:53–62.

Goth, Brenna
    2012   "Bollard Border Fence Draws Good Reviews on First Anniversary." *Nogales International,* August 17. www.nogalesinternational.com/news/bollard-border-fence-draws-good-reviews-on-first-anniversary/article_3c0e21c6-e884-11e1-aedc-001a4bcf887a.html.

Green Valley News
    2002   "Truck with Illegal Immigrants Rolls over on Arivaca Road." August 14.

Greenwald, Noah, Brian Segee, Tierra Curry, and Curt Bradley
    2017   *A Wall in the Wild: The Disastrous Impacts of Trump's Border Wall on Wildlife.* Center for Biological Diversity, May. https://www.biologicaldiversity .org/programs/international/borderlands_and_boundary_waters/pdfs /A_Wall_in_the_Wild.pdf.

Haddal, Chad C., Yule Kim, and Michael John Garcia
    2009   *Border Security: Barriers along the U.S. International Border.* Congressional Research Service Report to Congress. March 16. https://fas.org/sgp/crs /homesec/RL33659.pdf.

Haller, John S.
    1992   *Farmcarts to Fords: A History of the Military Ambulance, 1790–1925.* Carbondale: Southern Illinois University Press.

Hartman, Pamela
    1994   "INS Effort Stirs Mixed Feelings." *Tucson Citizen,* October 18. http:// tucsoncitizen.com/morgue2/1994/10/18/75116-ins-effort-stirs-mixed-feelings/.

1995   "Patrol Shores up Border." *Tucson Citizen,* October 13, 1995. http://
        tucsoncitizen.com/morgue2/1995/10/13/198044-patrol-shores-up-
        border/.

1999   "Suspected Drug Tunnel Ends below Church." *Tucson Citizen,* January 22.
        http://tucsoncitizen.com/morgue2/1999/01/22/109977-suspected-drug-
        tunnel-ends-below-church/.

Hattam, Victoria
2016   "Imperial Designs: Remembering Vietnam at the US–Mexico Border
        Wall." *Memory Studies* 9(1):27–47.

Herzfeld, Michael
1997   *Cultural Intimacy: Social Poetics in the Nation-State.* New York:
        Routledge.

Heyman, Josiah McC.
2000   "Respect for Outsiders? Respect for the Law? The Moral Evaluation of
        High-Scale Issues by US Immigration Officers." *Journal of the Royal
        Anthropological Institute* 6(4):635–52.

2002   "U.S. Immigration Officers of Mexican Ancestry as Mexican Americans,
        Citizens, and Immigration Police." *Current Anthropology* 43(3):479–507.

Hillinger, Charles
1986   "An International Tale of Two Cities: Separated by a Border, They Are
        United by History." *Los Angeles Times,* February 9. http://articles.latimes
        .com/1986-02-09/news/vw-6230_1_twin-cities.

Hitti, Miranda
2005   "Medical Radiation Scans Flag Airport Security." WebMD, July 21. www
        .webmd.com/heart/news/20070101/medical-radiation-scans-flag-airport-
        security.

Holley, Denise
2014   "Students Expand Kit Project That Can Save Lives in the Desert." *No More
        Deaths Newsletter,* November 23. http://forms.nomoredeaths.org
        /students-expand-kit-project-that-can-save-lives-in-the-desert/.

Hunter, Duncan
2006   Testimony at Joint Hearing before the Subcommittee on Economic Secu-
        rity, Infrastructure Protection, and Cybersecurity of the Committee
        on Homeland Security with the Subcommittee on Criminal Justice, Drug
        Policy, and Human Resources of the Committee on Government Reform,
        House of Representatives, 109th Congress, Second Session, July 20.

Hutchinson, John F.
1996   *Champions of Charity: War and the Rise of the Red Cross.* Boulder, CO:
        Westview Press.

Iglesias-Prieto, Norma
2017   "Transborderisms: Practices That Tear Down Walls." In *Borderwall as
        Architecture: A Manifesto for the U.S.-Mexico Boundary.* Ronald Rael, ed.
        Pp. 22–25. University of California Press.

Infante, César, Alvaro J. Idrovo, Mario S. Sánchez-Domínguez, Stéphane Vinhas, and Tonatiuh González-Vázquez
    2012   "Violence Committed against Migrants in Transit: Experiences on the Northern Mexican Border." *Journal of Immigrant Minority Health* 14(1):449–59.

Ingram, Paul
    2015   "Sonora Police ID 4 of 7 Tortured & Killed on Ranch Near Az-Mexico Border." *Tucson Sentinel,* October 26. http://www.tucsonsentinel.com /local/report/102615_bodies_id/sonora-police-id-4-7-tortured-killed-ranch-near-az-mexico-border/.
    2016   "9th Circuit Dismisses Terry Family's Lawsuit over BP Agent's Death." *Tucson Sentinel,* June 27. www.tucsonsentinel.com/local/report/062716_ terry_lawsuit/9th-circuit-dismisses-terry-familys-lawsuit-over-bp-agents-death/.

Isacson, Adam, Maureen Meyer, and Ashley Davis
    2013   *Border Security and Migration: A Report from Arizona.* Washington Office on Latin America, December 5. www.wola.org/analysis/border-security-and-migration-a-report-from-arizona/.

Janetsky, Megan
    2018   "Passage Prevented: How Trump's Border Wall Will Harm Arizona Wildlife." *Tucson Sentinel,* January 15. www.tucsonsentinel.com/local/report /011518_border_wall/passage-prevented-how-trumps-border-wall-will-harm-arizona-wildlife/.

Jiménez, Manuel
    2015   "Padre de jornalero sufre calvario por hallar a hijo." *El Imparcial,* June 22.

Jimenez, Maria
    2009   *Humanitarian Crisis: Migrant Deaths at the U.S.-Mexico Border.* American Civil Liberties Union. www.aclu.org/legal-document/humanitarian-crisis-migrant-deaths-us-mexico-border.

Johnson, Kevin
    2017   "The Arizona Lawman Challenging President Trump's Border Wall." *USA Today,* March 5. www.azcentral.com/story/news/2017/03/05/arizona-lawman-challenging-president-trumps-border-wall/98492128/.

Jusionyte, Ieva
    2015a *Savage Frontier: Making News and Security on the Argentine Border.* Oakland: University of California Press.
    2015b "States of Camouflage." *Cultural Anthropology* 30(1):113–38.
    2017a "Pain on the Border: Fieldnotes from a Migrant Aid Center in Nogales, Mexico." *ReVista: Harvard Review of Latin America* 16(1):46–49.
    2017b "The Wall and the Wash: Security, Infrastructure and Rescue on the US-Mexico Border." *Anthropology Today* 33(3):13–16.

2018   "Called to 'Ankle Alley': Migrant Injuries and Emergency Medical Services on the U.S.-Mexico Border." *American Anthropologist* 120(1):89–101.

Kafka, Franz

1931   *The Great Wall of China.* Trans. Ian Johnston. www.kafka-online.info/the-great-wall-of-china.html.

Kasulaitis, Mary

2002   "The Village of Arivaca: A Short History." *The Smoke Signal* 75.

Kenward, Alyson, Todd Sanford, and James Bronzan

2016   *Western Wildfires: A Fiery Future.* Climate Central Study, June. http://assets.climatecentral.org/pdfs/westernwildfires2016vfinal.pdf.

Kramer, Melody

2013   "Why Big, Intense Wildfires Are the New Normal." *National Geographic,* August 30. https://news.nationalgeographic.com/news/2013/08/130827-wildfires-yosemite-fire-firefighters-vegetation-hotshots-california-drought/.

Lacey, Marc

2010   "Water Drops for Migrants: Kindness, or Offense?" *New York Times,* September 26. www.nytimes.com/2010/09/27/us/27water.html?_r=0.

Lakoff, Andrew

2007   "Preparing for the Next Emergency." *Public Culture* 19(2):247–71.

Lewis, Patti

2004   "2 Saved, 1 Dies." *Nogales International,* July 28. https://www.nogalesinternational.com/news/saved-dies/article_8da647e9-66b6-52b3-a29c-21a1dbbe1750.html.

Lieberman, Amy

2014   "Arizona's Checkpoint Rebellion." *Slate,* July 20. http://www.slate.com/articles/news_and_politics/politics/2014/07/arizona_immigration_checkpoint_criticism_border_patrol_harasses_people_and.html.

Lomonaco, Claudine

2006   "Border Patrol, Migrant Aid Groups Brace for Desert Heat." *Tucson Citizen,* June 3.

Lovett, Ian

2012   "Border Cities Are Burdened with Calls for Help." *New York Times,* August 26, A16.

Luong, T.M., C.L. Castro, H. Chang, T. Lahmers, D.K. Adams, and C.A. Ochoa-Moya

2017   "The More Extreme Nature of North American Monsoon Precipitation in the Southwestern United States as Revealed by a Historical Climatology of Simulated Severe Weather Events." *Journal of Applied Meteorology and Climatology* 56:2509–29.

Lydgate, Joanna

2010   "Assembly-Line Justice: A Review of Operation Streamline." *California Law Review* 98(2). www.law.berkeley.edu/files/Operation_Streamline_Policy_Brief.pdf.

Magahern, Jimmy
  2013   "Arizona's Smallest Town." *Times Publications,* December 3.
Manaugh, Geoff
  2016   *A Burglar's Guide to the City.* New York: Farrar, Straus and Giroux.
Marsh, Charles P., Ellen G. Segan, Brian Temple, and Tod E. Kaspar
  1999   *Engineering Life-Cycle Cost Comparison Study of Barrier Fencing Systems.* Technical Report no. 99/28. US Army Corps of Engineers, February. https://www.dtic.mil/cgi-bin/GetTRDoc?AD=ADA360954.
Martínez, Oscar
  2014   *The Beast: Riding the Rails and Dodging Narcos on the Migrant Trail.* London: Verso.
Masco, Joseph
  2014   *The Theater of Operations: National Security Affect from the Cold War to the War on Terror.* Durham: Duke University Press.
Massumi, Brian
  2016   *Ontopower: War, Powers, and the State of Perception.* Durham: Duke University Press.
Mbembe, Achille
  2003   "Necropolitics." *Public Culture* 15(1):11–40.
McCain, John, and Jeff Flake
  2014   Letter to Denise Turner Roth, Administrator of the General Services Administration. July 14. https://www.mccain.senate.gov/public/_cache/files/9ba9b397-28c9-4208-ace8-94067f79c224/7.14.16-mccain-flake-nogales-tunnel-letter-to-gsa.pdf.
McCombs, Brady
  2008   "Mexico Ties Flooding in Nogales to U.S. Border Patrol-Built Wall." *Arizona Daily Star,* July 23. http://tucson.com/news/local/border/mexico-ties-flooding-in-nogales-to-u-s-border-patrol/article_a11265b0-17c3-5bed-b50a-72e5d17e1369.html.
McGuire, Randall H.
  2013   "Steel Walls and Picket Fences: Rematerializing the U.S.-Mexican Border in Ambos Nogales." *American Anthropologist* 115(3):466–80.
McIntyre, Erin Siegal
  2014   "Rape Another Threat on Migrant Women's Journey North." *Americas Quarterly,* September 16. www.americasquarterly.org/content/rape-another-threat-migrant-womens-journey-north.
McKinnon, Shaun
  2011   "U.S. Funds, Arizona Effort Help Mexico Trucks Pollute Less." *Arizona Republic,* April 11. http://archive.azcentral.com/news/articles/2011/04/11/20110411arizona-mexico-truck-pollution-regulation.html.
Meissner, Doris
  1995   Statement Prepared for the Hearing before the Subcommittee on Immigration and Claims of the Committee on the Judiciary, House of Representatives, 104th Congress, First Session, March 10.

Miller, Todd, and Alex M. Schivone

    2015   "Gaza in Arizona: The Secret Militarization of the U.S.-Mexico Border." *Salon,* February 1. www.salon.com/2015/02/01/gaza_in_arizona_the_secret_militarization_of_the_u_s_mexico_border_partner/.

Montoya, Aaliyah

    2016   "Border Patrol Works to Combat Advanced Activity." *Douglas Dispatch,* February 16. https://www.douglasdispatch.com/news/border-patrol-works-to-combat-advanced-activity/article_6179208a-d4d7-11e5-bf9a-d7b6ad5c0444.html.

Montoya, Nancy

    2015   "Sheriff Challenges Governor's DPS Border Drug Strike Force." Arizona Public Media, November 24. https://news.azpm.org/s/35441-sheriff-challenges-arizona-governors-border-drug-strike-force/.

Morris, Rosalind C.

    2010   "Accidental Histories, Post-Historical Practice? Re-reading Body of Power, Spirit of Resistance in the Actuarial Age." *Anthropological Quarterly* 83(3):581–624.

Morris, Tirion

    2016   "TMC Wants to Recycle, Reuse Your Old Car Seats." *Tucson Sentinel,* February 25. www.tucsonsentinel.com/local/report/021716_car_seats/tmc-wants-recycle-reuse-your-old-car-seats/.

Mumme, Stephen P., and Oscar Ibáñez

    2009   "US-Mexico Environmental Treaty Impediments to Tactical Security Infrastructure along the International Boundary." *National Resources Journal* 49(3):801–24.

National Academy of Sciences, Division of Medical Sciences, National Research Council

    1966   *Accidental Death and Disability: The Neglected Disease of Modern Society. Washington DC.* September. http://www.ems.gov/pdf/1997-reproduction-accidentaldeathdissability.pdf.

Nevins, Joseph

    2010   *Operation Gatekeeper and Beyond.* 2nd ed. New York: Routledge.

Nogales International

    2011   "Bull Fire Exhibiting 'Extreme Fire Behavior'; Three Homes Threatened." April 30. https://www.nogalesinternational.com/news/breaking_news/bull-fire-exhibiting-extreme-fire-behavior-three-homes-threatened/article_224df152-bc27-5d5e-9bc4-9b945528143b.html.

    2015a "BP Agent from Rio Rico Accused of Transporting Cocaine." November 24. https://www.nogalesinternational.com/news/bp-agent-from-rio-rico-accused-of-transporting-cocaine/article_d8118456-9311-11e5-8b9e-1bd2140370cb.html.

    2015b "Storm Claims Woman's Life in Nogales, Sonora." July 28. https://www.nogalesinternational.com/news/storm-claims-woman-s-life-in-nogales-sonora/article_fe89b930-35a8-11e5-9504-5fa10dfc65eb.html.

2016a "CBP: Nogales Man Tried to Smuggle Meth in Tortillas." October 31. https://www.nogalesinternational.com/news/cbp-nogales-man-tried-to-smuggle-meth-in-tortillas/article_3a21e442-9fe6-11e6-9c34-9b4ff2a84bef.html.

2016b "CBP Seizes $4.5-Million Pot Load at Mariposa Port." May 13. https://www.nogalesinternational.com/news/cbp-seizes-five-ton-pot-load-at-mariposa-port/article_b5b5e03c-bda9-11e6-a07b-77b444fbeec7.html.

2016c "Senators Call for Action on Drainage Tunnel under Port." July 18. https://www.nogalesinternational.com/news/senators-call-for-action-on-drainage-tunnel-under-port/article_85154a58-4d2e-11e6-b805-7354e2645ebd.html.

2017 "Air Pollution Advisory Issued for Nogales on Friday." December 28. https://www.nogalesinternational.com/news/air-pollution-advisory-issued-for-nogales-on-friday/article_96db4648-ebf2-11e7-9dc7-534a48355e6a.html.

NPR (National Public Radio)

2017 "PHOTOS: The Many Possible Shapes of Trump's Border Wall." April 5. www.npr.org/sections/thetwo-way/2017/04/05/522712279/photos-the-many-possible-shapes-of-trumps-border-wall.

Nuñez-Neto, Blas, and Stephen R. Viña

2005 *Border Security: Fences along the U.S. International Border.* Congressional Research Service Report for Congress. January 13. https://fas.org/sgp/crs/RS22026.pdf.

Pallack, Becky

2005 "1 Dead, 7 Critical in Entrants' Crash." *Arizona Daily Star,* January 11. http://tucson.com/news/local/crime/dead-critical-in-entrants-crash/article_92af95c3-fbb5-52a1-afdb-176a762ce88e.html.

Pao, Christine, and Jana Tran

2017 "Firefighters and Trauma: Addressing Post-Traumatic Stress Disorder in the Fire Service." *Fire Rescue Magazine,* March 28. www.firerescuemagazine.com/articles/print/volume-12/issue-3/features/firefighters-and-trauma.html.

Pavlakovich-Kochi, Vera

2014 *Maquiladora Related Economy of Nogales and Santa Cruz County.* www.azeconomy.org/2014/04/technology/maquiladora-related-economy-of-nogales-and-santa-cruz-county/.

Pestano, Andrew V.

2016 "Mexico Recovers Stolen Radioactive Material after Container Left on City Bench." United Press International, August 8. https://www.upi.com/Top_News/World-News/2016/08/08/Mexico-recovers-stolen-radioactive-material-after-container-left-on-city-bench/4611470669863/.

Pineda, Paulina

2015 "Artist Uses Paint to 'Erase' Border Fence." *Nogales International,* October 14. https://www.nogalesinternational.com/news/artist-uses-paint-to-erase-border-fence/article_9c6d89b8-72a0-11e5-87f9-57978b03f324.html

2016 "Woman Dies after Apparent Fall from Border Fence." *Nogales International,* June 21. https://www.nogalesinternational.com/news/woman-dies-after-apparent-fall-from-border-fence/article_1d0d569e-37f8-11e6-aadc-339f19764309.html.

Prendergast, Curt
2014 "NFD Making Regular Trips to BP Station." *Nogales International,* June 27. https://www.nogalesinternational.com/news/nfd-making-regular-trips-to-bp-station/article_5db40ab8-fe0b-11e3-837c-0019bb2963f4.html.

Pruitt, Lisa R.
2014 "The Rural Lawscape: Space Tames Law Tames Space. In *The Expanding Spaces of Law: A Timely Legal Geography.* I. Braverman, N. Blomley, D. Delaney, and A. Kedar, eds. Pp. 190–214. Stanford: Stanford University Press.

Rael, Ronald, ed.
2017 *Borderwall as Architecture: A Manifesto for the U.S.-Mexico Boundary.* Oakland: University of California Press.

Ralph, Laurence
2014 *Renegade Dreams: Living through Injury in Gangland Chicago.* Chicago: University of Chicago Press.

Redfield, Peter
2005 "Doctors, Borders, and Life in Crisis." *Cultural Anthropology* 20(3):328–61.

Reeves, Madeleine
2014 *Border Work: Spatial Lives of the State in Rural Central Asia.* Ithaca: Cornell University Press.

Rochford, Richard
2009 "Hydrogen Cyanide: New Concerns for Firefighting and Medical Tactics." *Fire Engineering,* June 29.

Rodriguez, Marisol, and Hector Rivero
2011 "ProNaF, Ciudad Juarez: Planning and Urban Transformation." *ITU Journal of the Faculty of Architecture* 8(1):196–207.

Romero, Alex R.
2005 "83 Vehicles Charred in Nogales, Sonora, Fire." *Nogales International,* May 11. www.nogalesinternational.com/news/vehicles-charred-in-nogales-sonora-fire/article_d01204fa-382f-515d-a9ee-a891e12c0fe8.html.

Rosas, Gilberto
2012 *Barrio Libre: Criminalizing States and Delinquent Refusals of the New Frontier.* Durham: Duke University Press.

Ross, Brian, Brian Epstein, and Paul Blake
2017 "Retiring Border Chief Calls Trump's Wall a Waste of Time, Money." ABC News, January 23. https://abcnews.go.com/Politics/trumps-border-wall-waste-time-money-retiring-border/story?id=44978156.

Rothenbuhler, Eric
2005 "Ground Zero, the Firemen, and the Symbolics of Touch on 9/11 and After." In *Media Anthropology.* E. Rothenbuhler, W., and M. Coman, eds. Pp. 176–87. Thousand Oaks, CA: Sage.

Rotstein, Arthur H.

2003 "Fake Border Blast Triggers Massive Terror Response Drill." *Arizona Daily Sun,* November 16. https://azdailysun.com/fake-border-blast-triggers-massive-terror-response-drill/article_75f293be-c323-57f9-a3d8-1d68219a7083.html.

Rowley, Heidi

2008 "Feds to End Funding of ER Care for Migrants." *Tucson Citizen,* August 28. http://tucsoncitizen.com/morgue/2008/08/28/95093-feds-to-end-funding-of-er-care-for-migrants/.

Rubio-Goldsmith, Raquel, M. Melissa McCormick, Daniel Martinez, and Inez Magdalena Duarte

2006 *The "Funnel Effect" and Recovered Bodies of Unauthorized Migrants Processed by the Pima County Office of the Medical Examiner, 1990–2005.* Tucson: Binational Migration Institute, University of Arizona.

Sahuarita Sun

2000 "12 Injured in Rollover." June 21.

Schlyer, Krista

2017 *Embattled Borderlands.* http://storymaps.esri.com/stories/2017/embattled-borderlands/index.html.

Schmitt, Carl

2005 *Political Theology: Four Chapters on the Concept of Sovereignty.* Chicago: University of Chicago Press.

Schwartz, Alexandra

2017 "The Artist JR Lifts a Mexican Child over the Border Wall." *New Yorker,* September 11. www.newyorker.com/news/as-told-to/the-artist-jr-lifts-a-mexican-child-over-the-border-wall.

Secretaría de Gobernación

2016 *Coordinación Nacional de Protección Civil emite alertamiento por robo de fuente radiactiva en Querétaro.* Bulletin no. 118/16. February 28. www.gob.mx/segob/prensa/la-coordinacion-nacional-de-proteccion-civil-emite-alertamiento-por-robo-de-fuente-radiactiva-en-queretaro?idiom=es-MX.

Sessions, Jeff

2017 "Attorney General Jeff Sessions Delivers Remarks Announcing the Department of Justice's Renewed Commitment to Criminal Immigration Enforcement." Nogales, AZ, April 11. www.justice.gov/opa/speech/attorney-general-jeff-sessions-delivers-remarks-announcing-department-justice-s-renewed.

Siegel, Greg

2014 *Forensic Media: Reconstructing Accidents in Accelerated Modernity.* Durham: Duke University Press.

Simpson, Connor

2013 "They Found the Stolen Truck Filled with Radioactive Material." *Atlantic,* December 4. www.theatlantic.com/international/archive/2013/12/radioactive-material-stolen-mexico-worries-iaea/355773/.

Slack, Jeremy, and Howard Campbell

    2016   "On Narco-Coyotaje: Illicit Regimes and Their Impacts on the US–Mexico Border." *Antipode* 48:1380–99.

Slack, Jeremy, and Scott Whiteford

    2011   "Violence and Migration on the Arizona-Sonora Border." *Human Organization* 70(1):11–21.

Smith, Dylan

    2016   "Former Border Agent Sentenced to 8 Years for Pot Smuggling." *Tucson Sentinel,* February 18. www.tucsonsentinel.com/local/report/021816_cbp _sentencing/former-border-agent-sentenced-8-years-pot-smuggling.

Smith, Kim, and Dan Shearer

    2017   "Border Patrol Says Off-Duty Agent Tied to Sawmill Fire." *Green Valley News,* April 27. https://www.gvnews.com/free_access/update-border-patrol-says-off-duty-agent-tied-to-sawmill/article_fe0cf892-2b9b-11e7-81ea-9329eb1765cc.html.

St John, Rachel

    2011   *Line in the Sand: A History of the Western U.S.-Mexico Border.* Princeton: Princeton University Press.

Stephenson, Hank

    2011   "Nogales Border-Fence Revamp under Way." *Nogales International,* February 14. https://www.nogalesinternational.com/news/nogales-border-fence-revamp-under-way/article_0611f70c-ac45-5844-8ec3-780b1e7c27f1 .html.

Stevens, Kevin

    2006   Testimony at the Joint Hearing before the Subcommittee on Economic Security, Infrastructure Protection, and Cybersecurity of the Committee on Homeland Security with the Subcommittee on Criminal Justice, Drug Policy, and Human Resources of the Committee on Government Reform, House of Representatives, 109th Congress, Second Session, July 20.

Stuesse, Angela, and Mathew Coleman

    2014   "Automobility, Immobility, Altermobility: Surviving and Resisting the Intensification of Immigrant Policing." *City and Society* 26(1):51–72.

Taussig, Michael

    1992   *The Nervous System.* New York: Routledge.

Tebeau, Mark

    2003   *Eating Smoke: Fire in Urban America, 1800–1950.* Baltimore: Johns Hopkins University Press.

Teibel, David L.

    2003   "13 from 'Deep Mexico' Hurt in Arivaca Rollover." *Tucson Citizen,* February 22.

Terry, Jennifer

    2017   *Attachments to War: Biomedical Logics and Violence in Twenty-First-Century America.* Durham: Duke University Press.

Ticktin, Miriam

    2011   *Casualties of Care: Immigration and the Politics of Humanitarianism in France*. Berkeley: University of California Press.

Trevizo, Perla

    2015a "Border Apprehensions at 'Unheard of' Lows." *Arizona Daily Star*, September 5. http://tucson.com/news/local/border-apprehensions-at-unheard-of-lows/article_aa27cbde-0826-52f7-98d2-884e11c97295.html.

    2015b "Border Fence Jumpers Breaking Bones." *Arizona Daily Star*, July 4. http://tucson.com/news/border-fence-jumpers-breaking-bones/article_ed0f14a0-3eee-5877-9166-3397881cc8b5.html.

    2015c "Officials: Past Border Tech Efforts Failed, but This One Won't." *Arizona Daily Star*, December 26. http://tucson.com/news/local/officials-past-border-tech-efforts-failed-but-this-one-won/article_2192fa1f-47b6-5954-8575-8a74fc691820.html.

    2016a "Arivaca Residents Monitoring Border Patrol Checkpoint on AZ 286." *Arizona Daily Star*, February 3. http://tucson.com/news/arivaca-residents-monitoring-border-patrol-checkpoint-on-az/article_e3a9e9e1-0706-5c59-bdf7-fae183140a29.html.

    2016b "Arrests in Border Patrol's Tucson Sector at 20-Year Low." *Arizona Daily Star*, January 16. http://tucson.com/news/arrests-in-border-patrol-s-tucson-sector-at—year/article_3278f9c2-cb73-555a-90b3-a0f216bbe52d.html.

Trouillot, Michel-Rolph

    2001   "The Anthropology of the State in the Age of Globalization: Close Encounters of the Deceptive Kind." *Current Anthropology* 42(1):125–38.

Truett, Samuel

    2006   *Fugitive Landscapes: The Forgotten History of the U.S.-Mexico Borderlands*. New Haven: Yale University Press.

Tucson Citizen

    1998   "More Injured Illegal Immigrants Discovered after Truck Rollover." February 26. http://tucsoncitizen.com/morgue2/1998/02/26/41074-more-injured-illegal-immigrants-discovered-after-truck-rollover/.

Urrea, Luis Alberto

    2004   *The Devil's Highway: A True Story*. New York: Little, Brown.

US Army Corps of Engineers Los Angeles District and the International Boundary and Water Commission

    2004 [revised January 2005] *Ambos Nogales Special Flood Damage Reduction Study*. September. www.ibwc.state.gov/Files/Amb_Nogales_Flood_Reduction_Study_rev_January_2005.pdf.

USBP (US Border Patrol)

    1994   Border Patrol Strategic Plan, 1994 and Beyond. July. www.hsdl.org/?view&did=721845.

US CBP (US Customs and Border Protection)

    2017   Solid Concrete Border Wall RFP. Solicitation no. HSBP1017R0022. March 17.

US DOT, PHMSA (US Department of Transportation, Pipeline and Hazardous Materials Safety Administration)

    2016   *Emergency Response Guidebook.* Washington, DC: US Government Publishing Office.

US EPA (US Environmental Protection Agency)

    1983   La Paz Agreement. August 14. https://www.epa.gov/sites/production/files/2015-09/documents/lapazagreement.pdf

    2008   Mexico–United States Joint Contingencies and Emergencies Plan for Preparedness and Response to Events Associated with Chemical Hazardous Substances in the Inland Border Area. September 4.

US EPA and SEMARNAT (US Environmental Protection Agency and Secretaría de Medio Ambiente y Recursos Naturales)

    2012   *Border 2020: US-Mexico Environmental Program.* www.epa.gov/sites/production/files/documents/border2020summary.pdf.

van Stralen, Daved

    2008   "The Origins of EMS in Military Medicine: How Combat Medicine Influenced the Advent of Today's EMS Model." *JEMS: Journal of Emergency Medical Services* 32(10):11–15.

Vélez-Ibáñez, Carlos G.

    1996   *Border Visions: Mexican Cultures of the Southwest United States.* Tucson: University of Arizona Press.

Virilio, Paul

    2011   *The Original Accident.* Cambridge, UK: Polity.

Wacquant, Loïc

    2010   "Crafting the Neoliberal State: Workfare, Prisonfare, and Social Insecurity." *Sociological Forum* 25(2):197–220.

Wagner, Dennis

    2009   "I-19 Checkpoint near Tubac Angers Locals." *Arizona Republic,* July 16. http://archive.azcentral.com/arizonarepublic/news/articles/2009/07/16/20090716checkpoint0716.html.

Weber, Max

    2012   "The Fundamental Concepts of Sociology." In *Max Weber: The Theory of Social and Economic Organization.* Talcott Parsons, ed. Mansfield Center, CT: Martino Publishing.

Weizman, Eyal

    2007   *Hollow Land: Israel's Architecture of Occupation.* London: Verso.

    2014   *Forensis: The Architecture of Public Truth.* Berlin: Sternberg Press.

    2017   *Forensic Architecture: Violence at the Threshold of Detectability.* New York: Zone Books.

Williams, Jill M.

2015   "From Humanitarian Exceptionalism to Contingent Care: Care and Enforcement at the Humanitarian Border." *Political Geography* 47:11–20.

Woodhouse, Murphy

2015a   "Big-Ticket Ladder Truck Takes on Many Roles." *Nogales International,* January 30. https://www.nogalesinternational.com/news/big-ticket-ladder-truck-takes-on-many-roles/article_fdfdb15c-a88f-11e4-b85b-a396ffb0f7e5.html

2015b   "Nogales Is Still Tunnel Capital, despite Decline in Busts." *Nogales International,* October 2. https://www.nogalesinternational.com/news/nogales-is-still-tunnel-capital-despite-decline-in-busts/article_db33c082-6890-11e5-a3d4-b78ca081ea7c.html.

2016   "Mayor Blasts Patagonia for Aggressive Ticketing of Mexicans." *Nogales International,* March 17. https://www.nogalesinternational.com/news/mayor-blasts-patagonia-for-aggressive-ticketing-of-mexicans/article_ada84400-ec96-11e5-9238-5b18acb5d5fa.html.

Ybarra, Megan

2017   *Green Wars: Conservation and Decolonization in the Maya Forest.* Berkeley: University of California Press.

Zeiderman, Austin

2016   *Endangered City: The Politics of Security and Risk in Bogotá.* Durham: Duke University Press.

Ziegler, Zachary

2015   "International Port Grows as Gateway for Mexican Produce." Arizona Public Media. May 18. https://news.azpm.org/p/news-splash/2015/5/19/64112-international-port-grows-as-gateway-for-mexican-produce/.

Zink, Brian J.

2006   *Anyone, Anything, Anytime: A History of Emergency Medicine.* Philadelphia: Mosby Elsevier.

INDEX

wildfires, 167, 176, 177. *See also* unauthorized migrants
Border Crossing Card, 53, 92, 215, 243n61
border fence: art, 211; border security, 7, 13, 19, 36, 46, 64fig, 85; construction, 45, 59; failure to stop mutual aid, 99; Grupo Beta, 194fig; injuries, 221; labeling, 56; migrants tied up against, 174; narratives, 50, 61, 62, 63, 78, 132, 137, 190, 191, 201. *See also* border wall
Border Patrol. *See* United States Border Patrol
border security: Border Patrol, 13; militarization, 13, 138–39; narratives, 172; post 9/11, 10, 24, 214; radiation, 129; Secure Fence Act, 44, 241n41; temporality, 51; urban areas, 42. *See also* tactical infrastructure
border wall: art, 210; border security, 20, 86; brotherhood, 225; deaths, 63; injuries, 54, 57, 62, 65; labeling, 56; narratives, 3, 18, 29, 95, 122; politics of wounding, 212; topography, 216
BORSTAR, 170, 196, 249n22
Bowden, Charles, 147, 190
Boundary Monument 122, 58, 243n70
boundary treaties, 69
Bourdieu, Pierre, 21, 22
Bracero Program, 185
Buena Vista Ranch, 3, 9
Buenos Aires National Wildlife Refuge (BANWR), 177, 183, 184, 191
bulletproof vests, 8, 76, 77, 97, 102, 173
Bureau of Land Management (BLM), 184, 185
burns, 24, 38, 69, 110, 238n74

C4, 70, 71, 110, 122, 132, 244n96
Caborca, Sonora, 120, 121, 192, 124, 194, 196, 197
cacti, 56, 121
Calderón, Felipe, 77
California, 41, 59, 69, 83, 113, 117, 124, 177
Calle Internacional, 18, 65, 72, 74map, 94, 95
camaraderie, 99, 214, 218
carbon monoxide, 24, 107, 109, 246n19
cartels, 76, 77, 161, 184, 196–98, 201, 212

cattle tanks, 156, 164, 202
CBRNE (chemical, biological, radiological, nuclear, and explosive), 129, 134
cell phones: communications, 49, 162; dead battery, 162; humanitarian volunteers, 195, 200; inability to navigate, 70, 189; lack of coverage, 35, 113, 114, 148, 157, 173, 176, 187, 190, 193; pictures, 161, 162; towers, 86
Cemetery Wash, 72
Central America, 6, 41, 151, 181, 185, 197, 200
cervical collars, 48, 86, 103, 218
checkpoints: Amado, 29, 145; avoidance by border crossers, 10, 14; benefits, 152–53, 156; demonstrations, 53, 147; humanitarian volunteers, 196; inspections, 84; Mexican army, 119; Nogales, 33; questioning of firefighters and paramedics, 22; radiation detection, 130; Sasabe Highway, 170; security strategy, 5, 7, 44, 52, 146; sick persons, 65, 186; SR 86, 123; Tubac, 4, 29, 52, 54, 119, 120
chemicals: ammonia, 38, 118, 127–28; border security, 214; chlorine, 38, 117, 118, 133–34; cyanide, 106, 108–110, 112, 113; emergencies, 19, 116, 117, 139; hydrogen sulfide, 107, 134; maquiladoras, 108, 140; mercury, 131; sodium hydrosulfide, 134; spills, 10, 18, 38, 85, 115, 139, 140; storage, 38; sulphuric acid, 18, 34, 38, 109, 113, 117, 119, 132, 133; terrorism, 17; testing kits, 118; trains, 34, 38, 133; training, 125, 129, 135; United Nations hazmat placard system, 109
chickenpox, 79
child car safety seats, 105, 119, 124, 141
chlorine, 38, 117, 118, 133–34
citizenship, 22, 53, 237n60
Ciudad Juárez, Chihuahua, Mexico, 66, 77, 201
civil defense, 17, 107, 139. See also *protección civil*
civil initiatives, 185
Civil War (American), 16
Clorox, 173, 205
cocaine, 3
Cold War, 17, 129, 213

comedor, 30, 183, 184, 199, 200, 202, 204, 222. *See also* Kino Border Initiative

Community-Integrated Paramedicine program, 175

Computer-Aided Management of Emergency Operations (CAMEO), 116

CONAFOR, 178, 179

congressional hearings. *See* United States Congress

constitutional rights, 53, 66

Constitution-free zone, 19

contraband, 75, 76, 193. *See also* smuggling

copper, 10, 18, 34, 108, 109, 134

Coronado National Forest, 177, 178, 189, 191

cough drops, 200, 205, 222

coyotes (human smugglers), 51, 202. *See also* human smugglers

coyotes (wildlife), 145

CPR, 69, 214, 222

crime: border security, 43, 139, 215; circumvention of boundaries, 223; humanitarian aid, 170, 184, 186, 195; injuries as evidence, 14, 15, 24; scenes, 218; stealing cacti, 121; tactical infrastructure, 50; Three Points, 170; transporting undocumented aliens, 168; violent, 77

Cruz Roja (Red Cross): humanitarian volunteers, 157, 195; injuries, 110; Mexico, 236n45; mobile clinic, 197; narratives, 61, 68, 70, 103, 104, 108, 110, 122, 124, 127, 201; port of entry, 67; skills, 112; training, 117, 125, 135

custody, 70, 152, 162, 163, 166, 170, 171, 182

customs: brokers, 34; bypassed, 90, 100, 135; donations, 103, 104, 105; drugs, 8, 29; Ellis Fire, 92; emergencies, 75; narratives, 78, 126, 193

Customs and Border Protection (CBP). *See* United States Customs and Border Protection (CBP)

cyanide, 106, 108–110, 112, 113

DACA, 211, 251n6

de León, Jason, 85

dehydration: border crossers, 14, 28; BP Strategic Plan, 43; deaths and hospi-

talization, 56, 67, 151, 186, 199; narratives, 80, 157, 164, 165, 202

DeConcini port of entry, 35, 59, 72, 132, 137

dentistry, 106. *See also* toothache

deportation: Alien Transfer Exit Program, 200; Border Patrol, 81; deportees, 60, 199, 200, 201; el comedor, 199; El Sásabe, 198; humanitarian volunteers, 187; medical care, 52, 211

Operation Streamline, 183, 250n35

detention centers, 81, 86, 161, 168, 191, 199, 211

deterrence. *See* "prevention through deterrence" strategy

Dewachi, Omar, 15

DHS. *See* United States Department of Homeland Security (DHS)

disappearance, 43, 50, 52, 60, 203

disaster, 4, 10, 98, 129, 137, 139, 199, 214, 215

disease, 17, 19, 131, 139, 174, 235n21

distraction fires, 178

diversionary fires, 178

domestic violence, 29, 169, 172

domino effect, 197

donations: child car seats, 105; equipment, 102–105, 118; medical supplies, 102–104

dosimeters, 130

Douglas, Arizona: border fence, 45; donations, 104, 120; medical services, 13, 15, 17, 61; narratives, 29, 97, 103; "prevention through deterrence", 185; sending firefighters to Mexico, 101; split city with Agua Prieta, 18, 21map, 95; training, 134, 135

Douglas Fire Department, 101, 134, 246n16

drones, 38, 44, 51, 52, 190, 242n57

drowning, 14, 15, 28, 43, 56, 75

drugs: cartels, 76, 77, 184, 196–98, 201, 212, smuggling, 55, 178, 183, 197, 250n38; trafficking, 3, 8, 17, 19, 45, 77, 118, 123. *See also* cocaine, marijuana, mules

drug mules, 4, 14, 37, 173

drug war, 9, 21, 77, 147, 248n46

Dunn, Timothy, 28

economy, 9, 14, 28, 37, 128

Elbit Systems, 45

electricity. *See* public utilities

electrolyte solution, 195, 201

Ellis Fire, 90–92, 99, 119

El Paso, Texas, 41, 42, 50, 236n41

Elena Rodríguez, José Antonio, 65, 66fig

Eloy (detention center), 184

El Salvador, 56, 63, 181, 199, 203, 245n106

El Sásabe, Sonora, 21map, 161, 162, 192–98

Emergency Health Services Furnished to Undocumented Aliens, 169

emergency: drills, 110, 117, 125, 134; management, 17, 19, 20, 35, 97, 115, 122, 127, 133, 136, 139, 214

emergency medical services (EMS): bomberos, 111; border policing, 15; history of, 16; post 9/11, 21; narratives, 30, 69, 124, 149, 160, 169; standards, 16, 84, 235n28

emergency medical technicians (EMTs): Arivaca, 166; Border Patrol, 15, 164, 168, 169;

fence, 65; firefighters, 12, 149; narratives, 5, 25, 26, 63, 150, 151, 155, 156, 157, 159, 167, 170, 217; post 9/11, 214; standards and training, 72, 112, 177, 180, 185, 235n28

Emergency Medical Treatment and Active Labor Act of 1986 (EMTALA), 55

Emergency Planning and Community Right-to-Know Act, 37, 112, 239n14

emergency responders: binational cooperation, 96, 99; Border Patrol relations, 45, 182; car seats, 105; challenges, 21, 22, 84, 104; criticism, 168; deaths, 172, 209; drug trafficking, 8;

duties, 12; first to the scene, 12, 20; Good Samaritan law, 72; hazardous materials, 24;

insurance, 99; knowledge, 23, 37, 86, 89; medical services, 67; reporting patients, 65, 167, 171; rural communities, 154, 169; safety issues, 148, 212; training, 19, 111; bulletproof vests, 76

emergency response guidebook (ERG), 109

environment: ecosystems, 86; EPA, 20, 98; falls, 85; field causality, 12; hazards, 116; La Paz Agreement, 18; manmade, 85; natural, 20, 30, 37, 73, 138, 140, 212; Nogales fire station placard, 213; sur-

vival, 56; urban, 42, 113, 219; violence, 13; wall, 210

EPA. *See* Border 2020 program, United States Environmental Protection Agency

Estrada, Tony, 36, 174

ethics, 23, 27, 166, 214, 221

ethnography, 6, 220

E-Verify, 167

exposure: carbon monoxide, 24; cyanide, 110; environmental hazards, 8, 139; heat and cold, 43, 170, 156, 162; public, 55; radiation, 129, 130; rebar, 131; TB, 163

Fassin, Didier, 22

Father Kino, 197

fear, 3, 15, 52, 129, 198, 202, 212, 214, 217

Federal Emergency Management Agency (FEMA), 100 136, 139, 222, 226

Feldman, Allen, 11

female. *See* women

femur fractures, 62, 150

fence jumpers, 13, 46. *See also* border fence, fractures

fence. *See* border fence, border wall

Fernandez, Ana Teresa, 59, 60

Ferromex, 18, 113

field causality, 11–12

firefighters: hoses, 19, 90, 95, 96; hydrants, 3, 19, 40, 90, 94, 95, 112; ladders and ladder companies, 47, 50, 51, 91, 94, 95, 102, 103, 209; stations 25, 58, 90, 102, 103, 106, 111, 113, 124, 137, 141, 146, 169, 175; trucks, 6, 9, 19, 22, 47, 49, 90, 95, 99, 170, 209. *See also* structure fires, wildland fires

first aid, 15, 16, 30, 68, 107, 109, 183, 185, 203, 226

flags, 166

Flake, Jeff, 132

floods: arroyos, 68; donations to victims, 120; drowning, 14; flash, 4, 10, 18, 85, 137;

hazard mitigation plan, 131; narratives, 217; Nogales, 72, 73; sewer water, 39; tactical infrastructure, 139; TTX, 136; warning sign, 145

Florida, 5, 25, 220, 222

littering, 184, 185
López Mateos, Adolfo, 72
low-intensity conflict, 28

M8A1, 59, 243n75
Madrid, Miguel de la, 18
mafia. *See* cartels
manpower, 15, 89, 92, 93, 98, 128, 170, 179, 181
maquiladoras: 39, 86, 103, 105–110, 112, 117, 140, 204, 240n22, 246n18
Mara Salvatrucha, 181
marijuana, 3, 8, 34, 38, 41, 148, 154, 175, 193
Mariposa port of entry, 34, 47, 74map, 117, 140, 202
mask, 110, 159, 161, 219
Masco, Joseph, 138
Massumi, Brian, 139
materiality, 10, 20, 26, 138
Mbembe, Achille, 11, 85
McCain, John, 132, 135
McFarland, USA (movie), 83
McSally, Martha, 132, 135
mechanism of injury, 11, 48, 65, 146, 212
media, 12, 39, 57, 96, 106, 129, 134, 147, 155, 210. *See also* journalists
medical examiner's office, 35, 199
Medicare, 55, 169
Mediterranean Sea, 15
Meissner, Doris, 41, 42, 59
mercury, 131
methamphetamines, 4, 29, 34, 170
methane, 107
Mexican Consulate, 56, 57, 65, 73, 80, 93, 104, 118
Mexican Revolution, 39, 58, 101
Mexico City, 71, 104, 115, 159, 161
Micanopy Fire Department, 26, 220
migrant deaths, 6, 43, 63, 69, 77, 131, 153, 154, 155, 165
militarization, 13, 138–39
mining, 109, 130, 131, 134, 146, 189
Mobile Army Surgical Hospitals (MASH), 16
MOLEX, 108
monsoon rains, 10, 35, 54, 189, 234n15
Montana Peak, 189
moral injury, 27, 238n76

Morley Tunnel, 39, 72
morphine, 48
motor vehicle accident (MVA), 152, 153, 154, 181
mountain lions, 4, 7. *See also* wild cats
MS-13 (Mara Salvatrucha), 181
mules (drug smugglers), 4, 14, 37, 173
Murphy Complex Fire, 179–80

Napolitano, Janet, 212
narcoguerra, 9, 13. *See also* drug war
National Academy of Sciences, 84
National Emergency Training Center, 136, 222
National Highway Traffic Safety Administration, 16
narrative, 11, 26, 28, 29, 30, 61, 209, 210. *See also* storytelling
New York City, 17, 161
Newton's laws of motion, 12, 85
night vision goggles, 145, 166, 169
NFPA, 93, 105, 112, 118, 219
No More Deaths, 157, 167, 168, 184, 185, 200, 205, 249n16
Nogales, Arizona: fence, 58, 64fig; firefighters and federal agents, 45, 51; hospital, 69; Independence Day parade, 91fig; mutual aid by firefighters, 90, 93, 99, 126, 215; narratives, 46, 47, 49, 50, 52, 70, 71, 73, 98, 101, 103, 106, 114; train, 132; training, 117
Nogales Border Patrol station, 13, 41, 74map, 78
Nogales Fire Department: history, 36; mutual aid, 62, 90, 95, 108; narratives, 8, 40, 46, 58, 63, 77, 79, 98, 114, 129, 133, 180
Nogales International, 95, 222
Nogales Suburban Fire District, 3, 30, 63, 90, 155, 222
Nogales Wash: Army Corp of Engineers, 131; Arroyo Chimeneas, 72; contamination, 133; drowning, 14; emergency response plan, 138; flooding, 114, 137; Santa Cruz River, 35; tunnel, 39
Normandy barriers, 4, 44fig, 190
North American Free Trade Agreement (NAFTA), 34

toxic substances, 117, 125, 131, 134, 140. *See also* chemicals

tracheostomy, 205

Traffic Incident Management Systems, 124

trafficking: criminal offense, 14; drugs, 3, 8, 9, 17, 19, 45, 77, 118, 123; human, 3, 56, 195

train derailment, 18, 113

transport authorization request (TAR), 163, 169

trauma: assessment, 27; border-related, 13, 85; calls, 170, 212; center, 49, 52, 55, 62, 65; chest, 16; dressings, 60; exaggeration, 61; head, 63; human rights, 14; kinematics, 11, 12, 84, 86; mechanism of injury, 146; post 9/11, 214; sensationalizing, 26; patients, 61; physical barrier, 67; politics, 28; surgeons, 54, 55

trinational plan, 121

Treaty of Guadalupe Hidalgo, 9, 185. *See also* boundary treaty

Trump, Donald, 36, 210, 211, 213, 233n4, 236n37

Tubac: Border Patrol, 29, 33, 52, 120, 189; funding, 37; mutual aid, 91; narratives, 54, 63, 96, 119, 148; refusal of medical treatment, 84

Tubac Fire District, 97, 127, 155, 172, 179

turberculosis (TB), 159, 162, 163

Tucson: border control, 193; EMTs, 167; hospitals, 49, 56, 67, 68, 69, 104, 105, 152, 153, 154, 192, 201; humanitarian volunteers, 149, 182, 185; Mexican Consulate, 57; narratives, 22, 29, 30, 52, 63, 76, 120, 121, 127, 128, 151, 158, 159, 162; Operation Streamline court, 183

shopping, 196; training, 117

Tucson Samaritans, 30, 146, 183, 191, 200, 222

Tucson Sector (Border Patrol), 6, 15, 41, 42, 43, 44, 199, 222

tunnels: border control, 5, 24, 45; collapse, 38; drones, 51; Nogales Wash, 14; narratives, 218; trainings, 5, 125, 141

tunnel vision, 138

Tychem suits, 110

UAVs, 38. *See also* drones

unaccompanied minors, 79

unauthorized border crossers, 3, 41, 46, 167, 170, 176, 177, 183

unauthorized migrants: accidental violence, 83; checkpoints, 52, 156; deaths, 10, 14, 35, 176; EMTs, 167; ethics, 166; medical treatment, 169, 171; narratives, 151, 153, 170; Proposition 187, 41; tactical infrastructure, 139; Tucson Samaritans, 146; viewed as criminals, 15; war on drugs, 147

UDAs (undocumented aliens), 78, 85, 151, 156, 164, 166, 167, 170, 173

Union Pacific, 18, 34, 36

United Nations hazmat placard system, 109

United States Border Patrol: 911 calls, 15; ambulances, 166; deportation, 81; EMTs, 15, 164, 168, 169; frontline, 50; helicopters, 15, 43, 201; images of, 15; relations with emergency responders, 45, 182; strategic plan, 42, 43, 146; women officers, 120, 16. *See also* border security, checkpoints, tactical advantage

United States Border Patrol Search, Trauma, and Rescue unit (BOR-STAR), 170, 196, 249n22

United States Bureau of Land Management (BLM), 184, 185

United States Congress, 43, 50, 59, 60, 132

United States Customs and Border Protection (CBP): authority, 19, 52; humanitarian parole, 215; illegal aliens designation, 46; image of, 15; narratives, 53, 66, 68, 82, 192; Nogales, 20, 34; politics of verticality, 51; protocols, 10, 44, 67, 92, 130, 178, 191; recruitment, 45; training, 35, 135, 137; wall, 210

United States Department of Homeland Security (DHS), 10, 17, 19, 44, 51, 136, 139, 212

United States Department of Justice, 167, 249n35

United States Environmental Protection Agency (EPA), 19, 20, 97, 98, 114, 117, 118, 128, 140. *See also* Border 2020 program

United States Fish and Wildlife, 183, 184, 185
United States Forest Service, 4, 18, 19, 101, 175–78, 180, 189
United States Government Accountability Office (GAO), 43, 177
United States Immigration and Customs Enforcement (ICE), 191, 198, 211
United States-Mexico boundary commission, 59
University Medical Center (UMC), 55, 56, 69, 153, 154, 162, 249n22
University of Arizona, 54, 131, 205
Urrea, Luis Alberto, 6
US-Mexican War, 9, 57

VADER (Vehicle and Dismount Exploitation Radar), 52
Valenzuela Hermanos (VH) supermarket, 90
vanishing, 51, 52, 211
vests, 8, 76, 77, 97, 102, 173
Vietnam War, 13, 16, 23, 59, 60, 170, 243n75
violence: binational security, 17, 23, 24; border wall, 209, 211, 212, 213, 218; crime 77; domestic, 29, 169, 172; drug and human trafficking, 3; ecosystem, 195; gangs, 181, 202; human rights, 185; political, 15; smugglers, 8; state, 12; structural, 28, 235n25; topographic, 11
Virgen de Guadalupe, 37, 70–71, 221
Virilio, Paul, 84

wall. See border fence, border wall
war on drugs, 9, 21, 77, 147, 248n46
war on terror, 9, 17, 209
Warsaw Canyon, 190

war zone, 15, 27, 62, 155, 157, 196
warehouse, 34, 38, 41, 79, 95, 102, 127, 140
wash. See arroyo, Nogales Wash
watchouts, 175–77
water: bottles, 50, 106, 125, 183, 184; hydrants, 3, 19, 40, 90, 94, 95, 112; pressure, 10, 19, 94
weapon: border infrastructure, 28, 86; narratives, 77; Nogales, 33, 36; smugglers, 193; tactical infrastructure, 50; terrain, 7, 9, 11, 211, 213. See also WMDs
weaponization, 211
weather, 7, 10, 17, 26, 39, 119, 136, 137, 155
WebEOC, 136
Weber, Max, 22
"wetback," 50, 185, 242n51
Weizman, Eyal, 12
Westphalian system, 20
wildland fires: across the border, 10, 18, 96; definition, 160; Forest Service, 18, 175, 178; hazard mitigation plan, 131; narratives, 5, 13, 25, 47, 54, 113, 175, 222; suspected causes, 13, 177; temperate increase, 4; training, 180; TTX, 136
wild cats, 4, 6, 7, 145, 172
WMDs, 17, 98, 117, 129, 134, 138, 214
women: border patrol officers, 120, 163; cramps, 41; detainees, 81; firefighters, 151, 172; injuries, 57; paramedics and emergency responders, 84, 172–73, 223; sign, 79. See also sexual assault
World War II, 16, 139
wounds, 14, 15, 61, 62, 65, 129, 135, 200, 212. See also injury, trauma

x-ray device, 24, 119, 128, 129